HARD CHOICES, LOST VOICES

Hard Choices, Lost Voices

. . . .

How the Abortion Conflict Has Divided America,
Distorted Constitutional Rights,
and Damaged the Courts

DONALD P. JUDGES

CHICAGO • *Ivan R. Dee* • 1993

Grateful acknowledgment is made to Keith L. Moore and the W. B. Saunders Company for permission to reprint illustrations and tables from The Developing Human: Clinically Oriented Embryology (4th edition, 1988).

Library of Congress Cataloging-in-Publication Data:
Judges, Donald P.
    Hard choices, lost voices : how the abortion conflict has divided America, distorted constitutional rights, and damaged the courts / Donald P. Judges.
        p. cm.
    Includes bibliographical references and index.
    ISBN 1-56663-016-9 (alk. paper)
    1. Abortion—Law and legislation—United States. 2. Abortion—United States—Moral and ethical aspects. I. Title.
KF3771.J83 1993
363.4'6—dc20   92-44593

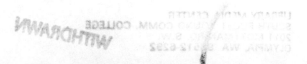

To the memory of Diane Shelledy
(July 7, 1961–May 15, 1992)

We may never know when life begins,
but she understood what it is for.

045316

Contents

Preface

This book is the result of a process of discovery that began for me when the Supreme Court announced its 1989 decision in *Webster v. Reproductive Health Services*. The media reported that the Supreme Court had substantially relaxed constitutional limits on state regulation of abortion, and that we had entered a new era of abortion rights. Developments over the next two years focused attention even more closely on the Supreme Court's position on abortion rights: Justice William Brennan and then Justice Thurgood Marshall announced their retirements; the ensuing confirmation hearings of Justices David Souter and Clarence Thomas attempted to probe their views on abortion rights; the Court issued a series of opinions demonstrating that *Webster* had indeed signaled a judicial retreat from *Roe v. Wade*; Operation Rescue escalated its campaign against abortion clinics; and the Court was asked by both sides in *Planned Parenthood of Southeastern Pennsylvania v. Casey* to decide whether *Roe* was still the law of the land.

As I observed the media's coverage of the issue, tried to help my students understand the Court's cases, and discussed the abortion issue with family, friends, and acquaintances, I discovered that this divisive question involves gaps in more than just opinion and belief. For an issue that provokes such strong emotions, there seems to be a substantial information gap as well. Many people I have talked with, even some who are actively involved in the abortion issue, seem to know little about it. In a nation that performs one and a half million legal abortions annually, in which informed sources estimate that almost half of all women can be expected to have at least one abortion in their lifetime, and which is stirred to such violent passions about the issue, closing that information gap is essential. This book is intended to be one step in that direction.

Abortion is more than a moral or religious issue: it touches many areas unfamiliar to the average layperson. Among other things, abortion is very much a legal issue; but most people have only the fuzziest idea of what the legal problems are. While the media told the public that *Webster* changed the law, I suspect that many people, including some lawyers, did not really understand how it did so or what the basis was for the larger constitutional dispute surrounding *Roe v. Wade*. Indeed, it seems likely that many people are unfamiliar with abortion's historical context and *Roe*'s relationship to that history.

Abortion is also a social issue. It is practiced in a social context by various classes of women, for a variety of reasons, and under a number of constraints. Yet there seems to be popular misunderstanding or ignorance about that context as well. Real women living in real-life circumstances have abortions, yet the issue is often discussed in sterile, abstract terms. And abortion is obviously a medical issue as well. But again it seems likely that many people have never set foot in an abortion clinic and only vaguely understand what the procedure involves.

As I explored this issue I discovered other gaps as well. It is scarcely news that people are deeply divided over abortion, but it takes some study to realize just how wide the gulf is that separates them. Laurence Tribe's 1990 book characterized the abortion dispute as the "Clash of Absolutes." He might more accurately have described it as the absolute of clashes. Domination of one side by the other, not reconciliation, seems to characterize most efforts at resolution. When the issues are as directly antagonistic as the core claims of the pro-life and pro-choice sides, compromise threatens to be put out of the question. Not only does the ideological divide seem unbridgeable on its own terms, but the intensity of the emotional conflict often precludes real dialogue. Talking all too often degenerates into shouting, and reasoned discussion often is displaced by slogans and dogma.

Even when opposing views are not shouted, a wide gap often appears between statements and facts. For example, there seems to be a disparity between what people say they believe when arguing about abortion, and what they actually do when confronted with the decision. Arguments from both sides of the issue often turn reason and reality upside down. Laws that interfere with one of the safest medical procedures today are defended by anti–abortion rights advocates in part as necessary to protect women's health. Arguments against the unborn's legal and moral status—that in any other context would be rejected out of hand by many "liberals" as morally inadmissible—are routinely deployed by pro–abortion rights advocates. And the Supreme Court's struggle to compromise the competing claims has satisfied neither side.

Also striking, and deeply troubling, is the growing gap between the issues that everyone seems to care so passionately about and the factors that actually determine who has access to abortion services. As a practical matter in the United States today, access to abortion depends far more on factors such as a woman's financial status, where she lives, whom she knows, and how much vexation she can tolerate than it does with any important moral, legal, or philosophical questions about prenatal life and the woman's claim to liberty. In real-life terms, arbitrariness rather than principle often determines the question of choice.

Finally, I found a gap where I least expected it—but it is the one that gives me real hope for the outcome of the abortion conflict. I began this project burdened by at least as much ideological baggage, misinformation, and ignorance as I imagine many other people bring to the formation of their opinions on abortion. The more I learn about this difficult subject, the more I find that I must question my own assumptions and conclusions, and the more I yearn to find a way to think about the problem that does not require me to discount the convictions of others or to invest more energy in conflict, hostility, and divisiveness.

My other discoveries have led me to suspect that, quite apart from the question of who, if anyone, ultimately has the correct answer to the problem of abortion rights, something is seriously wrong with our society's approach to the problem. In the name of God and righteousness, people throw dead fetuses at others, blockade and bomb doctors' offices, and harass patients. Otherwise "liberal" people refuse to come to grips with basic claims of equality, justice, and nonviolence or to confront abortion's truly disturbing images. Our highest judicial officers quarrel bitterly among themselves and offer patently self-contradictory or implausible justifications for their decisions. The conflict's practical impact has less and less to do with any principle that matters in the debate. Doctors have been directed in some circumstances not to speak openly with their patients, and poor women are denied the health care they need. And the very meaning of fundamental constitutional rights has been undermined in the name of preserving a fragment of one particularly problematic right.

When we have reached such a state of affairs it is time to begin looking for a fresh approach. Working on this book has helped me to appreciate more fully the claims of people whom I earlier regarded as opponents to overcome rather than as individuals to understand, and to begin thinking about alternatives to the current adversarial, conflict-oriented debate.

Unlike many others on the subject, this book does not tackle the ultimate question of abortion rights. It recognizes that such rights exist and tries to fill some of the gaps described above. First, to set the abortion issue in its social, medical, and historical context, Part One provides an overview of the images, tone, and character of the debate itself; a description of who has abortions and in what circumstances; a brief explanation of abortion's medical aspects, including a description of gestation, viability, and the procedure itself; and a summary of abortion's historical background.

Part Two addresses abortion as a legal issue. It explains *Roe v. Wade* in terms of its constitutional law context, including the problems of constitutional interpretation raised by *Roe*, the decision itself, and the principal criticisms aimed at it. Part Three describes the Supreme Court's sixteen-year enterprise of filling in the contours of abortion rights and dealing with the state legislative efforts to restrict those rights.

With the foregoing as background, Part Four describes and

comments on the Court's transition from elaborating abortion rights to contracting them in *Webster* and ensuing cases. Part Four also discusses the issues involved in overruling *Roe*. Part Five describes and criticizes the Court's current phase of redefining abortion rights in *Casey*. As argued there, the Court's current approach is perhaps the worst possible resolution of the conflict in constitutional terms from either side's perspective.

Part Six then steps back to take stock of the issue and hazards speculation on future developments while political power apparently is shifting toward the pro-choice side of the conflict. It concludes by suggesting ways we might begin to redefine the abortion issue in terms of our similarities rather than our differences.

The purpose of this book is to inform and to stimulate thought, not to persuade anyone one way or the other on the ultimate question of abortion rights. It attempts an ambitious experiment—a balanced and informed treatment of the issue that does not shy from critical examination of shortcomings on either side of the conflict or in the nature of the conflict itself. Readers who have already made up their minds on the issue may nevertheless find useful information. At the least, this book may help them to understand better what they are talking—or shouting—about. For readers whose views are not predetermined, this book may contribute to an appreciation of how complex and highly contextual the issue is. And I hope it helps such readers to develop their own inquiries and insights about abortion. Perhaps what we need most in this area are more questions and fewer answers, more informed doubt and less uninformed conviction. My goal is to help open minds on this issue, not close them, and to bridge gaps rather than create them.

Acknowledgments

This book would never have been written without the support and assistance of many friends. David Shelledy's and Mark Killenbeck's generosity with their time, formidable analytical ability, and clarity of expression has greatly aided this project. Many eight-and-a-half-mile discussions with Paul Schwartz have helped me to think about the abortion problem, and his constant support has helped me to sustain the pace to the finish. William Harrison, M.D., a quiet man who understands this issue better than most who shout about it, has been a valuable resource. And I am grateful to Dr. Keith L. Moore for his advice and permission to use his illustrations.

I especially wish to thank Chandana Becker. Her insightful comments certainly improved the manuscript. Much more than that, she has shared a dozen years of love, laughs, and learning, and put up with far too many late nights, unruly dogs, off-key flute sonatas, and lost turtles.

I am indebted for research assistance to Barbara Lingle and Lorre Moore, and to Joann Slocum for secretarial help. Sine qua non, if ever there was.

I also wish to thank Ivan Dee for his steady and sure editorial hand. His guidance has made this a much better book.

Finally, I wish to thank the other friends who have supported me in this and other writing endeavors. Linda Weinstein's faith in this project helped to get it off the ground. John Watkins has been a reliable source of encouragement and advice since I began my academic career. Len Strickman has provided, among other things, the wherewithal for this project. Richard Atkinson provided particular help. And thanks to S.H. for more than I can say.

D. P. J.

Fayetteville, Arkansas
January 1993

HARD CHOICES, LOST VOICES

Nobody's right if everybody's wrong.

Stephen Stills with Buffalo Springfield, 1967

Part One

. . . .

THE ABORTION WARS: ISSUES, FACTS AND FIGURES, AND HISTORY

1. The Nature of the Debate

· ·

Abortion. It is one of the most divisive issues of our time. It has been compared with the regional conflict over slavery that erupted into the Civil War.[1] While that comparison may be exaggerated, there is no denying the depth of feeling the issue elicits. To some it is nothing less than the slaughter of millions upon millions of the most innocent and vulnerable of all victims, and thus stands as the most monstrous moral outrage in human history. To others it tests our society's commitment to fundamental principles of individual liberty, personal autonomy, and women's welfare.

Stripped to its essentials, the conflict seems intractable: pregnancy can have only one of two possible outcomes. The issue is who gets to decide between them. The powerful claims asserted by the state on behalf of the unborn child appear to collide head-on with the pregnant woman's understandable assertion of a right to choose the outcome of her pregnancy. In such a bitter contest, where both sides champion compelling but opposing claims, partial or total victory for one side or the other may be more a function of "might" than "right."

As we pass the twentieth anniversary of the United States Supreme Court's landmark decision in *Roe v. Wade*, there is cause to wonder whether reasoned dialogue about this incendiary issue will ever be possible. As the legal scholar Ronald Dworkin has observed, "No judicial decision in our time has aroused as much sustained public outrage, emotion, and physical violence, or as much intemperate professional criticism."[2] The various sides of the debate appear largely to be shouting past one another and do not even share a common vocabulary—especially about the most central matters. Neutral terms are elu-

4

sive. An embryo or a fetus is alternatively "an unborn child" or "a product of conception." A "pro-life" person implicitly, and often quite explicitly, calls his or her opponent "pro-death." "Pro-choice" advocates characterize their opponents as "fanatics," "fascists," and "misogynists." Abortion is alternatively a "simple surgical procedure" or "murder." A doctor's office becomes an "abortorium," the doctor becomes a "baby killer." Abortion rights advocates ask how anyone who sends death threats to physicians who perform abortions, threatens their children and bombs their clinics, or would force women to bring to term pregnancies of children who are unwanted and will be uncared for, can seriously claim to be "pro-life" and "pro-child." And they complain of the opposition by anti-abortion forces to government-subsidized contraception and postnatal care. Anti-abortion advocates demand to know what "choice" abortion leaves the unborn child.

The images of this conflict are no less searing and divisive than its rhetoric. The media almost daily present pictures of Americans—including young children—screaming at and shoving one another, blockading abortion clinics, rushing or restraining blockades, and thousands upon thousands marching in demonstration or being arrested. Protesters dogged both Republican and Democratic candidates throughout the 1992 presidential campaign.

A particularly disturbing image is that of anti-abortion protesters repeatedly confronting people, including candidates for public office, with fetal remains. In one gruesome scene in front of a Buffalo, New York, abortion clinic, Operation Rescue's Reverend Robert Schenck held out to a clinic defender what he claimed, according to *Life* magazine, was "my friend baby Tia, a beautiful little girl who was aborted." *Life* describes how "suddenly, a hand is grabbing. Schenck bobbles the fetus. It falls to the sidewalk and the police, pro-choicers and pro-lifers plunge to the ground, like football players scrambling for a fumble." The county coroner later concluded that the remains were of a fetus stillborn at no earlier than twenty weeks' gestation.[3]

Political candidates have also sought to capitalize on the

impact of such images. Unsuccessful congressional candidate Michael Bailey pioneered the use of television ads featuring graphic photographs of bloody fetuses to dramatize his anti-abortion position in Indiana's 1992 Republican primary. Numerous complaints prompted broadcasters to ask the Federal Communications Commission to declare such ads indecent. The FCC refused, but a federal court ruled that a broadcaster could decline to air the ads during prime time. At least twenty other candidates expressed interest in Bailey's offer to make the film available for campaign use. Daniel Becker, unsuccessful GOP candidate for Congress in Georgia, carried a pocket-sized plastic model of a fetus to demonstrate the reality of abortion.[4]

Such incidents surely reveal something about the nature of this debate; but, characteristically, the message is in dispute. To zealous anti-abortion activists like Reverend Schenck and Operation Rescue founder Randall Terry, such tactics are necessary to shock complacent Americans into an awareness of abortion's horrors. "If you can't bear to look at it," Schenck explains, "it shouldn't be tolerated in this country."[5] To others, however, such conduct, especially in pursuit of elected office, reflects a grotesque and hypocritical exploitation of the very kind of wrongdoing that anti-abortion advocates decry. It demonstrates how the extremism that dominates the abortion conflict can dehumanize its participants.

THE ABORTION WARS: CONFLICT AS IRRESPONSIBILITY?

From this book's perspective, incidents like these are among many indications that something is seriously wrong with America's approach to the abortion issue. Some critics say that the problem is the Supreme Court's godlessness or its blindness to the killing of unborn children; others blame the Court's frustration of the democratic process. Still others accuse the Court and politicians of insensitivity to women's needs and concerns.

A more fundamental problem may be that as a society we have largely approached the abortion problem—like most other social issues—as a power conflict. Both sides in the struggle seem to avoid responsibility for the impact of the conflict. By approaching the issue as a kind of small-scale, only partly unarmed civil war, the abortion warriors seem to ignore the consequences of their bitter strife. Perhaps some social problems, including abortion, simply are not appropriate for resolution through the familiar process of competing power factions—whether the battleground is the courthouse or the statehouse. The adversarial approach is so much a part of our culture, politics, and thinking that this suggestion may strike some as heresy, visionary, or meaningless. One goal of this book, in addition to providing important information about one of the great issues of our time, is to ask whether the current struggle between pro– and anti–abortion rights forces— particularly in the courts—ultimately may prove to be fruitless and even harmful. The conflict has divided the people, produced judicial decisions that distort the fabric of constitutional law regardless of one's position on the underlying issue of abortion rights, and has interfered arbitrarily with the access of disadvantaged women to abortion services.

One indication that the approach may be part of the problem is the way in which the debate, especially in the legal sphere, has come more and more to resemble Alice's Wonderland. Each side seems to gain the most only when it relies on its weakest arguments. Thus anti-abortion forces have had some success in limiting abortion by advocating restrictions enacted largely in the name of protecting women from the procedure's physical and psychological risks. In view of abortion's relative safety, however, that argument is far from convincing. Another relatively successful tactic for anti-abortion protesters has been the sometimes violent and unlawful harassment and intimidation of abortion patients and providers. Although most Americans find such conduct abhorrent, and it seems cynically at odds with a "pro-life" ethic, such harassment may be succeeding (at least indirectly) in making access to abortion services more difficult.

The strongest anti-abortion argument on its face would appear to be that abortion takes the most innocent of human life without sufficient justification. Yet one objection to that

argument's corollary—that a fetus is a "person" in any meaningful sense of the word—is that it proves too much to be tolerated. And the historical roots of restrictive abortion policy in
America and elsewhere do not reveal a clear commitment to the
protection of fetal life. Finally, the "baby killing" accusation is
one that makes many people uncomfortable.

On the other side, pro–abortion rights advocates have largely
succeeded, at least until recently, where their claim is relatively
weak. In view of the serious interpretive problems presented by a
constitutional claim to abortion rights, the more convincing pro-
choice arguments would seem to be based on women's welfare
and autonomy as a matter of policy rather than constitutional law.
This is not to imply that *Roe v. Wade* was wrongly decided; that is
a complex and difficult question. The point is that an objective
approach must acknowledge the difficulties of the arguments on
both sides of the debate. In *Planned Parenthood of Southeastern
Pennsylvania v. Casey*, a badly divided Court overruled precedent,
announced a hopelessly vague and indeterminate new standard,
and cut back abortion rights while simultaneously extolling the
virtues of consistency, certainty, and individual liberty.

Another problem with the extremists of the current controversy is that they seem to accuse those individuals who reserve
judgment, weigh the merits and deficiencies of both sides, and
wish to talk—rather than shout—about it, of moral inadequacy.
This implicit accusation does not just criticize those who refuse
to join the fray; it strikes at the heart of reasoned discourse and
reflective thinking about such difficult issues. At the least, the
debate's polarized atmosphere creates a natural tendency toward
extremism and in-group identification.[6] Warriors from either
camp in this battle appear to enjoy an enviable clarity of conviction and a comforting sense of solidarity. They know where they
stand, what they are about, and who their friends and enemies
are. Many seem strikingly untroubled by abortion's agonizing
moral conflicts: each side appears quite prepared to discount the
core claims of the other. Unencumbered by soul-searching
doubts, they devote all their attention to tactics. Since they
already know what is right and what is wrong, they need only

concentrate on how to win. Reasons and arguments proceed from, rather than lead to, conclusions. And some individuals seem mainly to enjoy the sense of self-righteousness, solidarity, and excitement of battle that front-line activism offers. For them, satisfaction comes from taking sides and heaping abuse—verbal and physical—on an identified enemy.

For many people, however, the ultimate rightness or wrongness of abortion is far from self-evident. And it sometimes appears that the closer the two sides engage each other at the front line, the further they seem to move from what matters most. There is much to question on both sides of the issue. Although some individuals arrive at their position on abortion through a leap of faith that tolerates little equivocation, many others regard the issue as complex and highly contextual. This ambivalence is reflected, for example, in opinion polls, which typically show a sizable majority of Americans favoring protection of abortion rights in at least some circumstances, but less agreement about what those circumstances ought to be. What's more, attitudes expressed through surveys and polls do not square with the actual behavior of people faced with a personal abortion decision.

For people who see the abortion conflict as more than a one-dimensional question, the outcome of which is predetermined by religious, philosophical, or political absolutes, an important threshold problem is determining the *kinds of issues* abortion raises: How are we to think about abortion? What ought we consider important in coming to grips with it? What kinds of facts and arguments ought we pay attention to, and what kinds can we safely disregard? What tests will sort the serious from the silly?

FRAMING THE ISSUES: THE ABORTION CONFLICT'S IMPACT IN AND ON THE COURTS

This threshold problem is central to one highly important arena where the battle has been fought during the last two decades.

Although abortion may be a public health, religious, moral, philosophical, and political issue debated in conferences, the pulpit, and the academy, in the United States it is also very much a *legal* issue decided in the courthouse. Courts must grapple not only with the fundamental problem of whether some basis in law exists for claims to abortion rights, but also with determining the parameters of those rights. In deciding such questions, courts necessarily must decide what counts as meritorious argument, which claims are legitimate, who bears the burden of proof, and by what standards these matters are to be measured.

In the twenty years since *Roe v. Wade* the federal judiciary has both shaped and been shaped by the debate. With its 1992 decision in *Planned Parenthood of Southeastern Pennsylvania v. Casey,* the Supreme Court has decided more than twenty abortion rights cases involving more than twice as many written opinions. Those opinions have had a major influence on the arguments in the abortion debate as well as a more diffuse impact on constitutional law generally and even on the membership of the federal bench.

In *Roe* the Court cast the abortion debate in terms of individual liberty. The *Casey* decision, whatever questions it may have left unanswered or raised itself, kept the debate there. Constitutionalization of the abortion debate has profoundly affected both its direction and outcome. First, the immediate constitutional question has been the scope of governmental (both state and federal) authority to regulate abortion and abortion-related activities, or, put the other way, the scope of individual abortion rights. Thus the question—at least in theory—is not whether particular measures, such as parental consent or notification requirements or even outright prohibitions on abortion, are sound or wise *policy*, but rather whether they are *constitutional*. In other words, the legal issue is not whether government *ought* to enact a particular measure; it is whether government has the *power* to do so. As we shall see, a point of bitter contention in the constitutional debate is whether the Supreme Court has really been answering the "ought to" question in the guise of ruling on the "power to" question.

Second, as the last point suggests, the abortion debate must

10

now make room for the entire controversy about constitutional interpretation. Although constitutional scholars disagree about the extent to which constitutional law (especially as it concerns abortion rights) is a matter of coherent principles, arguments to the Court about abortion must at least be presented in the context of recognized interpretive theory. This constraint means that advocates' arguments will include references to sources that mainstream constitutional theory deems relevant. Those sources include the text of the Constitution itself, to the very limited extent that it can be said to speak even implicitly to the issue; historical sources such as past custom, practice, and legal treatment of abortion; generalizations about traditions concerning individual liberties and their meaning; generalizations about the propriety of the judiciary recognizing or declaring rights not specifically provided for in the Constitution; current social mores and their relevance to the constitutional question; the practical impact of a given regulation on the exercise of the right; and the force of the asserted government interests at stake.

Third, just as advocates must frame their arguments in constitutional terms, the Court makes constitutional law each time it speaks on the abortion issue. Like the Heisenberg Uncertainty Principle, the Court cannot look at the fabric of constitutional law without changing it. The Court's resolution of the constitutional questions raised by abortion—such as the basic questions of whether and how to infer rights from the Constitution, who is entitled to invoke the courts' jurisdiction, the balance of power between the federal and state governments, and the appropriate reach for the Court in reviewing legislative enactments—has profound implications for the entire body of constitutional law quite beyond the specific issue of abortion rights.

Less directly but no less importantly, the abortion controversy has become a rallying flag in a larger struggle over the ideological direction of the country, and gaining control of the appointment of federal judges has been a key strategic goal in that struggle. In grossly simple terms, the conflict is between a preference for institutional, authoritative regulation of many aspects of an individual's personal life (especially those concerning sexu-

ality and family matters), and a preference for relatively unconstrained individual discretion over such matters. The origins of
the authoritarian stance often can be found in organized religion, and the ideas reflect cultural homogeneity. The opposite
position reflects an increasingly secular, pluralistic society.

Researchers Ron Lesthaeghe and Jon Surkyn have studied the
secularization of Western European society through the use of a
survey which touches on values in religion, education, politics,
materialism, and marital and family values.[7] They conclude that
the long-term trend in Europe has been toward secularization
and individual discretion. Building on that research, the sociolo-
gists Alice Rossi and Bhavani Sitaraman have suggested that the
United States is following a similar but less advanced path
toward secularism and individualism, and they have argued that
such a trend includes attitudes toward abortion.[8]

Whether they are correct about America's ideological future
remains to be seen, but their characterization of the opposing
sides in the abortion debate has some support in fact. For example, here is how they report on a survey of Missouri abortion
activists:

> Other values antiabortion advocates ranked high were family
> security, national security, and inner harmony. Values the pro-
> choice advocates ranked high were equality, accomplishment,
> pleasure, freedom, an exciting life, and a comfortable life.
> Across the two profiles, one can sense the predominance
> among the prochoice activists of a secular, highly individualized
> orientation and among the right-to-life advocates the predomi-
> nance of the traditional orientation that gives primacy to family
> rights and communal obligations over individual rights.[9]

This split is also illustrated by the frequency with which ultra-
conservative politicians and candidates invoke "traditional family
values" and by controversies over matters such as school prayer.

The roster of organizations submitting *amicus curiae*, or friend
of the court,* briefs to the Supreme Court in the 1989 case of

---

*An *amicus curiae*, or "friend of the court," is a person (not a party) with a strong
interest in a case who asks the court for permission to file a brief.

12

Webster v. Reproductive Health Services, which was a turning point for abortion rights, also in part reflects this ideological divide. *Webster,* discussed in detail in Part Four, involved a challenge to several provisions of Missouri law concerning the definition of when life begins, the use of public facilities and employees for abortions, and the determination of fetal viability. The parties to the case, and many friends of the court, also argued for and against overruling *Roe.* Those friends of the court opposing *Roe* included a number of religious and conservative organizations in addition to single-issue pro-life groups.* Friends of the court supporting *Roe* and the challengers to Missouri's laws, on the other hand, predictably included liberal and libertarian groups.† A similar lineup developed in response to the nomination of Robert Bork to the Supreme Court, motivated in part by his opposition to *Roe v. Wade.*

This division of attitudes is also reflected at the personal level in the orientations of individual activists. Operation Rescue's Randall Terry, for example, has insisted that the "underpinnings of the republic have got to be what God gave Moses on Mount Sinai and confirmed through the Lord Jesus." For Terry the problem can be traced back to the Renaissance, which "sought to make man autonomous from God and from moral absolutes." Terry believes that "married couples who confess to be followers of the Lord Jesus should leave the number of children they have

---

*Among the religious and conservative groups were the Catholic Health Association of the United States, the Catholic Lawyers' Guild of the Archdiocese of Boston, Catholics United for Life, Christian Advocates Serving Evangelism, Focus on the Family, the Holy Orthodox Church, the Knights of Columbus, the Missouri Catholic Conference, the New England Christian Action Council, the Lutheran Church—Missouri Synod, Roman Catholic Bishop Austin Vaughn and the Crusade for Life (a Protestant evangelical organization), and the United States Catholic Conference. Examples of pro-life groups against *Roe* were Birthright, Inc., the National Right to Life Committee, the American Life League, and the Rutherford Institute.

†Among those groups were the American Civil Liberties Union; the National Education Association; People for the American Way; the Newspaper Guild; the National Writers Union; Canadian Women's Organizations; Committees on Civil Rights, Medicine and Law, and Sex and Law of the Association of the Bar of the City of New York; a group of American law professors; the National Association of Women Lawyers; the National Council of Negro Women; the National Family Planning and Reproductive Health Association; the National Organization for Women; and Americans United for the Separation of Church and State.

13

in the hands of God." Contraception and abortion are tools of Satan, and secular education is "some godless curriculum or setting, where [children's] minds are filled with pollution." To Terry the struggle is no less than a "cultural civil war."[10] Other anti-abortion activists are also absolutists on sexual morality. Judie Brown, the founder of the American Life League, believes premarital sex is sinful, "birth control leads to abortion," and the solution is abstinence.[11]

On the side of abortion rights, an example of someone who believes in individual discretion in matters of lifestyle and sexuality is National Organization for Women President Patricia Ireland. Indeed, for some individuals in the conflict an underlying dynamic may be not so much abortion but sexuality itself.[12] According to one researcher, "Authoritarianism is based in part on guilt and anxiety about sexuality. One of the concerns of authoritarians is the disapproval of sexual stimulation, 'unacceptable' sexual expression, and a desire to control the sexuality of others."[13]

The Reagan and Bush presidencies, the rise of the Moral Majority in the 1980s, and the influence of the fundamentalist Christian movement in part testify to this broader ideological conflict and to a noticeable rightward movement in the United States. And the abortion issue was a key factor in mobilizing political support for those administrations. After a series of post-*Roe* losses in the Supreme Court, anti-abortion activists concentrated their forces on electing presidents who would nominate jurists likely to reject abortion rights and to favor institutional authority, at least in areas of individual morality and religion. Taking the long view, Rossi and Sitaraman regard these developments as part of the "fits and starts in a dialectic process [of political and social change] necessarily subject to deflections and vacillations."[14] Their prediction may find some confirmation in another powerful political movement which the abortion issue, and other events such as the Clarence Thomas hearings, has helped to fuel: the acceleration of women's entry into politics.

Certainly the larger battle is also being fought over the status of women in American society. Some observers believe that women's gains toward equality have precipitated a backlash, often couched in terms of protecting "traditional family values"—which values would place women in their stereotypic role as homemaker and mother.[15] At least some of the impetus against abortion rights has been along those lines. The growing power of women is perhaps the strongest indication that Rossi and Sitaraman are correct. As more and more women enter Congress, boardrooms, cabinet positions, police forces, and businesses, their political and economic power will continue to grow. In an era when women fly spacecraft, pilot assault helicopters, and enter Marine combat divisions, it is hard to imagine they will long tolerate a retrenchment of an important aspect of their independence.

But one must take a long view to see past the influence of the Reagan-Bush era, at least as far as the judiciary's interpretation of the Constitution is concerned. Presidents Reagan and Bush have appointed more than 60 percent of all sitting federal judges.[16] Many of those jurists are relatively young, and their conservative influence will be felt well into the next century across a broad spectrum of substantive areas that go far beyond abortion—including free speech, separation of church and state, the free exercise of religion, criminal justice, gay rights, affirmative action, judicial review of administrative agency action, the scope of congressional powers (especially relative to the states), and statutory interpretation. Thus the abortion controversy has been at the center of a movement to redirect the orientation of the federal judiciary distinctly rightward: and so the issue has shaped the federal courts.

LOOKING PAST THE STEREOTYPES

In discussing the abortion issue, trying to make general appraisals can instead produce misleading oversimplifications. Some observations about trends may be possible, but it would be a serious mistake to believe that people on either side of the issue are homogenous on any dimension, including ideology, religion, or party affiliation. For example, some committed civil libertarians, such as Nat Hentoff, are ardently opposed to abortion.

Moreover, neither religion in general nor Christianity in particular are the exclusive province of abortion's foes. For example, filing or joining *amicus curiae* briefs in opposition to the Missouri laws in *Webster* and in defense of *Roe* were numerous groups representing a variety of sincerely held religious convictions.* They explained, "Because the amici recognize the many divergent theological answers to the questions raised by abortion, the amici agree that each woman should be free to consult with her religious convictions, as well as her best medical advice, without governmental coercion or constraint when exercising religious and personal conscience in making a decision whether to terminate her pregnancy."[17] One review of the literature has found "Protestant-Catholic differences [in attitudes toward abortion] to be minimal, once a measure of religiosity is introduced: Regular church attendance is more specifically related to abortion attitudes than religious affiliation per se."[18] And, as mentioned, data discussed in the next chapter show a surprising divergence between attitude and conduct when people are actually faced with the abortion decision.

Similarly, members of the health-care establishment, according to the *Webster* brief of the American Medical Association and other organizations, "hold widely divergent views on the various issues raised in *Roe v. Wade....*" The AMA's brief, joined by seven other mainstream health-care organizations, including the American Academy of Child and Adolescent Psychiatry, the American Academy of Pediatrics, the American College of Obstetricians and Gynecologists, and the American Psychiatric Association, sought to inform the Court about the relative

*Those groups included Agudath Israel of America (a national grassroots Orthodox Jewish organization), the American Jewish Congress and American Jewish Committee, the American Friends Service Committee, the Board of Homeland Ministries—United Church of Christ, the Episcopal Diocese of Massachusetts—Women in Crisis Committee, the Episcopal Diocese of New York—Episcopal Women's Caucus, the General Board of Church and Society—the United Methodist Church, the National Assembly of Religious Women, the Anti-Defamation League of B'nai B'rith Women, the Presbyterian Church (U.S.A.) by James E. Andrew as Stated Clerk of General Assembly, the St. Louis Catholics for Choice, Women in Ministry—Garrett Evangelical Seminary, the Unitarian Universalist Association, Catholics for a Free Choice, and numerous individual clergy.

16

health risks of abortion and childbirth while taking a noncommittal position on the central constitutional issue. "Our members all agree that every individual has a fundamental right to make an individual medical decision free of state interference unless the state has a compelling justification for the restrictions it imposes," said the brief, but it avoided taking a position on the crucial question of *which* state interests (such as protecting postviability fetal life) are compelling.[19] The American Psychological Association, the American Nurses' Association, and the American Public Health Association also filed *Webster* briefs in support of challenges to the Missouri laws.

Other organizations of health-care professionals, most formed in reaction to *Roe*, are outspokenly anti-abortion. For example, groups supporting the Missouri law in *Webster* and condemning *Roe* included the American Association of ProLife Obstetricians and Gynecologists, founded in 1973 in the wake of *Roe v. Wade*, the American Association of Pro-Life Pediatricians, and the American Academy of Medical Ethics, which describes itself as "an educational and legislative lobbying organization with approximately 20,000 physician members...[formed] in response to an adversely changing medical and ethical climate in the American Medical Association and the American College of Obstetricians and Gynecologists."[20]

The legal profession, though generally a force for the liberalization of abortion laws in recent decades, also has long been divided over the issue of abortion. The American Bar Association proposed a Uniform Abortion Act in the 1960s which would have liberalized the laws in many states if adopted, and which strongly influenced legislative reform efforts under way in several states when *Roe v. Wade* was decided. The Uniform Act's provisions, seen in the light of *Roe*'s standards, seem restrictive today. In 1990 the American Bar Association's House of Delegates substantially liberalized its position on abortion, opposing legislation or other government action that would interfere with a woman's right to terminate her pregnancy "at any time before the fetus is capable of independent life," or thereafter as necessary to preserve the woman's health.[21] The 1990 vote was so controversial

17

that the House of Delegates revisited the issue in 1992 and again endorsed abortion rights.[22] Several thousand lawyers have resigned their membership in protest.

Although both political parties had opposing platform planks on the abortion issue in 1992, with the Democrats endorsing abortion rights and the Republicans taking an anti-abortion position, the issue is not solely one of partisan politics. Surveys have shown that attitudes toward abortion do not correlate significantly with party affiliation: a majority of voters from either party takes a generally pro-choice position.[23] Both parties faced dissension on the issue in 1992: Republicans were confronted with forceful insurgencies by Republicans for Choice and another pro-choice group called Women in the Senate and House (WISH); Democrats denied party stalwart Governor Robert Casey of Pennsylvania the opportunity to address the 1992 convention with his plea to add the unborn to the party's "natural constituency" of "the powerless and the voiceless."[24]

Finally, although some individuals' views on abortion derive from bedrock moral or religious convictions, it is incorrect to assume that everyone's position is carved in stone. One may not be surprised to learn that George Bush's stance on the issue changed (more than once) over time, or that both Bill Clinton and Al Gore have taken positions in the past that could be construed as anti-abortion; they are, after all, political survivors. But other individuals also have experienced a profound change of heart. A striking example is Bernard Nathanson, M.D. Dr. Nathanson's brief in support of Missouri's law in *Webster* described his own experience:

> I was co-founder of the National Association for Repeal of Abortion Laws (now the National Abortion Rights Action League) in 1969, and served as medical consultant to that organization until my resignation in 1975. As one of the key architects of abortion political strategy in the United States I was responsible for the coining of many passwords and shibboleths, such as "freedom of choice" and "a private matter between a woman and her doctor," which have too long passed for serious argument in this infinitely complex and incendiary issue.

I was also the world's leading abortionist. I did abortions in New York when they were illegal by claiming that they were necessary to preserve the patient's life. When abortion became legal, I presided over the world's largest abortion clinic. It did 60,000 abortions in the 19 months I presided....

But the more I learned, the more I moved from pro-choice to pro-life. I now urge this Court to declare what medical science has known for generations, that the not yet born human is an individual and therefore a person.[25]

Dr. Nathanson's conversion to the anti-abortion camp resulted in his production of two influential films, "Silent Scream," which depicts a suction curretage abortion, and "Eclipse of Reason," which portrays a dilation and evacuation abortion.

VOICES IN THE STORM: REAL EXPERIENCES WITH ABORTION

Experiences like Dr. Nathanson's poignantly illustrate what may be the single incontrovertible truth in the entire abortion controversy: discussion and debate, however heartfelt and passionate, are not the same as direct personal experience. One can never be sure how one will decide until actually confronted with abortion. Bringing the question home has a way of testing one's abstract principles. Examples from the 1992 presidential campaign illustrate how even a hypothetical situation, involving a loved one, can moderate strongly professed beliefs. When he was asked during a live interview, "What if your daughter grew up and had a problem, came to you with that problem? How would you deal with it?" arch-conservative and anti-abortion advocate Vice President Dan Quayle replied, "I hope that I never do have to deal with it. But obviously...I would counsel and talk to her and support her on whatever decision she made." Interviewer Larry King pressed the point: "And if the decision was abortion, you'd support her, as a parent?" Quayle replied, "I'd support my daughter."[26] Later George Bush also said that while he would attempt to talk his granddaughter out of an abortion, it would be *her* decision, and if she so chose, he would stand by her.[27]

Even here, individual reactions diverge. For example, both sides in the *Webster* case presented moving personal accounts by women who have had abortions. The individual stories are compelling. It is important to hear from people whose lives have been directly touched by abortion, for such real voices are easily lost in lawyers' arguments in the rarified atmosphere of the Supreme Court or between the shouting and shoving mobs outside an abortion clinic.

On the pro–abortion rights side, Ellen Messer and Kathryn E. May have collected pre-*Roe* accounts in *Backrooms: Voices from the Illegal Abortion Era* (1988). As one might expect, the anecdotes describe hemorrhages, infections, and bloody coat hangers. But they also tell of the emotional wounds women suffered: their feelings of isolation, degradation, fear, desperation, helplessness, and being trapped by a hostile, male-dominated system. One woman tells of her experience as a rape victim for whom the abortion option was unavailable, the rejection and hostility she endured, and the pain of putting her child up for adoption.[28] Other women describe covert meetings in shabby hotel rooms, sleazy abortionists, and always the terrible feeling of aloneness.

One woman relates how, after a saline injection administered in a seedy house by an abortionist who doubled as a bookie, she later aborted alone in her dormitory room and then hemorrhaged "more blood than I ever imagined. I used one of these metal waste baskets...and I remember it being filled up." She continued to bleed almost to death over the next month—"terrified of [obtaining urgently needed medical attention] because I didn't want my parents to find out and I didn't want to be arrested." She concluded:

> I certainly wouldn't want anyone to have to live through the experience that I lived through. There's no need for it. I did make choices: I considered and chose not to choose marriage. I chose not to be an unwed mother. Abortion was the option of last resort, but I chose it because it seemed the only option that would allow me to go on with my life, even at the risk of losing it.[29]

20

Refreshingly, *Backrooms* also includes the story of a young man's experience. He speaks eloquently of how frightening, confusing, and painful it was to be fifteen with a pregnant fourteen-year-old girl friend. His story reveals the especially difficult plight of teens, both male and female, faced with unwanted pregnancy under pre-*Roe* law.

> It really wasn't a joke, even though there really wasn't any responsibility I could bear except for guilt. I mean, what could I do? I couldn't give her money, I couldn't marry her. I couldn't do anything except say goodbye [when she went away to have the baby and put it up for adoption]....
>
> Not that abortion is an easy way out, but it's easier than something that wasn't her choice.... There was no option. No option whatsoever. A fifteen-year-old kid at that time—it was hard enough to know what was going on, much less to try and negotiate the criminal aspect of dealing with something like abortion. How could a fifteen-year-old move into the crime world and make a deal and be assured of her safety?...
>
> [After she went away] I was really grieving—it really was very hard. When she came back, I couldn't handle my feelings, or the situation, and she couldn't either. We had no knowledge, we didn't know what we should feel, or why, or who was lying, which everybody was. Nobody told us—useful information was not available to us, on an emotional basis or a practical basis, there wasn't anything. Even my peers that knew about it, who wanted to be supportive, had no idea either, so they were supportive by saying things like, "Ha ha ha, you got away with it," which, of course, made me want to puke.[30]

In *Webster*, 2,887 women who had had abortions joined a brief arguing that *Roe v. Wade* was "a wise and just" decision, necessary to the safety and well-being of women, and that the abortion/childbirth decision is a profoundly personal one and is therefore better left to an individual woman instead of to legislators. Attached to the brief were selected letters. One woman's letter compared the agony she felt at putting her daughter up for adoption in 1962, when abortion was illegal, with the "great relief" she felt after a "safe, legal abortion" in 1977: *"There is no comparison between the loss of a fetus to an abortion and the loss of my real baby girl to adoption."*[31] Another woman shared a stereotype-defying experience which in some respects is the reverse of Dr. Nathanson's:

> In 1977, I became active in the anti-abortion movement. By 1978 I had been elected [to a national office of a national anti-abortion group]....
>
> In 1980, I found myself pregnant as a result of a forced sexual encounter. All my "pro-life" beliefs flew out the window when I realized that my life was also a "human life," and that I knew I simply *could* not bear a child from such an ugly experience!
>
> I went to a clinic in my city (one which I had even picketed at one time) and I had the abortion there. Strangely I had no misgivings afterward, and no guilt. (I had assumed I'd become suicidal.) I was surprised by how easy it was, both physically and emotionally....
>
> Since my abortion (quite some time later), I became a born-again Christian. Strangely (to *most* people, anyway), I find my faith in Christ strengthens my pro-choice commitment. Jesus Christ tells me as a Christian to "judge not, that ye be not judged" (Matt. 7:1). I think that all who pass judgment on women who have abortions should take His words to heart.[32]

As in *Backrooms,* some of the *Webster* letters describe women's experiences with illegal abortion. They tell of shame, degradation, exploitation (including sexual abuse), fear, isolation, rejection, and serious physical injury. One fifty-eight-year-old grandmother, for example, related her two experiences with illegal abortion in the 1950s. One of the men from whom she sought an abortion subjected her to a painful pelvic examination (during which he sexually molested her), then exposed himself to her and proposed various sexual encounters in exchange for the abortion service. Another man invited her to participate in live sexual performances and pornographic productions as part of the abortion procedure. Her first abortion resulted in a "crippling infection," the second subjected her to a near-fatal injection of antibiotics. In addition to her physical trauma, she also describes her "psychic scars" and the harm to her children that resulted from her ordeal to obtain an abortion.[33]

It takes a heart of brass not to be moved by such acccounts, but in one sense they bring us back to the intractability of the debate. The anti-abortion side points out that the real horror stories belong to the most voiceless and vulnerable victims—the millions upon millions of aborted children. They will never be heard from, for their voices have been forever silenced by abortion. The pro–abortion rights side immediately replies that the same could be said for all the women who died from illegal, substandard abortions.

The anti-abortion side can also point to moving accounts of women's unfortunate experiences with abortion, collected in *Aborted Women, Silent No More* (1987). Some of these stories are excerpted by anti-abortion forces, including Women Exploited by Abortion of Greater Kansas City, who presented their own anecdotes in the *Webster* briefs. These women describe feeling pressured into having an abortion, being inadequately informed and positively misled about the procedure, experiencing psychological scarring, and suffering physical complications (including subsequent infertility).

One woman described her two abortions. The first was as a sixteen-year-old newlywed under pressure from her husband. The second was three years later, after she had been raped at gunpoint while at work. She described how the doctor told her "my only choice...was an abortion," and how he failed to describe the risks. After the abortion "the 'oh-so-rare' physical complications began immediately. I began hemorrhaging and cramping severely and was given an injection to lessen the bleeding...." Ultimately she had an emergency dilation and curretage, which left her with a scarred uterus causing her later pregnancies to be difficult and high risk, and eventually requiring her to have a hysterectomy. Still, her worst scars may be emotional:

> While studying fetal development [in nursing school], I realized that I had been lied to. At eight weeks, those "clusters of cells" had a remarkable resemblance to a baby. They had

hands and feet, a heartbeat and brainwaves, which meant that those babies did indeed feel the pain of their horrible deaths....

Had I been told the truth about the risks that I was taking with my body and about the developing person inside of me, I know that I would not have made the decision to destroy life. There are those people who can deliberately take the life of another person, but that is not my nature. Yet I must live with the truth, because of what I have done.[34]

Another letter is from the parents of a twenty-year-old woman who died from an abortion. She had stopped breathing during a legal abortion performed at a clinic under general anesthesia when she was twenty-one weeks pregnant. Resuscitation efforts failed, and she died some twelve hours later in a hospital. The parents first learned of their daughter's pregnancy and abortion when they were summoned to the hospital's critical-care unit. They reported that the doctors at the hospital "told my husband and me with tears in their eyes, please do not let them get away with this; get something done for they butchered your daughter." The parents concluded, "Young girls as well as women like our daughter are not aware that there are unclean, unsafe clinics that go unnoticed."[35] Another woman described what she witnessed as an owner/operator of several abortion clinics:

I saw women lied to about the development of her "product of conception."

Doctors commonly rushed in the clinic, asking, "How many do we have today"—interested only in how much money they would make that day.

Doctors rush from room to room sometimes bragging about how fast they "could kill a baby." One doctor claimed to be able to do a two to three minute abortion, but missed one of each five. One patient of this particular doctor came in at six weeks for her abortion. She called back some time later to say she felt a "foot in her vagina." Upon arrival, she was examined by a physician who found her to be 20 weeks pregnant, an

24

incomplete abortion, and the baby's foot was extended out of her cervix into her vagina....

I believe I became involved in the abortion industry in an attempt to justify my own abortion. I believed I was "helping women" with the "safe, legal choice" of abortion. What I saw was that women were being injured or died at alarming rates.[36]

Yet another set of stories, only recently uncovered, involves the experiences of women in "bogus abortion clinics." Congressional hearings in 1991 investigated allegations that some anti-abortion groups misleadingly portray themselves as abortion providers, lure pregnant women seeking an abortion into their facility, present false and disturbing information about abortion and its risks, and pressure these distraught women to forgo "murdering their children."

One North Little Rock, Arkansas, woman, trying to raise her seventeen-month-old daughter on $3,500 a year, discovered in December 1990 that she was again pregnant. She decided to seek an abortion. She told the House Subcommittee on Regulation, Business Opportunities, and Energy that she looked for an abortion provider in the Yellow Pages, tried to distinguish abortion from adoption providers, and finally contacted an entity that advertised free pregnancy testing and abortion information. When she arrived at the "clinic," her daughter was kept in a lobby area while she was taken to another room and told "I was about to watch a film on a news report—it was a news reporter type film—and [the "clinic" representative] said that I would enjoy this film....I felt forced to view this film to receive the results of my pregnancy test." The woman testified,

The film showed saline abortions, which is something that I was not there for. The film said that abortions caused women to bleed to death, never have children again, and women have hysterectomies. After I had my abortion at Little Rock Family Planning, I knew that this was not true....

I was very scared, and I was very concerned about myself and my daughter at this time when I realized that I was in the wrong place.

The woman went on to testify that the "counselor" "argued with me pretty much...that I should not have an abortion." She said the counselor "was telling me a lot of stuff that would happen to me if I had an abortion...she was trying to bring me down, trying to make me not have an abortion." According to the testimony, representatives from the "clinic" "called my mom's house," after which the woman felt forced to disclose her abortion to her mother. The testimony concluded:

> I advocate against this business existing, because women like me go into these clinics expecting them to be abortion clinics, and they're not, and [we're] fooled. They step all over your feelings, and I don't want any other woman to have to go through what I had to go through, because it was a horrible experience.[37]

Another woman, a subcommittee investigator, posed as a pregnant woman to investigate allegations that a Virginia facility calling itself the AAA Women for Choice was operating a bogus clinic. The investigator described experiences similar to those of the North Little Rock woman: the offer of a pregnancy test, graphic films of abortions, photographs of bloody fetuses, accusations of the murder of babies. The investigator concluded that, although she (unlike the "clinic's" usual "client") knew what she was in for,

> I was still completely shocked and upset by my experience. A younger woman, less informed and emotionally distraught about the possibility of being pregnant, is even more vulnerable to this manipulation than I was.
>
> By the time a woman realizes what is happening to her, she has usually sat uncomfortably through a counseling session and at least part of an explicit and graphic film. Even if a woman is able to walk out of this clinic, resisting a counselor's pleas, pressure, and in some cases physical restraint, the experience stays with her.[38]

Once again, the other side can reply that any momentary discomfort inflicted on these women is nothing compared with the enormity the "clinics" seek to prevent. If abortion is murder, they might argue, the steps taken by such organizations are not only justified but inadequate. Many such organizations also say they do not misrepresent the nature of their activities.

DIMENSIONS OF THE DEBATE

These stories from both sides bring us to a final introductory observation. Taken simply on its most basic moral terms, abortion presents an apparently irreconcilable dilemma of profound depth. But when one looks at the range of considerations which the courts have weighed in reaching legal conclusions about abortion rights, the problem begins to seem almost as wide as it is deep. As we shall see, the Court in *Roe v. Wade* regarded the constitutional issue from several perspectives: the pregnant woman's privacy or autonomy interest in making her own reproductive decisions; both the woman's and the state's interest in her physical and mental health; and the state's interest in the life (or "potential" life) of the fetus. Much of the original debate about *Roe* focused on the conflict between the first and third interests: the woman's privacy versus fetal life.

Since *Roe* the debate has broadened to include the *woman's* welfare. One striking aspect of the arguments in *Webster* is the volume of material devoted to the impact of abortion on the woman's mental and physical health. Groups calling themselves "feminists" against abortion, recalling the position of some feminists of the previous century, now argue that liberal abortion laws reflect simply one more instance of male domination of and violence against women. These developments have led to the enactment of numerous laws regulating the abortion procedure in the name of protecting maternal health, many of which have been challenged in the courts under *Roe*, as well as to calls for the near-total abolition of abortion.

At least some of these laws are part of the anti-abortion movement's increasingly sophisticated post-*Roe* strategy of "incrementalism." Some anti-abortion activists have concluded that legislators and the public, far from being persuaded by "bloody

27

fetus" tactics, are quite alienated by them. Turning from the "abortion is murder" approach, these activists have advocated a variety of limitations on abortion—such as viability testing, parental notification and consent requirements, bans on public funding, informed-consent laws, facility and second-physician requirements, waiting periods—all of which can add to the cost, delay, and difficulty of the procedure. Although none of these measures in itself will stop abortions, the hope is that collectively they will substantially reduce the number. And if anti-abortion activists succeed in overruling *Roe* and restrict abortion to cases of rape, incest, and real danger to the pregnant woman, very few legal abortions will be performed. Conversely, abortion rights advocates, who for years had relied on the courts to protect abortion rights, have recognized the need for political mobilization that their opponents saw decades ago, and they are working to catch up.

The battle has thus intensified. In the past few years it has been waged in the streets, as Operation Rescue escalated its campaign dramatically in Kansas City and elsewhere and as more than half a million pro-choice demonstrators, most of them women, marched in Washington, D.C., on April 5, 1992. In the political arena abortion was a large issue in the 1992 election campaigns, a number of states enacted laws governing abortion, and advocates pressed Congress to enact the Freedom of Choice Act.

After the Court's decisions in *Webster* and *Casey*, in which the Court preserved some core aspects of *Roe* but substantially enlarged the scope of permissible government regulation, these developments mean that the courts will continue to play a central role in defining the extent of abortion rights. That process will become more and more complex as the abortion debate expands across many fronts.

2. The Demographic and Social Context: Who Has Abortions, When, and Why

. . . .

As the abortion debate becomes more complex, and the central questions remain as controversial as ever, the demographic and sociological aspects of abortion have received greater study. Information about women who have abortions is collected and reported by several organizations, including the United States Centers for Disease Control (CDC), the Alan Guttmacher Institute (AGI), and the National Center for Health Statistics. Until recently, data were obtained from limited information reported to the CDC by state health agencies from approximately forty-five states and the District of Columbia, and by hospitals and other medical facilities for a handful of other areas.[1] The National Center for Health Statistics has also compiled data from certain states; its 1990 report presents data through 1987 on a number of characteristics from up to fourteen reporting states. AGI has significantly expanded the range of available information through its periodic direct surveys of abortion providers, and, through them, of abortion patients. In addition to the ongoing surveillance work by entities such as CDC and AGI, other studies have examined matters such as attitudes toward abortion and the reasons women obtain abortions.

MILLIONS AND MILLIONS OF ABORTIONS

Not surprisingly, the data show that *Roe v. Wade* has dramatically affected the rate of legal abortion in the United States. The number of legal abortions almost doubled on the heels of the Court's 1973 decision in *Roe* and continued to increase for the next seven years. In 1972, when the legality of first- and second-trimester abortions was a function only of state law, 586,800 legal abortions are estimated to have been performed in the United States on women aged 15 to 44 years.[2] In 1975, 1,034,200 legal abortions were performed. The annual number climbed steadily until it peaked at 1,577,300 in 1981, dipped and then peaked again in 1985 at 1,588,600, and then declined to 1,559,100 in 1989.

To control for changes in population size, the frequency of abortion also is reported in terms of the abortion rate (abortions per 1,000 women aged 15 to 44) and the abortion ratio (abortions per 1,000 live births).* In 1972 the abortion rate was 13.2 and the ratio was 184. By 1975 the rate had risen to 21.7 and the ratio had risen to 331. The rate climbed steadily to a high of 29.3 in both 1980 and 1981, and then declined gradually to 27.1 in 1987. The ratio peaked twice, once at 430 in 1981 and again at 436 in 1983, and then declined to 406 in 1987.[3]

As with so much else in the abortion controversy, the significance of these data depends on one's position on the overall issue. To someone who believes abortion is murder, any abortions are intolerable; but an *annual* death rate of 1.5 million is an enormity beyond belief. According to available data, at least some of which has been said to underreport abortions substantially,[4] between 1975 and 1987 a total of 19,016,500 legal abortions were performed in the United States. That total eclipses the Nazi Holocaust (6 million), the casualty rate for World War I (between 8 and 9 million), and the death toll from the Stalinist collectivization (10 million), and it approaches the

---

*The compilation of abortion ratios is lagged by six months to make them comparable with abortion rates.

30

casualty rate for World War II (estimated between 35 and 60 million).[5] To an abortion rights supporter, on the other hand, the data indicate the number of women's lives that have been spared either the risks of illegal abortion or the traumas of unwanted parenthood, and reemphasize the need to leave the choice to the individual woman. Pro-choice advocates also take the rate of abortion as evidence of abortion's compatibility with prevailing moral standards. Regardless of one's position, the numbers plainly demonstrate that abortion is an issue of immense proportions and a widespread practice.

To place the data in perspective, it is worth noting that abortion is a truly global phenomenon. It has been estimated that between 40 and 60 million women each year seek to terminate pregnancy.[6] The United States is by no means the world's leader in the number, rate, or ratio of abortion, but it appears to be among the top ten. According to a 1990 AGI study, "In 1987, an estimated 26 to 31 million legal abortions and 10 to 22 million clandestine abortions were performed worldwide. Legal abortion rates ranged from a high of at least 112 abortions per 1,000 women of reproductive age in the Soviet Union to a low of 5 per 1,000 in the Netherlands." Other statistics indicate that China performed 10,394,500 abortions in 1987 alone. Incomplete statistics indicate that 6,818,000 abortions were performed in the Soviet Union in 1987; and estimates based on surveys and other data show 2,250,000 abortions in Japan in 1975 and 11 million abortions in the Soviet Union in 1982.[7]

Rate and ratio information allow more useful comparisons between countries of different population sizes. Of the 23 countries for which AGI reports data believed to be reliable, seven had higher abortion rates (reported as the number of abortions expected to be had by 1,000 women during their reproductive lifetimes, based on age-specific abortion rates) than the United States (28 in 1985): Bulgaria (64.7 in 1987), China (38.8 in 1987), Cuba (58 in 1988), Czechoslovakia (46.7 in 1987), Hungary (38.2 in 1987), Singapore (30.1 in 1987), and Yugoslavia (70.5 in 1984). Incomplete data show higher rates for Rumania (90.9 in 1983) and the Soviet Union (111.9 in 1987). And estimates show higher rates for Japan (84 in 1975), South Korea (53 in 1984), the Soviet Union (181 in 1982), and Turkey (46 in 1987). Rates for other countries that may be of interest are: England and Wales (14.2 in 1987, counting residents only), Canada (10.2 in 1987), East Germany (26.6 in 1984), West Germany (6.7 in 1987, based on incomplete data), and Australia (16.6 in 1988).[8]*

According to anthropologists, "voluntary abortion is and has been a common practice in a majority of cultural traditions of mankind." For example, one study found more than three hundred separate tribal or cultural groups practicing induced abortion. The same study "found only a single group where induced abortion could confidently be said to be unknown."[9]

Another perspective on the prevalence of abortion in the United States examines the percentage of American women who experience unintended pregnancy, unintended births, and abortion in their lifetimes. One AGI study estimates that 46 percent of American women aged 15 to 44 have had at least one unintended pregnancy. AGI estimates that 25 percent of women have had an unintended birth and 21 percent of women of reproductive age have had an abortion. These estimates, however, are based on historical data that include women who came into reproductive age when neither contraception nor abortion were as available as they are today. Adjusting for those factors, AGI estimates that if current abortion rates continue,

> *nearly half of U.S. women can be expected to undergo an abortion at least once during their lives.* Furthermore, if the lifetime rate of unintended pregnancy remains at the 65 percent level estimated for women aged 40–44 in 1982, then the current abor-

---

*The same AGI study reports abortion ratios per 1,000 known pregnancies (legal abortions plus live births, unlagged because birth data was generally unavailable). Complete statistics indicate eight countries with ratios higher than the United States (297 in 1985): Bulgaria (507 in 1987), China (314 in 1987), Cuba (453 in 1988), Czechoslovakia (422 in 1987), East Germany (297 in 1984), Hungary (402 in 1987), Singapore (327 in 1987), and Yugoslavia (488 in 1984). Incomplete statistics show the Soviet Union (549 in 1987) and Rumania (567 in 1983) at the top of the list; and estimates place Japan (550 in 1974), South Korea (430 in 1984) and the Soviet Union (680 in 1982) in the lead.

tion rates imply that about *70 percent of women who experience an unintended pregnancy will have at least one abortion.*[10]

Once again, both sides in the debate can base competing arguments on these estimates; the difference is largely a function of one's premises. Pro–abortion rights advocates can point out that it is difficult to invoke prevailing community norms to deny a choice that so many women apparently conclude is best for them. They might further contend that, in view of such frequency, any conception of personal autonomy that takes serious account of women's interests must protect the abortion choice. Anti-abortion advocates might reply that those estimates only show both the extent to which liberalized abortion has corrupted morality and the urgent need for limitations on abortion.

THE TIMING OF ABORTIONS

Another focal point in the abortion debate—particularly under the Court's approach in *Roe v. Wade*—is the timing of the abortion procedure. Two items stand out. First, the overwhelming majority of abortions are performed early in pregnancy. Second, the trend since 1973 has been toward a larger share of abortions being performed earlier in pregnancy. In 1973, 85.4 percent of abortions were performed in the first twelve weeks of pregnancy, or the first "trimester." Since 1980 the number has been at 90 percent or higher. More than 77 percent of abortions since 1980 were performed within the first ten weeks, and more than 50 percent were performed at less than nine weeks' gestation.[11] The National Center for Health Statistics reports a similar pattern from a thirteen-state reporting area for 1987. Almost nine of ten abortions occurred in the first trimester, approximately 49 percent were for pregnancies of eight weeks' gestation or less, and 41 percent were in the nine- to twelve-week range.[12]

The data on gestational age are relevant to several issues. First, they temper the relevance—though perhaps not the impact—of those anti-abortion "bloody fetus" images that rely on late-term abortions. Second, gestational age is a crucial factor in the health risks which abortion poses to women; those risks increase dramatically the later in pregnancy that abortion is per-formed. Third, and related to the second point, is the impact of delay-producing regulatory provisions, such as waiting periods and notification or consent requirements involving parents or spouses. That impact provides fuel for pro–abortion rights argu-ments in the name of women's welfare.

CHARACTERISTICS OF AMERICAN ABORTION PATIENTS

Arguments for or against abortion rights also rely on assump-tions about the characteristics of women who seek abortions, such as their age, race, socioeconomic circumstances, and prior contraceptive use. For example, abortion is sometimes character-ized as the last resort of the irresponsible, as an illegitimate sub-stitute for contraception, or as a flight from real-life obligations of family. To develop a more informed picture, a 1988 AGI study surveyed a nationally representative sample of abortion patients at 103 facilities (21 hospitals and 82 nonhospital facilities), gath-ering data on age, race, ethnicity, and Medicaid status for 10,289 women and additional information on 9,480 of them. The sur-vey describes the typical 1987 abortion patient as aged 20 to 24 (33.1 percent of all abortion patients, with a total of 55.4 per-cent of abortion patients aged 20 to 29), never married (63.3 percent), white (68.6 percent), childless (52.4 percent had zero live births), no particular income level (roughly 33 percent for each of three income levels), and no prior induced abortions (57.1 percent). Most women who have abortions (69.7 percent) report an intention to have children.[13]

The profile changes substantially when each subgroup is indexed to account for its proportion of the overall population (a process that closely approximates abortion rates). A high index for a given subgroup means that members of that group are much more likely than other women to have an abortion. The highest rates are among young, nonwhite, Catholic, sepa-rated, lower-income, working women. This adjustment produced a strong effect for age, with the index being highest for women

34

18 to 19 years of age and then declining precipitously after age 24.

Indexing also yielded a marked difference for ethnicity. Although most abortion patients have always been white, the percentage of abortion patients who are not white far exceeds the proportion of all nonwhite women of reproductive age. For example, the AGI index shows the highest abortion rate for 1987 was among nonwhites, next highest among Hispanics, and lowest among whites. Other data show that the abortion ratio for nonwhites also has greatly exceeded that of whites since 1973 (252 nonwhite to 178 white in 1973, 392 to 274 in 1980, 397 to 265 in 1985, and 393 to 252 in 1987).[14] The National Center for Health Statistics' report from fourteen states showed that the abortion rate for black women in 1987 was 2.25 times that for white women, and that "for almost every age group, ratios for black women were higher than for white women."[15]

AGI's data for 1987 on religious affiliation are different from what stereotypes might suggest. Indexing showed that Catholics are at least 30 to 38 percent more likely than Protestants to have abortions (even standardizing for ethnic and age differences). Further, women who describe themselves as Born again/Evangelical do indeed have abortions (15.8 percent of abortion patients in the sample aged 18 to 44 described themselves as Born again/Evangelical), but at a lower rate. A large percentage of all abortion patients (22 percent) report no religious affiliation, and 1.4 percent are Jewish.[16]

Although never-married women are the largest percentage of the marital-status characteristic, indexing showed that women who are separated have the highest abortion rates. When standardized for age, separated women still had the highest abortion rate. Further, "Widows and separated, divorced and never-married sexually active women had abortions at 4-5 times the rate of married women living with their husbands." And "cohabiting women had the highest abortion index of any group examined...almost five times the overall abortion rate, and nine times that of currently married women."[17]

The abortion rate was highest among working, low-income women. Although employment patterns roughly tracked population figures, the percentage of lower-income and Medicaid-covered women having abortions is much larger than their proportion among all women of childbearing age. Most women who have abortions are employed (68.1 percent), and the abortion rate for employed women exceeded that for unemployed women even when standardized for age. The abortion rate for women in school also was substantially higher than the rate for women not in school. Women whose income is less than $11,000 had a much higher abortion index than higher-income groups. A similar pattern appears for women covered by Medicaid. AGI notes, "Women covered by Medicaid have a number of characteristics that may contribute to their relatively high abortion index. For example, they are disproportionately nonwhite, unmarried and poor, all characteristics associated with high abortion rates."[18]

Subgroup differences also emerge on the question of the timing of abortions. According to the National Center for Health Statistics, younger women tend to have abortions later in pregnancy than older women: "For women under 20 years of age, the median gestational period was 9.8 weeks, almost 1 week longer than the 8.9-week period for women aged 20 years and over." Further, "black women at every age had longer gestational periods prior to induced termination than white women."[19] Delayed abortion also correlated with lower educational attainment, although the difference was less dramatic when standardized for age.

The 1988 AGI study also examined prior contraceptive use among women who have abortions. The absence of national data on contraceptive use by women who have abortions, noted by AGI, is striking. Given the frequency of sweeping arguments about sexual responsibility in the abortion debate, this gap is surprising. It is unlikely that protection of women's privacy precludes information gathering, for data can be collected from voluntary representative samples, as was done in the AGI study. In any event, AGI's observation counsels the need for skepticism about arguments that rest on unsupported assumptions.

AGI found that many of the surveyed abortion patients had indeed tried to prevent pregnancy. In fact, 91 percent had used some method of contraception at one time; and 70 percent "either had used a method during the month in which they became pregnant or had discontinued use within three months of conception." AGI suggested that for many women, unwanted pregnancy results more from improper or inconsistent use than an unwillingness to practice contraception. Even pregnancy occurring soon after discontinuation of contraceptives may be more a case of extreme misuse than real nonuse—especially for women "caught" during a hiatus from the pill, given the popular but erroneous belief that the pill's reliability persists for several months after discontinuation. The study found "little evidence that women rely on abortion as their main method of avoiding unintended pregnancy...." AGI also found that abortion patients who were in school or employed were more likely to have been using contraception during the month they became pregnant. By contrast, "Nonuse is greatest among abortion patients who are young, poor, black, Hispanic or less educated."[20]

WOMEN'S REASONS FOR ABORTION

Another AGI study attempted to shed light on the reasons why women choose abortion, and the reasons why some women delay having the procedure. The study examined data from 1,900 abortion patients.[21] Several results stand out. First, for most women the decision to have an abortion is a complex one that rests on more than one factor. Many women cited three to five reasons, and some listed up to nine reasons. Among even the small percentage of women whose pregnancy resulted from rape or incest, 95 percent reported at least one additional reason for the decision to abort.

Six factors were mentioned most frequently: concern about how having a baby would change the woman's life (76 percent gave this as a reason), inability to afford a child right now (68 percent), problems in the relationship or not wanting to be a single parent (51 percent), not ready for the responsibility of parenthood (31 percent), not wanting others to know that the woman was pregnant or sexually active (31 percent), and not being mature or

37

old enough for a child (30 percent of the sample, but most common among the youngest patients). One-quarter of the women said they had all the children they wanted or had grown-up children, and 23 percent gave as a reason the husband's or partner's wish that she have an abortion.

When asked to rank the reasons in order of importance to their ultimate decision, the women in the sample most frequently cited not being able to afford a child and not being ready (equally so). When asked for more detail about their reasons, most of the women who expressed concern about how the child would affect their lives (67 percent of the subgroup, or about half the women in the survey) explained that having a child would interfere with their job or career. Half the women in this subgroup said that a child would interfere with school; 28 percent reported that a child would interfere with the woman's obligations to others who depended on her for care. The study also found, to the authors' surprise, that race and poverty were not significantly related to any of the reasons.

The survey also tried to determine the reasons for delay by women who had abortions later than sixteen weeks' gestation. The most common reason (71 percent) was the passage of time before the woman realized she was pregnant. Almost half the women having later abortions cited difficulty in making arrangements for the abortion, and 45 percent had first tried to obtain an abortion from another provider. Fear of telling a partner or parent was also a significant cause of delay (one-third of all women in the subgroup and 63 percent of the minors). Among the women who cited difficulty in making arrangements as a cause of delay, 60 percent reported that it took time to raise money to pay for the procedure; one-third had first contacted providers who did not provide abortion services; one-quarter did not have a provider nearby; and 20 percent said they did not know where to obtain an abortion.

DISCORD BETWEEN REAL-LIFE REASONS AND PUBLIC PERCEPTIONS

When compared with opinion polls, the AGI survey reveals a dramatic incongruence between the reasons women give for choosing abortion and the reasons that society seems willing to approve. When asked in a poll whether they approved of abortion in certain circumstances, most people disapproved the kinds of reasons frequently given by the women who had abortions. Polls have consistently indicated that while only a small and declining percentage of Americans believes that abortion should always be illegal, many think abortion should be legal only in certain circumstances. Men are slightly more liberal in their attitudes. For example, a 1990 Gallup poll showed that 31 percent of respondents thought abortion should be legal under any circumstances, 53 percent thought abortion should be legal only under certain circumstances, and 12 percent thought abortion should be illegal under all circumstances.[22]* Earlier polls are less tolerant—1988: 24 percent, 57 percent, and 17 percent;[23] 1981: 23 percent, 52 percent, and 21 percent; 1980: 25 percent, 53 percent, and 18 percent, respectively. Exit polls from the 1992 elections show that 34 percent believe abortion should always be legal, 39 percent believe it should be mostly legal, 23 percent believe it should be mostly illegal, and only 9 percent believe it should always be illegal.[24]

The 1988 poll asked the 57 percent subsample who thought that abortion should be legal only in certain circumstances whether they approved of abortion in specified circumstances. The replies indicate the degree of divergence between attitudes about abortion and actual conduct. Respondents overwhelmingly approved of abortion when the woman's life is endangered

---

*Because the question does not specify the circumstances, it is unclear whether gestation is to be considered a circumstance. In other words, one cannot tell whether the respondents would have given a different answer for very early versus very late abortions. The numbers here do not add up to 100 because I have omitted the "no opinion" response. A 1989 poll phrased the question somewhat differently, asking whether abortion should be legal as it is now; legal only in cases such as rape, incest, or to save the life of the mother; or not permitted at all. The answers were more liberal: 50 percent, 39 percent, and 7 percent, respectively.

(94 percent), her physical health seriously threatened (84 percent), or when the pregnancy is the result of rape or incest (89 percent).[25]* Yet those circumstances account for only a very small percentage of abortions; and, as the AGI survey demonstrates, even those few abortion patients almost always have additional reasons for aborting. A smaller majority of respondents endorsed abortion when there is any chance that the baby would be born deformed (60 percent). But a large majority—79 percent—*disapproved* of abortion for the reason that the family could not afford to have the child. More women disapproved of that reason than men, 80 percent to 69 percent. Yet inability to afford the child is a reason for abortion given by 68 percent of the women in the AGI study, and it is one of the reasons identified most frequently as the most important for women having abortions.

ABORTION IS ABOUT PEOPLE AS WELL AS ARGUMENTS

Again, either side in the debate can find ammunition in these data. Because the data show that most women's reasons for abortion are disapproved by a substantial portion of the public, anti-abortion forces can argue that most women having abortions, and the Supreme Court, are defying prevailing morality. Abortion rights advocates argue that the AGI survey results show the highly personal and individual nature of the abortion decision, how intertwined it is with every other aspect of the woman's life, and therefore that only the woman herself can make the appropriate choice. They further contend that anyone who speaks of the abortion decision as though it were made casually, or, as Justice Byron White implied in his *Roe v. Wade* dissent, on a "whim," could not be more wrong.

While there is force to both positions, the most certain con-

---

*The public as a whole has consistently approved of legal abortion in the case of rape. According to data provided by the National Opinion Research Center, approval ratings ranged from 75 and 83 percent between 1972 and 1985. One would expect these percentages to be somewhat smaller than those cited for the 1988 subsample because that subgroup had been preselected as indicating some approval of abortion.

clusion is that one's attitude about abortion, however strongly felt, must remain hypothetical until one must confront the decision. Abortion is an exceptionally serious decision for most women, arrived at after weighing numerous important considerations—many of which involve balancing a variety of responsibilities. The evidence suggests that people should be careful in judging a decision they have not personally faced.

These data illustrate the highly contextual nature of the abortion decision. Women having abortions—like women having children—are not faceless, anonymous figures who emerge silently from the shadows to have their abortions and then disappear. They are real people faced with real-life choices, and the available information shows that those choices are complex. Most of these women had been trying, albeit unsuccessfully, to avoid pregnancy. The women most likely to have abortions appear to have lives that are not easy, quite apart from an unwanted pregnancy. Rates are highest among minority women facing low-income jobs, poverty (evidenced by Medicaid status), and separation. Rates also are high among the young, for whom unwanted pregnancy imposes special burdens. And it appears that these women (young, minority, and poor) are at greater risk when they have abortions, for they tend to delay longer in pregnancy.[26]

In the tumult of the abortion debate it is easy to lose sight of these people. Their circumstances demonstrate the need to parse the issues carefully. For example, the information above helps to understand the nature of the pregnant woman's interest in making her own decision. Pro–abortion rights advocates contend that this decision is best left to the woman herself. After all, she must live within her circumstances. Anti-abortion advocates argue in response that none of those circumstances justifies the taking of fetal life. However one resolves this difficult conflict, it is essential not to ignore the considerations that give either side its significance. The phrase "abortion on demand," for example, is particularly unilluminating in view of the many factors that go into the decision. Just as pro–abortion rights advocates must not be allowed to disregard the silent but no less real presence of the fetus, the pregnant woman must not be rendered invisible by unacknowledged or uninformed assumptions about her circumstances.

Individual circumstances become more important as a combination of forces makes access to abortion services more difficult. The number of abortion providers in the United States has decreased, and they are not as evenly distributed geographically. AGI estimates that between 1982 and 1985 the number of providers declined by 5 percent.[27] By several measures, access to abortion services has become more difficult for many women living outside metropolitan areas. For example, 82 percent of American counties have no identified provider (up from 78 percent in 1982); yet 30 percent of women of childbearing age live in those counties. In 92 percent of the U.S. counties, where 43 percent of women live, there are no providers who perform more than four hundred abortions a year (providers who are much more likely to provide services on request as opposed only to a physician's established patients or only in limited circumstances). AGI also found that 79 percent of all nonmetropolitan women live in counties with no providers at all. Because "there is abundant evidence that the local availability of abortion services has an important effect on the utilization rate," the large disparity in abortion rates among states is added evidence of significantly unequal access to abortion services.[28] Many women in states that have only a handful of abortion providers for the entire population face substantial obstacles in obtaining access to abortion services.

Other factors also limit access. One is the shrinking number of hospitals that perform abortions and the limited number of all providers who perform late-term abortions. This factor is especially relevant to younger women, who more often seek late-term abortions. The cost of abortion services obviously is an important factor, particularly for the poor. The average cost in 1986 for a nonhospital abortion with local anesthetic was $213.[29] Now the average cost for a first-trimester abortion is $251.[30] In

the second trimester, as gestation progresses and risk of complication rises, the cost increases from almost $400 to more than
$1000. These prices include only the average cost of the proce-
dure itself and not ancillary costs, such as repeat visits to the
physician or transportation. For women in states with a poorly
developed transportation system, transportation costs are not
negligible, especially when laws or circumstances demand repeat
visits. Given the Supreme Court's current trend toward permit-
ting a variety of cost-increasing restrictions on abortion, it seems
likely that costs will continue to increase. And simple principles
of supply and demand dictate that declining numbers of
providers will cause prices to rise. One reason for delay in
obtaining abortions has been raising enough money: "women
who obtain abortions usually must pay for them with cash in
advance...."[31] Federal Medicaid funding for abortion has not
been available since enactment of the Hyde Amendment in
1977, and only a small number of states provide any state funds.

Regardless of whether the Supreme Court ever overrules *Roe
v. Wade*, access to abortion services probably will continue to
contract, especially for indigent women. The number of
providers will almost certainly continue to decrease. The number
of medical school obstetrics/gynecology programs that provide
training in first-trimester abortions has declined from nearly 25
percent in 1985 to 12 percent today. And only 7 percent offer
such training for second-trimester abortions.[32]

Harassment of abortion providers also is restricting accessibil-
ity. Although polls indicate that most people oppose such tactics, anti-abortion harassment is widespread in the United
States.[33] Harassment became more prevalent after candidates
attempted to exploit the abortion issue in the 1982 elections. It
has received some encouragement from Presidents Reagan and
Bush. In 1986 President Reagan promised to pardon such
demonstrators, a promise he ultimately did not keep.[34] And the
Bush administration took the position that harassment campaigns such as Operation Rescue do not interfere with federal
civil rights. The Supreme Court's 1993 ruling in *Bray v. Alexandria Women's Health Clinic*, agreeing with that position, will

probably stimulate an increase in harassment activity nationally.

Harassment campaigns frequently target stand-alone clinics, where most abortions are performed. Harassment ranges from peaceful picketing to blockades to firebombing and death threats.[35] Operation Rescue, in particular, has been active in campaigns in a number of cities, including Atlanta, New York, Buffalo, Wichita, and Baton Rouge. It seeks to overwhelm municipal law enforcement resources by making thousands of its demonstrators subject to arrest. Its campaigns have imposed substantial costs on target communities. The *Georgia State Bar Journal* describes Operation Rescue's tactics during the "Siege of Atlanta" in the summer of 1988:

> Demonstrators arrived en masse, swarming onto the private property of the clinics, sometimes invading the clinic by deception or force. Then, locking arms, sitting down, crawling and sprawling, they refused to move or allow any person access into or out of the clinics for hours at a time. Meanwhile, hundreds of demonstrators unwilling to risk arrest marched, chanted, screamed, and prayed for the television cameras amidst gory pictures, plastic fetuses, and graphic placards.[36]

Dr. William Harrison is the only remaining abortion provider in northwest Arkansas. His Fayetteville Women's Clinic, which offers a general OB/GYN practice that includes abortions, has been twice vandalized and once firebombed. Protesters have congregated in front of his clinic and screamed at his patients. He has suffered numerous threats against his life, several in person and apparently serious. According to Dr. Harrison, who personally has delivered more than six thousand babies, the firebombing was done by a fourteen-year-old boy who, after being shown the film "Silent Scream" and being told that babies were being killed in the clinic, placed an incendiary device in the clinic's basement window.

Dr. Harrison notes that before the harassment began in earnest in Fayetteville, thirteen physicians openly provided abortion services in northwest Arkansas. As a result of harassment, Dr.

Harrison has lost two partners (neither of whom performed abortions) and two employees. Although well respected in the local medical community, he remains unable to attract a partner because of the threat of harassment. His casualty insurance was canceled after the second vandalism attack, and he was unable to obtain replacement coverage for four years; his premium now has increased sixfold.

Dr. Harrison belongs to the dwindling pre-*Roe* generation of physicians who remember the harm inflicted on women by illegal abortion. His willingness to endure the disruption, discomfort, abuse, and danger of extended harassment derives from his commitment to the welfare of his current patients and his memory of the harm suffered by his past patients. He has concluded that speaking out publicly on the abortion issue is the best antidote to harassment, and his willingness to do so—along with community opposition to harassment and vigorous enforcement of criminal trespass laws—has played a large role in the decline of anti-abortion harassment in Fayetteville.

But an entire generation of physicians has now entered the profession without Dr. Harrison's perspective. They certainly did not make enormous sacrifices for medical training so they could expose themselves to death threats, hate campaigns, and firebombs. In the short run the easiest course for physicians must seem to be to insulate themselves from the entire controversy: not to perform abortions openly, and to keep quiet about the issue generally.

How effective these harassment campaigns are depends on what standards one uses to judge them—which depends, of course, on one's perspective. While these campaigns have been largely unsuccessful in closing clinics, it seems likely that both abortion and nonabortion patients are scared away or delayed. And such tactics surely cause health-care providers to think twice before entering the field. For example, Operation Rescue's extended "Summer of Mercy" campaign in Wichita, Kansas, failed to close any clinics; but it focused wide media attention on its cause and is estimated to have stopped at least twenty-nine abortions.[37] Its leaders count the campaign a success for having prevented that many "murders." More recently Operation Rescue has encountered growing police, municipal, and abortion rights opposition and dwindling public support. Its Buffalo campaign was labeled "Operation Fizzle" by *Time* magazine, and its Baton Rouge campaign was defeated largely by a tall chain-link fence erected around the target clinic.[38]

For a picture of harassment activity nationally, AGI surveyed providers in 1986, receiving responses from 722 hospitals and 927 nonhospital facilities. AGI reports that, in addition to being the target of picketing,

> almost half (42–48 percent) [of respondents] reported such activities as distribution of antiabortion literature inside the facility, bomb threats, physical contact with or blocking of patients by picketers, numerous no-show appointments made to disrupt the scheduling of legitimate patients and demonstrations loud enough to be heard inside the facility. Twenty-nine percent of facilities were invaded by demonstrators in 1985, and almost as many were vandalized. More than 20 percent of facilities had their telephone lines jammed.... Nineteen percent of the providers said their staff members had received death threats, and 16 percent reported that the homes of staff members had been picketed. Sixteen percent of the providers reported that patients had been harassed with phone calls or visits at home....[39]

According to the National Abortion Federation:

> Between 1977 and 1990, 829 acts of antiabortion violence were reported to NAF: 34 clinics were bombed, 52 clinics were the targets of arson, and 43 more clinics were the targets of attempted bombings or arson. In the first three months of 1991, two more clinics were firebombed and two others had been destroyed or damaged by arson.... In addition, there were 266 clinic invasions, 269 incidents of vandalism, 64 assaults and batteries, 77 death threats, 2 kidnappings and 22 burglaries.... While the total cost of this reign of terror is difficult to determine, it is estimated that antiabortion violence has resulted in $7.6 million in direct damages. This figure

does not even include the number of facilities that have been totally destroyed by antiabortion violence.

The NAF also states that since 1987 harassment has increasingly concentrated on the clinic blockade tactics of Operation Rescue and the Lambs of Christ.[40]

Much of this harassment obviously constitutes both civil and criminal wrongdoing. The question of whether abortion patients can claim the protection of federal civil rights laws is considered later. Here it is enough to see that such widespread and sustained harassment and intimidation is sure to drive away patients and providers alike. AGI concludes that "the effects of such harassment on women who are already undergoing a stressful experience can only be adverse. Since most of the health-care providers we surveyed also offer services other than abortion, patients seeking other types of care may encounter harassment as well."[41] An additional impact is increased costs for abortion providers, especially for security and legal services.

Harassment may combine with the distribution problem to limit access for more women than the numbers might first suggest. In the face of 1.5 million abortions a year, and thousands of providers, the destruction of a few clinics might seem small progress for abortion opponents. But in states that have only a few providers, the closing of even one clinic or the chasing out of one provider can have a devastating impact on access to abortion for the women who happen to live there.

Another problem encountered by abortion providers is cancellation of insurance or difficulty with local officials, including denial of necessary permits.[42] Approximately 32 percent of the providers in the AGI study were notified that their malpractice insurance was being canceled or not renewed; 22 percent faced a similar problem with their fire and casualty insurance. "Twenty-six percent said they had been asked to meet newly interpreted licensing requirements...."[43]

SUMMING UP: POWER, PRINCIPLE, AND ARBITRARY OUTCOMES

The access problem supports the contention that the abortion debate in America is more about power than principle. It is difficult for many people to discern a coherent principle when groups that call themselves "pro-life" resort to death threats and bomb attacks. More generally, the preservation of some measure of abortion rights does not mean that abortion is universally or even selectively available under any recognizable principle. While *Roe v. Wade* has greatly increased access to legal abortion, such access is haphazard. The availability of abortion in America is thus very much a practical as well as a legal problem, and it has been affected by the nature of the debate.

These practical problems—such as the shrinking numbers and uneven geographic distribution of providers, the absence of public funding for abortions, and harassment campaigns—combine to inject considerable chance and arbitrariness into the determination of which women succeed in obtaining abortions. Who is able to obtain services comes to turn less and less on principles—an individual woman's needs and claim to autonomy versus the morality of her abortion decision and claims to fetal life—and more and more on factors largely irrelevant to these issues, such as where she happens to live, how much money she happens to have, how her physician feels about abortion, how sophisticated she is, and whether her clinic (if she can find one) happens to be on the demonstrators' "hit list" that day. Moreover, even delaying rather than denying access to abortion creates the greater medical, legal, and ethical difficulties of late-term abortions—which both sides of the debate have an interest in avoiding.

3. The Medical Context

. . . .

Although the legal, philosophical, and religious aspects of abortion have dominated the debate in the United States in recent years, pregnancy and abortion are obviously health-care issues as well. The medical profession has been at the forefront of both the nineteenth-century rise of abortion regulation and twentieth-century pre-*Roe* abortion reform in this country. It is hardly surprising that the medical community, like every other sector of the population, is divided over the ethical questions raised by abortion. What is striking, however, is how matters of relatively objective medical judgment have become enmeshed in the polarized, adversarial atmosphere of the abortion controversy.

Anti-abortion forces' strategy of "incrementalism," which advocates restrictions and requirements that can add to the cost, delay, and difficulty of the abortion procedure, relies in part on arguments about the health impact of abortion. It challenges assumptions about the relative risks to women's health of abortion and childbirth. The Court's reasoning in *Roe v. Wade* rested in part on these risk assessments, and abortion rights advocates continue to rely on them.

A key medical issue in the abortion controversy concerns fetal development and viability. One aspect of this issue is the determination of when "life" begins, and the relationship between the fetus and the pregnant woman. More concretely, the determination of when the fetus is capable of survival outside the uterus—viability—has profound legal as well as medical consequences. The Supreme Court continues to regard viability as a legal milestone after which the state may prohibit abortion except to save the life or health of the pregnant woman.

49

Just as the circumstances of women who actually have abortions are easily overlooked in the dispute, a clear picture of the other subject of the procedure also is often missing from the debate. Abortion rights advocates like to focus attention outside the uterus while anti-abortion forces prefer to exaggerate developments inside (typically by misleading descriptions of the stages of fetal development). An informed view of the abortion issue must include a basic understanding of the products and processes of pregnancy. Most of the information here is drawn from *Williams Obstetrics*, the standard obstetrical text.[1]

Because fetal development is described in terms of gestational age, it is first necessary to define how that age is measured. One method estimates age from the first day of the last normal menstrual period (LMP), which precedes ovulation and fertilization by about two weeks and implantation by about three weeks. Obstetricians typically use LMP as the reference point for gestational age because it is much more certain. This is the sense in which gestational age is used in this book, unless otherwise indicated. The other method, used by embryologists, dates gestation from ovulation or conception ("ovulation age" or "fertilization age").

The medical term for all products of conception, including the fetus and the placenta, is the conceptus. Development of the conceptus begins in the fallopian tube with fertilization of the ovum by a spermatozoan within minutes (and no more than a few hours) after ovulation, producing the zygote cell. For the next three days or so, the zygote undergoes mitotic cleavage (the nucleus divides) into daughter cells called blastomeres. This process produces a solid cluster of sixteen or so blastomeres called the morula, which enters the uterine cavity about three days after fertilization.

The morula cells then undergo further cleavage; fluid begins to accumulate around them; and cell differentiation can be detected. The product of this process is called the blastocyst. Its inner cell mass will become the embryo, and its outer cells will become the trophoblasts, which allow implantation (nidation) and contribute to the formation of the placenta and the amnionic and chorionic structures (the inner and outer membranes surrounding the embryo). *Williams* describes a presumably normal blastocyst found free in the uterine cavity five days after conception that consisted of eight embryo-forming cells surrounded by ninety-nine trophoblastic cells. The blastocyst measured 0.153 x 0.155 millimeters, which is roughly the size of the two-celled zygote produced by the first cleavage—about the size of the period at the end of this sentence. In other words, the blastocyst does not become bigger than the two-cell zygote, just more complex.

The next stage in conceptus development (approximately six days after fertilization) is implantation in the mucous membrane lining the uterine wall, called the endometrium. Eroding the surface, the blastocyst completely buries itself in the endometrium. According to *Williams*, "At the time of blastocyst implantation, the invading conceptus is very analogous to a locally invasive tumor, but a very unusual one...."[2] The trophoblasts on the innermost side of the blastocyst replicate to form one pole that ultimately will become the placenta. The trophoblasts of the other pole grow out toward the uterine cavity and eventually form the smooth chorion, or membrane that encloses the fetus.

Over the next week or so the yolk sac develops, primitive structures begin to form that ultimately will become the umbilical cord and placenta, the chorionic and amnionic structures form, and the embryonic cells begin to proliferate and differentiate into three germ layers which ultimately will produce the skin, various organs (heart, kidney, brain, etc.), and bodily systems (nervous, skeletal, muscular, vascular, etc.) of the fetus. The embryonic cells thicken at the embryonic disc, which is at the midpoint of the embryonic axis called the primitive streak. The formation of the embryonic disc marks the transition to the embryonic stage, at about three weeks after fertilization or five weeks LMP.

The embryonic period lasts until approximately the seventh

week after fertilization. Cells proliferate rapidly, spreading out from the primitive streak as the development of the embryonic structures proceeds first from the head (cephalic) to the tail (caudal) ends of the embryo. Neural folds arise and enclose a groove to form a tube, and the underlying germ layer begins to organize itself into the structures (called somites) that eventually will become connective tissue, muscles, and skin. The embryo's cardiovascular system is formed by the fourth week after fertilization, and true circulation begins. *Williams* describes the embryo at the fourth, sixth, and seventh weeks after fertilization:

> By the end of the 4th week after ovulation [six weeks' gestational age], the chorionic sac measures 2 to 3 cm in diameter, and the embryo about 4 to 5 mm in length. The heart and pericardium [the sac that surrounds it] are very prominent because of the dilation of the chambers of the heart. Arm and leg buds are present, and the amnion is beginning to ensheath the body stalk, which thereafter becomes the umbilical cord.
>
> At the end of the 6th week after fertilization, or about 8 weeks after the onset of the last menstrual period, the embryo is 22 to 24 mm in length, and the head is quite large compared with the trunk. Fingers and toes are present, and the external ears form definitive elevations on either side of the head....
>
> By the 7th week after fertilization, the neck can be recognized, the tail filament has disappeared, and the embryo can be identified as human.[3]

The fetal period begins in the eighth week after fertilization, or the tenth week gestational age. Remember that most legal abortions (at least 77 percent since 1980) in the United States are performed by this time (ten weeks' gestational age). Thus most abortions technically are not abortions of fetuses but rather of embryos in the last stages of embryonic development. As *Williams* notes, however, the boundary between the embryonic and fetal stages is somewhat arbitrarily drawn at eight weeks' ovulation age.

By the beginning of the fetal period most major structures are formed, and the process largely becomes one of achieving func-

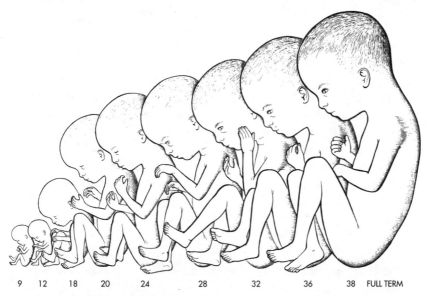

| 9 | 12 | 18 | 20 | 24 | 28 | 32 | 36 | 38 | FULL TERM |

The Fetal Period. The embryonic period ends at the close of the eighth week, by which time the beginnings of all essential structures are present. The fetal period—from the ninth week until birth—is characterized by the growth and elaboration of structures. These drawings are about one-quarter actual size.

Criteria for Estimating Fertilization Age During the Fetal Period

Age (weeks)	CR Length (mm)*	Foot Length (mm)*	Fetal Weight (gm)	Main External Characteristics
Previable Fetuses				
9	50	7	8	*Eyes closing or closed.* Head more rounded. External genitalia still not distinguishable as male or female. Intestines in the umbilical cord.
10	61	9	14	*Intestines in the abdomen.* Early fingernail development.
12	87	14	45	*Sex distinguishable externally.* Well-defined neck.
14	120	20	110	*Head erect.* Lower limbs well developed. Early toenail development.
16	140	27	200	*External ears stand out* from head.
18	160	33	320	*Vernix caseosa present.* Early toenail development.
20	190	39	460	*Head and body hair (lanugo) visible.*
Viable Fetuses†				
22	210	45	630	*Skin wrinkled* and red.
24	230	50	820	*Fingernails present.* Lean body.
26	250	55	1000	*Eyes partially open.* Eyelashes present.
28	270	59	1300	*Eyes open.* Good head of hair often present. Skin slightly wrinkled.
30	280	63	1700	*Toenails present.* Body filling out. Testes descending.
32	300	68	2100	*Fingernails reach finger tips.* Skin pink and smooth.
36	340	79	2900	*Body usually plump.* Lanugo hairs almost absent. Toenails reach toe tips. Flexed limbs; firm grasp.
38	360	83	3400	*Prominent chest;* breasts protrude. Testes in scrotum or palpable in inguinal canals. Fingernails extend beyond finger tips.

*Crown-rump and foot measurements are averages and so may not apply to specific cases; dimensional variations increase with age.

†There is no sharp limit of development, age, or weight at which a fetus automatically becomes viable or beyond which survival is assured, but experience has shown that it is rare for a baby to survive whose weight is less than 500 gm or whose fertilization age is less than 22 weeks.

tional milestones. By the eighth week gestational age, development has progressed to allow flexion of the neck and trunk. By ten weeks the fetus may respond to local stimuli by squinting, opening the mouth, incompletely closing the fingers, and flexing the toes. At eleven weeks the eyes are closing or closed and the intestines are in the umbilicus (but can undergo peristalsis, or waves of involuntary contraction). At twelve weeks, the end of the first trimester, the intestines are in the abdomen, fetal bone structures begin to solidify, digits differentiate and develop nails, and some hair appears. "A fetus delivered at this time may make spontaneous movements if still within the amnionic sac or if immersed in warm saline."[4] At sixteen weeks the gender of the fetus can be determined from examination of external genitalia, the head is erect, and the lower limbs are well developed. Swallowing of amnionic fluid (but not sucking), respiration, and complete finger closing may also appear by the sixteenth week. At the twentieth week the fetus weighs about 300 grams. *Williams* describes the fetal development over the next two lunar months:

> By the end of the 24th week, the fetus weighs about 630 g. The skin is characteristically wrinkled and fat is deposited beneath it. The head is still comparatively quite large; eyebrows and eyelashes usually are recognizable. A fetus born at this period will attempt to breathe, but almost always dies shortly after birth.
>
> By the end of the 28th week after the onset of the last menstrual period, a crown-rump length of about 25 cm is attained and the fetus weighs approximately 1,100 g. The thin skin is red and covered with vernix caseosa [an unctuous substance]. The pupillary membrane has just disappeared from the eyes. An infant born at this time in gestation moves his or her limbs quite energetically and cries weakly. The infant of this gestational age, with expert care, most often will survive.[5]

The fetus may be able to detect sounds as early as the twenty-fourth or twenty-sixth week, and the eye is sensitive to light by the twenty-eighth week gestational age.

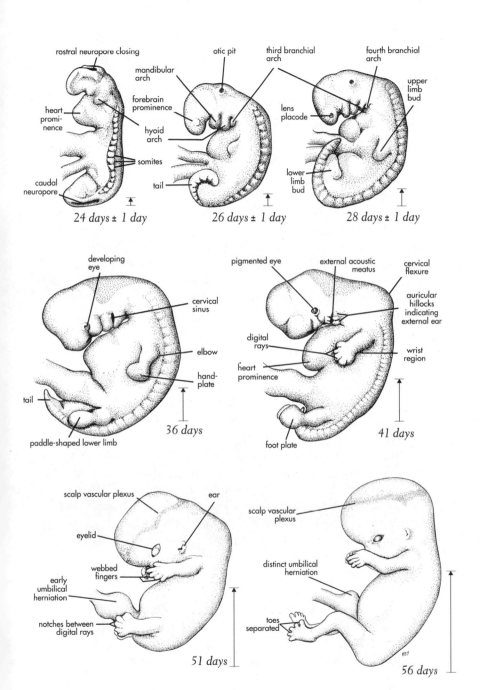

Embryos at Various Stages Between 24 and 56 Days (not to scale)
⬆ actual length

Turning for a moment to the legal implications of this development, the question whether the conceptus is in some sense a "person" is of paramount importance; for a positive answer could not only allow government to prohibit abortions but might even *require* it to do so. The condition of the conceptus also may be relevant to an evaluation of the state's interest in protecting it. Characteristically for the abortion debate, deriving criteria for addressing these questions is critical, yet there is no consensus on where those criteria should come from. Some abortion opponents find criteria in scriptural interpretations. Lawyers on both sides look to creative interpretations of legal precedents. Considering the attention the Supreme Court has devoted to other questions raised by abortion, its treatment of the personhood issue has been almost offhand. The Court's most detailed consideration of fetal development has focused almost exclusively on viability.

One can appreciate the Court's reluctance to set sail into these perilous seas without a compass. For those who believe—either as a matter of religious doctrine or as a consequence of deliberation—that a fertilized ovum or a zygote has the same moral standing as a fetus at seven months, a newborn at seven days, or a child at seven years, there is nothing left to debate on the personhood issue. For others, perhaps for many individuals, the conceptus at some stages of development bears such little resemblance to anything recognizably like a "person," as most people commonly use that term, that a different treatment may be justifiable. This approach requires its proponents to defend their criteria of the conceptus's functional and physical resemblance to the kinds of "persons" we normally see.

Even assuming such an approach can be defended, its application provides material for both sides. The pro–abortion rights side can argue that images of the zygote, morula, and blastocyst do not stir the conscience of most people to anything like the same degree as does an image of a twenty-four-week-old fetus. Demonstrators and politicians do not wave graphic "bloody blastocyst" pictures for the television cameras. Indeed, many people may not even be able to identify a picture of a preembryonic conceptus.

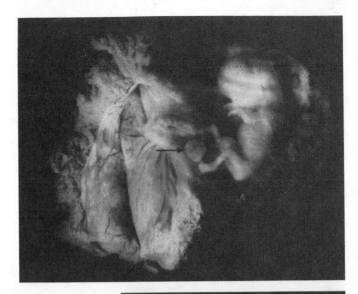

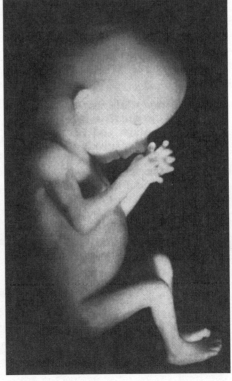

ABOVE: Photograph of a nine-week fetus in the amniotic sac exposed by removal from its chorionic sac. Actual size. The remnant of the yolk sac is indicated by an arrow. *(Photo by Jean Hay)*

BELOW: Photograph of a ten-week fetus, actual size.

RIGHT: Photograph of a thirteen-week fetus, actual size. *(Photo by Jean Hay)*

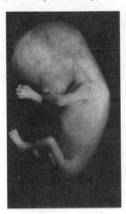

The embryo presents a more complex picture. At an ovulation age of three weeks (five weeks' gestational age), the embryo scarcely resembles a child or even a fetus. Many people may not even recognize it as human (especially if shown in its actual size). Embryonic development is rapid, however, and by the fourth and fifth weeks (ovulation age) structures recognizable to most persons are becoming more evident. By eight weeks' ovulation age (ten weeks' gestational age), the beginning of the fetal stage, appearance-based arguments seem more difficult to maintain, and the image of the embryo becomes disturbingly familiar. Nonetheless, even this image is not conclusive. A human embryo at this stage of development, although apparently recognizably human at first glance, is in fact difficult for a lay person to distinguish from other mammalian embryos.[6]

At some point after the tenth week of gestation, the fetus's appearance is sufficiently human to make the prospect of causing its death profoundly disturbing. The discomfort caused by the prospect reflects the acuteness of the abortion dilemma, even in the first trimester. One can see why abortion opponents have urged states to require that pictures of fetuses at various stages of development be made available to women contemplating abortion. And one can begin to appreciate the passionate opposition to second-trimester abortions that such images provoke. Although about half of all legal abortions are performed before nine weeks' gestational age, in 1987 26.7 percent were performed between nine and ten weeks' gestational age, with 12.5 percent being performed between eleven and twelve weeks. That translates into 416,280 abortions in 1987 between nine and ten weeks and 194,887 abortions between eleven and twelve weeks. And the 10 percent of abortions performed after thirteen weeks' gestational age in 1987 amounted to 155,910 procedures. To anyone who takes account of the outward appearance of fetal development in forming his or her position on abortion, the image of a fetus at eleven weeks' gestation or older can be extremely troubling. Yet such abortions in 1987 totaled 350,797.

Another consideration is the level of functional development of the fetal brain. One argument, advanced by Carl Sagan, is that

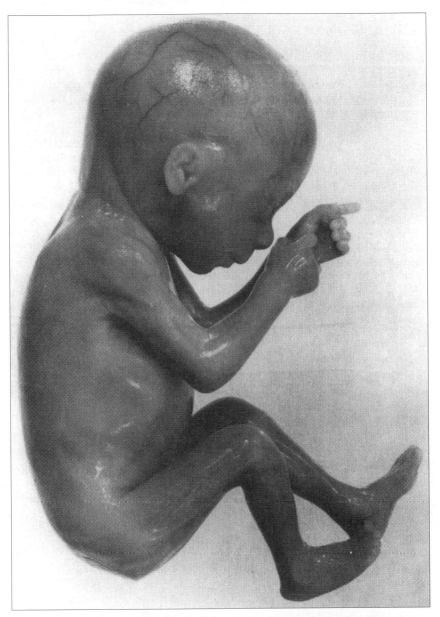

Photograph of a seventeen-week fetus, actual size. Note that the ears stand out from the head and that no hair is visible. Because there is no subcutaneous fat and the skin is thin, the blood vessels of the scalp are visible. Fetuses at this age are unable to survive if born prematurely, chiefly because their respiratory system is immature.

thinking is what separates humans from beasts, and that fetal brain development ought therefore to determine when the fetus has made the transition into personhood. There are powerful objections to this approach, discussed later, but first the facts.

As Sagan has pointed out, the lower brain structures are fairly well developed by the eighth week following fertilization, and the fetus is capable of responding reflexively to stimulation. Spontaneous fetal movement, or "quickening," usually does not occur until around the fifth month. But Sagan argues that motion and semiautonomic activity such as breathing are not characteristically human any more than is mere tissue growth. The characteristically human function, he contends, is thinking. The large-scale connection of neurons in the cerebral cortex that makes thinking possible does not occur until the twenty-fourth to twenty-seventh week of gestation.[7] Although the brain may exhibit some brain waves relatively early in pregnancy, as Bernard Nathanson has pointed out,[8] the regular wave patterns of the kind seen in human adults typically do not appear until the thirtieth week or so.

Sagan argues that young fetuses lack the necessary brain structures to think. In fact his description is conservative, he says, because regular brain wave activity is rare in fetuses. Therefore, erring on the side of fetal precocity, he concludes that drawing the line approximately at the end of the second trimester, as the Court did in Roe but for different reasons, is a workable solution to the "personhood" problem.

Other arguments about "personhood" and "life" contend that life demonstrably begins at conception because the fertilized ovum then becomes as genetically complete as an adult person, and because it then starts on the path that, barring abortion or other prenatal hazards, leads to birth. Again, everything turns on the determination of criteria and relevance, including the relevance of the question of when life begins. If determining the commencement of "life" is significant, and the indispensable element of "life" is the entity's ability to establish itself and to flourish, then there is some basis in medicine for the antiabortion point of view. This conclusion is supported by a brief review of what *Williams* refers to as the "dynamic role of the fetus in pregnancy." Although legal (and perhaps moral) conclusions are a separate matter, there is simply no denying that "after conception, the establishment and maintenance of pregnancy is highly dependent upon contributions made by the blastocyst, the embryo, and thence the fetus."[9]

The blastocyst and its products drive implantation, the subsequent development of the placenta, and maternal recognition of the pregnancy (which includes suppression of maternal antigens to allow implantation). "Thus, the blastocyst is an efficient, invasive, aggressive, dynamic force that directs the commencement of successful pregnancy." This process continues as the developing blastocyst and embryo form the two arms of the fetal-maternal communication system (the placental arm, the site of nutrient transfer and endocrine functioning, and the paracine arm, involving the fetal amnionic membranes). "The maternal organism is constitutively passive, responding to signals emanating from the fetus or extraembryonic fetal tissues, viz., the placenta and fetal membranes." Thus,

> The role of the fetus and extraembryonic tissues in pregnancy is not dissimilar to that of a nonmetastasizing, but rapidly growing, neoplasm. The developing embryo and fetus is very demanding; and, in general, its demands are met at whatever cost to the maternal organism by way of efficient placental mechanisms for nutrient uptake and transfer. But in other respects, the fetus is a benevolent, albeit self-serving, parasite in that it provides for the development of systems that facilitate maternal adaptation to the rapidly growing, semiallogeneic, tumorlike graft.[10]

Fetal contributions to the pregnancy process are prodigious. The "monumental and unprecedented" hormonal changes the woman undergoes in pregnancy are either directly or indirectly stimulated by the fetus. It is also likely that the fetus controls his or her own retreat from pregnancy and the timing of the birth process. The hormonal production that causes lactation before birth, and milk let-down thereafter, also probably is stimulated by the fetus. In sum, "the fetus enjoys a position of protection from the external environment that is never to be experienced again in life; but at the same time, it must be recognized that the fetus is the dynamic force in the orchestration of its own destiny."[11] "The maternal organism passively responds— even to the point of her own detriment."[12]

Now, *Williams Obstetrics* is written and edited by men, and some persons, particularly women, might strenuously object to *Williams's* description of women's role in pregnancy as "passive." Surely no mother would put it that way. Objection might also arise to *Williams's* reference to the fetus as a "tumor" or "parasite." While these word choices may seem unfortunate to lay persons, they must be understood in their medical context. The authors obviously do not mean to imply that pregnancy is a nonevent for women or that babies are a cancer. The point is that the conceptus is a quite vigorous, in some respects independent, actor in the pregnancy process, and is the biochemical initiator of many important events during pregnancy and childbirth.

In confronting the question of fetal development, the Court has seen the abortion issue as a contest between a woman's autonomy interests and the state's interests in protecting fetal and maternal life. Thus it has drawn a legal line at viability. After that point the state may prohibit abortion except as necessary to protect the life or health of the pregnant woman. The medical aspects of viability are therefore worth understanding.

The brief filed in *Webster* by the medical establishment— joined by the American Medical Association, the American College of Obstetricians and Gynecologists, and the American Academy of Pediatrics, among other organizations—provides a convenient summary. According to that brief, "Viability refers to the point at which the fetus would have a reasonable potential for survival if it were removed from the pregnant woman's uterus." "The earliest point at which a fetus can survive is 23–24 weeks." Medical technology has vastly improved the chances for survival of extremely low-birthweight babies (ELBW) who weigh between 500 and 1,000 grams. In the 1950s the survival rate was about 2 percent; by 1960 it had increased to 10 percent; by 1970 the figure was 20 percent; and "recent studies on the ELBW infants indicate that as many as 40–50% will survive." Fetal survival rates increase greatly (from 10 to 80 percent) as fetal weight increases from 500 to 1,000 grams (at 750 grams, about 26 weeks, approximately 50 percent survive) and gestational age increases from 24 to 28 weeks. "In short, if viability is defined as the point at which 50% of fetuses will survive, then it has moved from 28 weeks to 26 weeks since 1973. If viability is defined as the point at which a fetus has any prospect of extrauterine survival, then it has moved from 24 weeks to 23–24 weeks." The number of ELBW babies suffering major handicaps also has decreased from a majority to approximately 30 percent; but two-thirds will have significant educational problems.[13]

The current edition of *Williams* reports data collected at several hospitals on the survival rates of ELBW infants that refines this picture. For example, of 247 infants delivered between 1977 and 1981 in Providence, Rhode Island, who weighed between 500 and 900 grams, none survived in the 500–599 grams category; and only 3 percent weighing 600 to 699 grams survived. The average cost per survivor, which gives some indication of the measures required to save extremely premature infants and hence the extent of the risks they face, was $363,000. Of 79 infants in the 700–799 grams category, 24 percent survived at an average cost of $116,000 per survivor. Dallas's Parkland Memorial Hospital reports a 1985 survival rate of 13 percent for infants weighing 500 to 750 grams, 64 percent for infants weighing 751 to 1,000 grams, 88 percent at 1,001 to 1,250 grams, and 95 percent for 1,251 to 1,500 grams.[14]

While the legal issue, as the Supreme Court has defined it, is chiefly confined to the either/or question of survival, the medical profession necessarily takes a broader view. *Williams* points out, "Aside from survival, another important issue is the quality of life achieved by quite immature, extremely low-birthweight infants. It is apparent that appreciable compromise, both physical and intellectual, afflicts many such children." Here birthweight is not the only consideration. *Williams* notes that "in careful review of these extremely low-birthweight surviving infants, it was observed that they were typically growth retarded," that is, of greater gestational age at delivery than other fetuses of comparable weight. Survival prospects thus must also be considered in terms of gestational age and development, rather than birthweight alone. Summarizing the results of a Melbourne, Australia, study analyzing outcomes according to both birthweight and gestational age, *Williams* reports that

> survival as early as 23 weeks is possible; however, the prospects for survival without long-term sequelae [aftereffects] are remote. At best, no more than 6 or 7 of 100 surviving infants born at 23 to 25 weeks were free of subsequent impairment. *[The Melbourne study] emphasized that growth-retarded infants had significantly greater survival, but higher disability rates.*[15]

Physicians therefore must weigh several considerations. Another study cited by *Williams* reported results for infants in Cleveland who weighed less than 750 grams. None of the 56 infants who received no intensive care survived. Of the 41 admitted to intensive care, 11 survived; but "unfortunately, one third of these had moderate to severe neurosensory impairment." In another study, "active obstetrical management" improved neonatal survival for infants delivered at 24 to 26 weeks' gestational age to 28 percent, compared with a much greater survival rate at 27 weeks of 76 percent, but "there was similar long-term morbidity for each group at 2 to 4 years of age. This included bronchopulmonary dysplasia, cerebral palsy, blindness, and deafness." *Williams* concluded:

> Based on these results from San Antonio, Melbourne, Cleveland, and Halifax, as well as from our own experiences in Dallas, it appears that survival between 24 and 26 weeks gestation is possible, but that the long-term prognosis is decidedly guarded. Experiences such as these make it reasonable to set the gestational age for survival at 26 or 27 weeks, which is the current practice at Parkland Hospital.[16]

However one weighs these factors of mortality and morbidity to determine what survival means, the AMA brief in *Webster* explains that "there is an 'anatomic threshold' for fetal survival of about 23–24 weeks of gestation (500 grams). This is because the fetal lung does not mature sufficiently to permit normal or even mechanically-assisted respiration (i.e., breathing assisted by a ventilator) before 23–24 weeks of gestation." The problem is that "Until 23–24 weeks of gestation,...the network of air spaces and blood vessels is not extensive enough nor is the tissue barrier thin enough for effective oxygenation of the blood."[17] Functionally immature fetal lungs are especially susceptible to respiratory distress syndrome. A major factor in that condition is a deficiency in the biosynthesis of a complex lipoprotein called "surfactant," which lowers the surface tension at the air-tissue interface within the alveoli of the lung. Without enough surfactant, the alveolar-capillary exchange of oxygen and carbon dioxide is inadequate, resulting in potentially fatal extreme hypoxia (inadequate oxygen supply to the tissues) and acidosis (the accumulation of acid in the blood and tissues).[18] "Excoporeal membrane oxygenation" of the bloodstream can now be done by machine, but it cannot be used safely in infants of less than thirty-five weeks' gestational age or whose birthweight is less than 2,000 grams.

In sum, viability might best be thought of as a range. At one end is the twenty-three-week barrier of lung maturity, where fetal survival is possible but only at very high rates of mortality and morbidity. Mortality rates improve significantly from twenty-four to twenty-seven weeks, but long-term morbidity rates remain high. The legal consequences of the viability determination force the courts to look for a bright line, however; and the adversarial nature of the abortion debate creates pressures to draw that line earlier or later as the fortunes of one side or the other in the abortion debate prevail. Such pressures sometimes result in legislative interference with medical judgments concerning viability.

The term abortion technically refers to the "termination of pregnancy by any means before the fetus is sufficiently developed to survive." A substantial number of pregnancies terminate spontaneously, that is, without deliberate intervention. The number is difficult to estimate accurately, in part because of disagreement over when pregnancy commences (that is, whether at penetration of the ovum by the spermatozoan, at the first mitosis, at formation of the blastocyst, or at implantation) and in part because a number of pregnancies go undetected. *Williams* describes estimates of spontaneous abortion "between 20 and 62 percent with an average of 43 percent"; the embryologist Dr. Keith L. Moore estimates the number at 60 percent.[19]

The other kind of abortion, and the sense in which the word is commonly understood and has been used in this book, is induced abortion. Induced abortion is divided into two categories: therapeutic abortion, defined as "the termination of pregnancy before the time of fetal viability for the purpose of safeguarding the health of the mother," and elective or voluntary abortion, which is defined as "the interruption of pregnancy before viability at the request of the woman but not for reasons of impaired maternal health or fetal disease."[20]

The kinds of abortion techniques currently in use also fall into two categories, surgical and medical. Surgical techniques include surgical dilation and removal of the uterine contents, and laparotomy (hysterotomy or hysterectomy). Medical techniques include inducing labor by administering oxytocin, urea, saline, or prostaglandin. The antiprogesterone RU-486 also is used to prevent or to disrupt implantation.

The standard text for abortion providers is Warren M. Hern, *Abortion Practice*. *Williams* also contains a section on the subject. Hern's description of the general principles of abortion technique begins with a discussion of preoperative matters. The first is the practitioner's skill. Hern's comments underscore the hazards of illegal abortion and tend to rebut the claim of some abortion foes that the risks of the abortion procedure justify the reversal of *Roe*. Competency is a function of extensive practice, which became possible only after *Roe*. "Well-trained, highly experienced, and reputable gynecologists found, to their dismay, that when abortions became legal and they began performing them, the complication rates were frequently quite high," Hern writes.[21] He quotes one board-certified OB/GYN who did not begin to realize the extent of his ignorance about abortion until he had done five thousand procedures; only after twelve thousand did he begin to feel reasonably competent. Hern's second point is to emphasize that abortion in ambulatory clinics requires different, "no-touch" sterile techniques, if intrauterine contamination is to be minimized, from those used in sterile operating rooms where preoperative preparation and environmental control reduce the risk of infection.

The first step in surgical abortion is dilation of the cervix. Hern stresses the importance of using a dilation technique that is not traumatic. Some practitioners believe that for many women before ten weeks' gestation, dilation can be accomplished simply by using a mechanical dilator. For later abortions and for first pregnancies, however, mechanical dilation of an unprepared cervix can be painful and traumatic. It may therefore be necessary to prepare the cervix by first inserting a dilating and softening agent. One such agent is a laminaria tent (actually made of seaweed, or sometimes more recently of synthetic material), which absorbs fluid, swells, and partially dilates the cervix. Hern strongly recommends laminaria: "the exclusive overnight use of laminaria for cervical dilation has been a cornerstone of first-trimester abortion practice for us for 10 years. The exceedingly low complication rate confirms the acceptability of this practice" and more than offsets the disadvantages of two clinic visits and the risk of mild to severe cramping.[22] Another technique to prepare the cervix is to insert a prostaglandin suppository. Laminaria takes a minimum of six hours to work (and can take overnight); prostaglandins take about half that time.

Some physicians administer a mild tranquilizer, such as Valium, to help the patient relax, and an analgesic, such as Demerol. At the time of abortion the cervix is further prepared by administration of a local anesthetic to the cervical region and an antiseptic agent such as Betadine. Hern doubts "whether there is any justification, other than controlled epilepsy or agitated psychosis, for the use of general anesthesia in abortion."[23] The physician then probes the cervix to determine the size and position of the uterus.

Once the cervix is completely dilated, the most common method for evacuating its contents in the first fourteen weeks or so is vacuum aspiration. The physician inserts a vacuum aspirator suction curette into the cervix, taking extreme care not to perforate the uterine wall. According to *Williams:*

> Suction curettage is then used to aspirate most, if not all, of the pregnancy products. The vacuum aspirator is moved over the surface systematically in order to cover eventually all the uterine cavity. Once this has been done and no more tissue is aspirated, the procedure is terminated. Gentle curettage with a sharp curet is then utilized if it is thought that any placenta or fetal fragments remain in the uterus.[24]

Hern writes, "The physician will usually first notice a quantity of amnionic fluid, followed by placenta and fetal parts, which may be more or less identifiable. The patient usually experiences moderate to severe cramping at this point."[25] Hern recommends that, after completing aspiration, the physician explore the uterus for remaining tissue with forceps, followed by sharp curettage. According to *Williams,* the uterus also can be evacuated by using sharp curettage only, but "vacuum aspiration is generally preferable to mechanical curettage for abortion since it is quicker, has a lower perforation rate, induces somewhat less blood loss at operation, and there are fewer infections afterward."[26]

Another procedure known as menstrual extraction or menstrual induction is really an attempt at early abortion. The uterus is suctioned within one to three weeks of a missed menstrual period, using a flexible tube and a syringe. Although this is advocated by some individuals as a kind of home-remedy abortion, it is a risky and generally unsatisfactory procedure even when performed by a physician. According to *Williams,* "problems include the woman not being pregnant, the implanted zygote being missed by the [procedure], the failure to recognize an ectopic pregnancy, and, rarely, uterine perforation."[27] Although as a general rule earlier abortions are safer abortions, there is a point at which the risk of missing the conceptus becomes substantial. In Hern's view, "the risks of complications in the very early pregnancy termination (5–6 weeks from LMP) outweigh the benefits."[28]

The other surgical technique for accomplishing abortion is hysterotomy—in effect a kind of cesarean section, but with smaller abdominal and uterine incisions. Although the procedure may be indicated in a few cases for which curettage or medical induction of abortion is not appropriate, according to *Williams*, one study of seven hundred hysterotomies "rightfully concluded that the operation is now outdated as a routine method for terminating pregnancy."[29] Hern states, "The old method of hysterotomy with its extremely high morbidity and mortality had been abandoned [in the 1970s] except in the rarest of circumstances."[30] Hysterectomy, or the surgical removal of the uterus, of course effects an abortion; but hysterectomy is not indicated as a routine method of abortion.

According to Hern, although medical science has made exceptionally rapid progress in the technology of second-trimester abortions, the procedure at that stage of gestation presents difficulties not encountered during the first trimester, including enlargement of the uterus and fetus, psychological trauma for the patient, and "signs of fetal life on expulsion and the repugnance of dismemberment...."[31] Hern describes two basic categories of second-trimester abortion: induction of labor (accomplished by mechanical stimulation, amnioinfusion of drugs, or other agents) and surgical evacuation (dilation and evacuation, and the obsolete practice of hysterotomy).

Mechanical stimulation is both "one of the oldest methods for inducing abortion" and one of the more progressive. Insertion of a catheter into the cervix was a familiar practice among illegal abortionists. More recently the Japanese have had good results using catheters or similar devices with other materials such as laminaria.

Medical induction is another second-trimester induced labor

69

technique in the United States today. Hern describes three principal substances used in amnioinfusion procedures. One is replacement of a volume of amnionic fluid with a saline solution. Hern says the risk of complications associated with this method can be reduced substantially with proper technique, and that among its advantages are "its effectiveness, the reduced probability of signs of fetal life following expulsion, a relatively low rate of retained tissue, and availability."[32] Another substance used for amnioinfusion is a form of urea, sometimes accompanied by laminaria.

The third substance is some form of prostaglandin. Although prostaglandin avoids some of the complications of saline, it can create other risks. Physicians have obtained good results, however, with a combination of prostaglandin and saline or urea. Hern also reports that prostaglandin suppositories and other prostaglandin compounds have been used, but that their indication after sixteen weeks is questionable.

Williams takes a somewhat different position. According to that text, labor used to be induced by injection of saline or urea solutions into the amnionic sac. Because of this procedure's complications and the availability of safer methods, *Williams* reports, intra-amnionic instillation is rarely used today. Much more common in second-trimester abortions is prostaglandin induction. Prostaglandins are administered either in suppository form, as a gel injected by catheter into the cervical canal and lower uterus, or into the amnionic sac by amniocentesis. The technique produces cervical softening and dilation, uterine contraction, and expulsion of the conceptus from the uterus. Similar results are sometimes accomplished by intravenous administration of oxytocin, sometimes in conjunction with prostaglandin. It is not uncommon to use laminaria to assist dilation of the uterus in prostaglandin and/or oxytocin induction.

The surgical method of choice today for second-trimester abortions is dilation and evacuation (D & E). Its advantages are lower complication rates and avoidance of the protracted and painful labor accompanied by expulsion of the fetus (which may show signs of life) that can occur (sometimes when the patient

70

is unattended) from induction of labor. Its disadvantages are that it requires surgical skill and may be objectionable to physicians and assistants. Dilation is accomplished, according to Hern, through a much more involved procedure than in the first trimester. To accomplish a gentle, gradual, and sufficient dilation of the cervix, he employs multiple laminaria treatments, supplemented with mechanical dilation by Teflon dilators and sometimes infusion of a urea solution.

The actual evacuation procedure, as generally described by Hern, begins with the physician rupturing and draining the amnionic sac. The physician then inserts forceps gently (to avoid uterine trauma) and explores for fetal tissue: "As the forceps is closed, a solid feel will relay the information that the fetal parts are grasped. The forceps is gently withdrawn in a rotating motion [to determine whether the forceps have grasped 'the uterine wall instead of its contents']." After removing the fetus, the physician then removes or fragments the placental membrane with forceps. Evacuation is completed by gently stroking the uterus with a sharp curet, and then by application of the suction tube to "assure that the uterus is empty."[33]

Hern goes on to describe more specifically the procedures at different gestational ages, from thirteen to fourteen weeks up to twenty-four weeks. His descriptions are in appropriately clinical detail, explaining the different dilation techniques required, the proper instruments to use and how to use them, and the kinds of medications he has found to be indicated. It is easy to see how, in view of the greater complexity and difficulty of the procedures he describes, the risks of abortion to the pregnant woman increase dramatically as gestational age advances.

Hern's description of D & E procedures are a stark reminder that while abortion is clearly about women's reproductive autonomy and choice, it is also undeniably about the deliberate dismemberment of what in the second trimester looks very much like a tiny human being. Hern's description of second-trimester abortion techniques, written by a resolutely pro-choice physician to inform and not to shock or to dissuade, illustrates just how disturbingly real this aspect of the procedure is in the second trimester. For example, Hern provides the following account of D & E technique:

> At 16 to 17 weeks, fetal tissue is much more easily identifiable with the forceps and in some ways is easier to grasp and remove than in earlier gestations. The calvaria [upper, dome-like portion of the skull] is about the size of a Ping-Pong ball and usually can be grasped readily with the Bierer [forceps]. Collapsing it gives a definite sensation, which can be identified simultaneously with the appearance of the calvaria sign.[34]

Hern himself confronts this problem from the perspective of the abortion provider:

> It is clear that the D & E procedure places the responsibility for performance of the abortion squarely on the operating physician and those who are assisting, and this is an emotionally stressful experience for many. It is important to recognize this fact and to provide support for those who participate in the procedure. It is of the utmost importance to keep in mind the advantages that the procedure offers for patients and that the professional responsibilities of genuinely helping other people with difficult problems are frequently stressful. Those providing D & E procedures must be keenly aware of their level of commitment to the availability of choice for women in this stage of pregnancy. A strong commitment is as important here as is excellence in surgical technique.[35]

Once a clear image of the procedure is brought to mind, it is easy to understand some abortion opponents' stubborn invocation of the "bloody fetus" image, the depth of their outrage (particularly over second-trimester abortions), and why many pro-choice advocates prefer to focus attention on the interests of the pregnant woman rather than what happens in the clinic. Of course one must not lose sight of the pregnant woman's circumstances and needs if one really wants to come to grips with the abortion problem. But one also must not deny what actually happens during abortion—particularly later in the second trimester. Although the percentage of second-trimester legal abortions is relatively small (approximately 10 percent of all legal abortions), as already noted, the raw number is nevertheless substantial. In 1987 more than 156,000 legal second-trimester abortions were performed in the United States.

Finally, a recently developed technique for terminating pregnancy, currently not approved for general use in the United States, is administration of the antiprogesterone RU-486. By blocking the effect of progesterone, RU-486 interferes with implantation and produces a result similar to spontaneous abortion (miscarriage). According to AGI, RU-486 is used to perform 25 percent of abortions in France and has a 95 percent effectiveness rate when administered with prostaglandin within forty-nine days after the last menstrual period. The advantages of RU-486 are reduced risk of damage to the uterus, the elimination of anesthetics, and a greater sense of control for the woman. One disadvantage is that the course of treatment takes longer than surgical abortion.[36]

THE PHYSICAL AND MENTAL HEALTH CONSEQUENCES OF ABORTION

A surprising portion of the arguments in the *Webster* case concerns the health aspects of abortion. An unfortunate effect of the abortion controversy has been to create an ideologically driven and misinformed debate about the relative risks of abortion and childbirth. That debate appears to be a product of the politics of abortion, which have led abortion opponents to seek incremental regulatory measures that restrict or burden the availability of abortion, often justified as protecting women's health.

Several friends of the court in *Webster* argued that legal abortion presents grave risks to the health of American women. For example, the brief filed by Feminists for Life, Women Exploited by Abortion, the National Association of Pro-life Nurses, Let Me Live, and the Elliot Institute argued that "There is ample evidence in the medical studies and public health statistics cited herein that the unfettered right of abortion on demand foisted upon our society by the Court and by abortion advocates is a public health disaster the proportions of which we are just beginning to uncover."[37] The brief for Focus on the Family and the Family Research Council of America similarly argues that abortion has severe adverse health effects for women, and that those effects are underreported.[38] And the brief of the United States Catholic Conference argues that maternal death from legal abortion has replaced death from illegal abortion as the back-alley abortionist has moved into the clinic.[39]

Significantly, the briefs filed on behalf of the pro-life medical community (except the national Nurses for Life Association) did not make such arguments. For example, the brief of the American Association of Prolife Obstetricians and Gynecologists and the American Association of Pro-Life Pediatricians confines their arguments to the state's interest in protecting fetal life. And the brief of Doctors for Life, Missouri Doctors for Life, and Missouri Nurses for Life addresses the personhood issue, not maternal health.

Like any surgical procedure, abortion has some risk of complication, though usually less frequent and less severe than childbirth. About 12 percent of abortion patients experience complications more serious than the usual pain, headache, and nausea. About 0.4 percent suffer major complications such as perforation of the uterus or severe hemorrhage. Infection is also a risk. Rare but fatal complications include amniotic fluid embolism, pulmonary embolism, and massive blood clotting.[40]

Mainstream professional opinion, however, solidly recognizes abortion as an exceptionally safe surgical procedure. And, although conclusions about the psychological impact of abortion are somewhat less definite because of a shortage of adequate research, the weight of evidence appears to find abortion psychologically safe as well. It also appears beyond reasonable dispute that legalization of elective abortion has made the procedure much safer for women. The briefs filed in *Webster* by the American Medical Association, the American College of Obstetricians and Gynecologists, the American Academy of Pediatricians, the American Psychiatric Association, the American

Public Health Association, and the American Psychological Association strongly support these conclusions.

In *Roe v. Wade* the Court noted that maternal mortality rates for legal abortion were lower than for childbirth until the second trimester of pregnancy. Since 1973 mortality rates for both legal abortion and childbirth have declined, but the rate for legal abortion has declined more rapidly. The safety of legal abortion procedures thus has increased dramatically since *Roe v. Wade*. According to the American Public Health Association, "Between 1973...and 1985,...the death rate for legal abortions fell more than eighteen times from 3.4 to 0.4 deaths per 100,000 procedures.... Today, at *no* point in pregnancy is the risk of death from legal abortion higher than the risk of death from childbirth." In 1985 the death rate from pregnancy or childbirth was 6.6 per 100,000; the death rate was 0.4 per 100,000 legal abortions.[41] Not only is the risk of death greater in childbirth than in abortion, but childbirth also results in greater maternal morbidity. According to the brief of the American Medical Association, "While 63% of women suffered some adverse health effect during pregnancy,...approximately 12% of abortions result in some medical complication.... Moreover, the risk of major surgery is higher in childbirth." The greater risk of surgery results largely from the 25 percent incidence of cesarean section in childbirth, compared with less than 1 percent incidence of intra-abdominal surgery occasioned by abortion.[42]

According to the American Medical Association, pregnancy creates the risk of a number of adverse health effects, from nausea to death. Common problems include nausea, vomiting, fatigue, varicose veins, hemorrhoids, headache, and backache. More serious problems include hypertension (8 to 10 percent of pregnancies; usually controllable, but sometimes resulting in stroke, premature separation of the placenta from the uterus, and severe bleeding disorders); eclampsia (0.1 percent; this is a form of pregnancy-induced hypertension, discussed in *Casey*, and is accompanied by headaches, visual disturbances, abdominal pains, and seizures); hemorrhage during pregnancy, labor, delivery, and postdelivery (this can lead to kidney failure, stroke, loss of pituitary gland function, and death); and pregnancy-induced diabetes (1 to 3 percent of pregnancies) or pregnancy during previously diagnosed diabetes (1.5 million women of childbearing age), which greatly increases the risks of hypertension, infection, injury to the birth canal, cesarean section, and postpartum hemorrhage. Rare but life-threatening complications also include, as mentioned, amniotic fluid embolism, pulmonary embolism, and massive blood clotting. Cesarean section involves a 25 percent higher risk of death than vaginal delivery, and a 25 to 50 percent chance of complications, including infection; hemorrhage; laceration of the reproductive, urinary, or intestinal tract; and pulmonary embolism. Pregnancy also exacerbates preexisting diseases besides diabetes, including congenital heart disease, coronary artery disease, chronic renal failure, myasthenia gravis, and cancer.[43]

According to the American Public Health Association, three of ten women who undergo childbirth are treated for major complications, such as laceration of the pelvis's perineal muscle, cervix, or vagina, and severe postpartum hemorrhage. Some evidence indicates that the risks of pregnancy are greater for women carrying unwanted pregnancies to term. The risks include psychological damage, postpartum infection, hemorrhage, and depression. Conversely, there appears to be some health risk for women who do not bear children: increased risk of breast cancer, uterine cancer, colon cancer, and ovarian cancer.[44]

The American Public Health Association further states:

> Contrary to the assertions appearing in the brief of *amici curiae* Focus on the Family and Family Research Council of America, legal abortion does not adversely affect subsequent pregnancy outcomes, nor does it lead to an epidemic rise in miscarriages, premature births or low birthweight babies. Studies have shown no demonstrable increase in the frequency of fetal loss in any one of the trimesters of pregnancy among women who have previously had abortions. Nor is there any significant association between prior induced abortion and low birthweight, ectopic pregnancy, complications of pregnancy or labor, or congenital malformations.... To the contrary, by reducing the incidence of low birthweight babies,

the availability of legal abortion has significantly lowered the neonatal mortality rates in the United States.[45]

Williams also discusses a study that found no significant effect on subsequent fertility from elective abortion. In addition, there is no increased incidence of second-trimester spontaneous abortion, preterm deliveries, or low-birthweight infants in subsequent pregnancies if the abortion is performed by vacuum aspiration. And induced second-trimester abortions present little risk to later pregnancies provided injection techniques are used. The study also found, however, that forceful dilation of the cervix, in either the first or second trimester, increases the risks to subsequent pregnancies.[46]

Several factors account for the increasing safety of legal abortions. As Hern notes, *Roe v. Wade* has led to growing skill among physicians and the use of safer techniques. Like any delicate manual skill, surgery requires training and practice for proficiency. The primary risk in surgical abortion is perforation or scarring of the uterus, which can be minimized by proper technique; but mastery of that technique comes only when the procedure is done routinely. In addition, the great increase in legal abortion following *Roe v. Wade* has led to the relatively recent development of much safer surgical techniques, especially suction curettage, as abortion has entered the mainstream of legitimate modern medical practice.

Another important factor in the increasing safety of legal abortion, also as a consequence of *Roe*, is that the procedure is being performed earlier in pregnancy, when risks are significantly less. According to *Williams*, "The relative risk of dying as the consequence of abortion is approximately doubled for each 2 weeks of delay after 8 weeks of gestation."[47] And the American Public Health Association reports that the risk of complications increases by 20 percent for each week of delay.[48] According to an AGI study, "In the United States,...deaths per 100,000 legal abortions rise from 0.2 at eight or fewer weeks [LMP]...to 0.3 weeks at 9–10 weeks, 0.6 at 11–12 weeks, 3.7 at 16–20 weeks and 12.7 at 21 weeks or more."[49]

A third and especially significant factor, again directly following from *Roe*, has been the decline in the number of illegal abortions. Again according to the AMA brief:

> Between 1940 and 1972, more than 75% of abortion deaths were the consequence of unlawful abortions and, in 1972, women having unlawful abortions were eight times more likely to die than women having lawful abortions.... After *Roe*, abortion deaths dropped sharply. Between 1972 and 1974, for example, the total number of abortion deaths declined from 88 to 48, and deaths from unlawful abortions declined from 39 to 5.... In other words, 85% of the decrease in abortion deaths between 1972 and 1974 reflected reductions in mortality from unlawful abortions.[50]

According to the American Public Health Association, 193 women died from illegal abortions in the U.S. in 1965. In 1985, after the Supreme Court recognized constitutional protection for abortion rights, only two deaths occurred from illegal abortions. Six deaths resulted from legal abortions. One study estimates that without *Roe* as many as fifteen hundred women would have died in the 1970s from illegal abortions and that many thousands more would have suffered life-threatening complications. "In the 1960s, complications resulting from illegal abortions accounted for more than 20 percent of all pregnancy-related admissions to municipal hospitals in New York and California."[51] And deaths from illegal abortions are heaviest among minorities.[52]

In other countries with strict anti-abortion laws the death rate from illegal abortion remains high. AGI reports studies estimating the annual worldwide maternal death toll from illegal abortion at between 100,000 and 204,000.[53] For example, "In Latin America, complications of illegal abortion are thought to be the main cause of death in women between the ages of 15 and 39 years."[54] In Rumania, which set strict prohibitions on abortion in 1966, abortion mortality rose from 21 deaths to 128 deaths per 100,000 live births between 1965 and 1984. In 1984 alone, Rumanian registration data indicated that illegal abortion accounted for as high as 86 percent of maternal deaths in that country.[55] By contrast, in developed countries with legalized abortion, the aggregate mortality rate is 0.6 deaths per 100,000 legal abortions.[56]

The assertion in *Webster* by Focus on the Family that the hazards of abortion are underreported appears to be unfounded. The AMA points out in its *Webster* brief that the reported mortality figures for abortion may actually understate its relative safety because "mortality statistics published by the federal government underestimate the number of maternal deaths from childbirth by as much as 37%–50%.... The data on abortion mortality, on the other hand, are highly accurate. This is because efforts to detect maternal mortality from abortion have been very thorough."[57]

The brief for Focus on the Family also cites studies concerning adverse psychological effects of abortion, including guilt, anxiety, depression, and psychoses as well as delayed psychological consequences, suicide, isolation, alcohol and tobacco and drug abuse, and so-called Post-Abortion Syndrome. The brief also argues that abortion damages family relationships (especially the relationship with the assumed father) and causes serious sexual problems, divorce, and erosion of trust, communication, and problem-solving skills because of the inequality between the partners in the decision. The brief also reports studies of the adverse effects on surviving children (that is, older children in the family). Other pro-life *Webster* briefs make similar claims.

The health-care establishment takes sharp exception to these assertions. According to the AMA brief, which was joined by the American Psychiatric Association, "As others have observed, including the U.S. Surgeon General, the research on the psychiatric effects of abortion is not sufficiently rigorous to yield a complete understanding of the extent to which abortion results in psychiatric problems."* The AMA brief makes several observa-

*The reference to the Surgeon General refers to Everett Koop, M.D. In 1987 President Ronald Reagan asked Dr. Koop for an opinion that elective abortion was more psychologically harmful than giving birth to unwanted babies. Dr. Koop's letter in reply stated that, after extensive research, he had found insufficient data to support that conclusion. According to the *Washington Post*, administration lawyers later denied Koop permission to release the letter when it was forwarded to the president, promised to keep it confidential, and later released it to the press. Michael Specter, "Koop Upset by Release of Abortion Letter," *Washington Post*, January 13, 1989, p. A5.

tions. First, very few women develop severe psychiatric illness after either abortion or childbirth. Most women feel relief after abortion, and "the vast majority of women derived very significant emotional and psychological benefits from bearing and raising children." Second, mild, transient symptoms are not uncommon after either pregnancy or abortion. The incidence of postpartum depression, for example, may be as high as 20 percent; and 15 to 40 percent of women experience mild and transient feelings of guilt, regret, and sadness after abortion. Third, postpartum psychiatric disorder is more common than postabortion illness. Fourth, any psychiatric illness after abortion usually is temporary and limited to women who have a history of psychiatric illness or who abort to protect their own health rather than to terminate an unwanted pregnancy. Finally, women who are denied abortions are more likely than women who have them to suffer severe psychiatric distress and illness.[58]

The brief of the American Psychological Association also disagrees strongly with Focus on the Family. First, the APA observes that "in a review of thirty years of pre-*Roe* research, the authors noted that 'deeply held personal convictions frequently seem to outweigh the importance of data, especially when conclusions are drawn.'" Second, the APA criticizes the methodology of studies that find a significant incidence of psychological aftereffects. The APA concludes that

> five major reviews of the psychological and psychiatric literature published between 1975 and 1989 all confirm that for the overwhelming majority of women who undergo abortion, there are no long-term negative emotional effects. There is consensus among researchers that abortion—like any significant life event—has psychological implications. When women experience regret, depression, or guilt, however, such feelings are mild and diminish rapidly without adversely affecting general functioning. Severe emotional responses are rare, even in young women. To the contrary, the great majority of women who have had an abortion express feelings of relief.

The APA observes, "The focus of current research is on identifying the variables that predict diverse emotional responses to abortion. Abortion does not take place independently of a woman's intrapersonal and interpersonal context." In fact, data on the psychological risks of abortion tend to support an abortion policy based on choice and acceptance, rather than a reproachful one confined only to therapeutic abortion. Women are more likely to suffer psychological damage from abortion when the decision is forced on them by medical necessity or by someone else, and when their decision is not supported by people important to them. The APA argues that one can even find evidence of positive psychological changes after abortion, including stress reduction, increased use of contraceptives, and increased feelings of autonomy, self-directedness, and efficacy.[59]

Another health-care aspect of abortion is its impact on persons other than the pregnant woman. As mentioned, pro-life *amici* in *Webster* argue that abortion has adverse effects on surviving children—by weakening maternal ties, by fostering a societal attitude that children are "expendable," and by leaving them with a profound sense of insecurity about their own survival. Some briefs also contend that *Roe* has not mitigated the problems of unwanted children, out-of-wedlock births, and child neglect and abuse; to the contrary, each of those problems has become worse since 1973.[60]

The assumption underlying these arguments is open to question. While liberal abortion policy may not *solve* the problems of unwed motherhood, teenage pregnancy, child abuse, neglect, and abandonment (that abortion could do so has never been at the heart of the pro-choice argument anyway), which result from a combination of factors, it is difficult to see how prohibiting abortion by itself would do so. It is especially hard to believe that restrictions on abortion would notably improve parents' care and commitment for their children. To the contrary, several European studies indicate that the children resulting from unwanted pregnancies are at significantly higher risk for psychosocial problems during their developmental years—delinquency, inferior school performance, and treatment for nervous and psychosomatic disorders.[61]

Arguments have also been raised about abortion's impact on men—the feelings of powerlessness, of exclusion, and of a vaguely defined but compelling responsibility. In one eloquent study of this much-neglected aspect of abortion, the authors

> were struck during our own abortion experiences by certain stark and regrettable features of the scene—the absence of any helpful preparation for the experience; the embarrassment and uselessness men felt during their clinic vigil; the wish to talk about it versus the social pressure to tell no one; and the need to appear supportive regardless of one's own ambivalence and heartache.[62]

Here again the arguments raise important concerns but do not make a convincing case in themselves for prohibiting abortion. In view of what is at stake for the woman, it seems wrong to deny her an abortion just because it makes some men uncomfortable—after all, so do menstruation and childbirth. Instead these concerns indicate the need for greater sensitivity to the needs of everyone associated with the procedure.

4. The Historical Context

· ·

Approaching abortion as an historical issue raises difficulties similar to those encountered in considering abortion in its modern setting. Not surprisingly, the historical record has become one more battleground in the abortion wars: it offers more arguments than answers. Advocates from both sides invoke historical sources to support their claims. But the kind of historical picture one forms depends so much on what one is trying to accomplish. Modern anti-abortion advocates who want to demonstrate that abortion has been condemned throughout history, and thus is not part of our mainstream values and traditions, can cite numerous censorious references back to antiquity. The historian John T. Noonan, Jr., for example, cites Catholic theologians and moral philosophers to conclude that disapproval of abortion forms "an almost absolute value in history."[1] And the legal scholars Joseph Dellapenna and Robert Destro have argued that the common law has long condemned abortion.[2] Abortion rights advocates who wish to prove that abortion has been widely practiced and tolerated in the past can marshal evidence to support that claim as well. The legal scholar Cyril C. Means, for example, whose writings influenced the Court in *Roe v. Wade*, has argued that access to voluntary abortion was a common law liberty for centuries.[3]

Notwithstanding these conflicting conclusions, several general observations can be made. First, fertility control through contraception and abortion has been practiced since antiquity. Second, although abortion may have been tolerated in pre-Christian Greece and Rome, there is considerable evidence of later disapproval of the practice. The intensity of that disapproval varied, and abortion continued to be practiced.

83

Third, the English common law, which forms the basis of America's legal cultural traditions, apparently tolerated some forms of abortion. Although the record is ambiguous, it appears at the least that abortions performed before the first detectable fetal movements (referred to as "quickening," around the fifth month) were punished either less severely or not at all. Further, there is little conclusive evidence that voluntary abortion was of much concern to the common law.

Finally, American policy toward abortion has gone through several evolutionary stages, which are described in James Mohr's thorough work, *Abortion in America: The Origins and Evolution of National Policy, 1800–1900.* Preservation of fetal life did not become the driving concern of laws governing abortion until very recently. The first stage was characterized by the relatively tolerant English common law quickening rule. Second came a transitional phase, from 1820 to 1840, involving relatively weak legislative efforts to regulate postquickening abortion. The third phase, from 1840 to 1880, saw a proliferation of abortion practice and advertising for abortion services, rising concern with declining fertility among white, native-born, Protestant, upper- and middle-class married women, and a struggle for control of the practice of medicine in America. This period eventually yielded the restrictive laws that dominated American abortion policy for the next eighty years. The fourth phase was the beginning of a legislative reform effort in the 1960s to liberalize abortion laws. That phase was cut short, however, by the fifth and contemporary phase, in which the United States Supreme Court declared abortion to be a matter of constitutional law.

ABORTION IN THE ANCIENT WORLD

Abortion is hardly a modern invention: "it has always been available."[4] According to one source, "The oldest known medical texts citing abortion techniques appeared in China around 2737 B.C.E., more than 4,700 years ago."[5] Indeed, it seems likely that such practices are older than recorded history, given their ubiquity today—even among indigenous tribal cultures.[6] "To put it very mildly," writes one anthropologist, "these figures on distribution and frequency [of abortion among tribal cultures] suggest that the practice of voluntary abortion is and has been a common practice in a majority of cultural traditions of mankind."[7]

Abortion was a familiar practice in classical Greek and Roman times. A first-century gynecological treatise, for example, describes a variety of abortion methods, including vigorous exercise; bathing in or applying poultices or extracts of linseed, mallow, and wormwood; and being bled and shaken.

> The reasons for abortion were as various as the means. Soranus [c. 98–138 A.D.] notes three: to conceal the consequences of adultery; to maintain feminine beauty; to avoid danger to the mother when her uterus is too small to accommodate the full embryo. Plato and Aristotle thought of abortion as a way of preventing excess population. St. Ambrose was familiar with propertied families who practiced it in order not to divide their patrimony among too many children.[8]

Although the Hippocratic Oath contains a pledge not to "give a woman an abortifacient pessary," Hippocrates' contemporary culture apparently was quite tolerant of abortion. Hippocrates himself may even have prescribed an abortion-inducing procedure on occasion. According to the historian John Riddle, "Soranus interpreted Hippocrates to be referring [in the Oath] to drug-induced abortions because he knew the section in the Hippocratic treatise that prescribed a method to induce an abortion by manipulation."[9]

Other scholars point to ancient prohibitions on abortion. For example, one study observes that the ancient Persians and Assyrians punished abortion.[10] The same study also mentions the Code of Hammurabi (c. 1728 B.C.E.) and the Septuagint version of the Book of Exodus. Both texts, however, addressed only the unintentional causing of an abortion by a third party.

Riddle notes, "In Judaic scripture, the Talmud, Tosefta, and Midrash, abortions and 'root potions' for sterility are frequently enough mentioned that we can assume the practices must have been widespread and, to some degree, acceptable."[11] It appears that both the Jerusalem and Babylonian Talmud and the Mishna endorse the concept that the morality of abortion is determined by the point in gestation at which it occurs, and find that early abortions were acceptable. The Old Testament, as John Noonan observes, "has nothing to say on abortion."[12] The only directly relevant reference in the Bible is in Exodus 21:22–25, which states in the King James version:

> If men strive, and hurt a woman with child, so that her fruit depart *from her*, and yet no mischief follow: he shall be surely punished, according to as the woman's husband will lay upon him; and he shall pay as the judges *determine*. And if *any* mischief follow, then thou shalt give life for life, Eye for eye, tooth for tooth, hand for hand, foot for foot, Burning for burning, wound for wound, stripe for stripe.

Riddle reads the Hebrew text of the passage as accepting abortion implicitly by punishing it (*nefash tahat nefesh*, "life is given for life") only when the mother dies because of the procedure. The Septuagint translation of the passage "life for life" refers to imposition of the penalty after the conceptus is "formed." Once again, a gestational distinction appears. Riddle contends that although there was never absolute uniformity in Greek or Roman opinion, pagan belief, Judaism, or Christianity, "eventually, Hebrew, Greek, and Roman thought came nearly together on the point that prior to the fetus forming, feticide was not homicide." Riddle concludes:

> Clearly Hebrew, Greek, and Roman law did not protect the fetus, but there was a religious distinction made at the point when the fetus had formed recognizable features. Before that point women could either contracept or abort without religious or legal sanction. There were cases where the father had some legal interest in the decision and where a physician or *pharmakos* who gave *pharmakeia* (drugs, poisons) was denounced and, at times, legally punished (or so said the law) for a procedure that resulted in harm to the mother. Neither convention

86

nor the law protected the unborn and the unconceived. Accord-ing to convention and the law, ancient women could employ contraceptives and early stage abortifacient virtually without consequences. The same was true in medieval Islam and to some degree in Christian society during the Middle Ages.[13]

Noonan concludes, "Abortion, indeed, according to contempo-rary observers, was practiced very generally in the Greco-Roman period." Christian teachings, however, according to Noonan, stand in sharp contrast to the Greco-Roman toleration of abor-tion; he argues that those teachings are "certain, comprehensive, and absolute" in their condemnation of abortion.[14]

CHRISTIAN—PRINCIPALLY CATHOLIC—VIEWS ON ABORTION

Condemnations there certainly were, but they are far from uni-formly "certain, comprehensive, and absolute"—at least not until very recently. The Bible, which offers numerous specific, detailed injunctions on a variety of subjects from diet to deco-rum, is remarkably silent on an issue that some modern Christ-ian leaders regard as akin to murder. Noonan's case for biblical views on abortion, apart from Exodus, rests on inferences from the New Testament: benevolent references to children, such as "suffer little children, and do not prevent them coming unto me" (Matthew 19:14, Mark 10:14, Luke 18:16); reverential refer-ences to the life in Mary's womb (Matthew 1:18; Luke 1:40, 42); and generalities about loving one's neighbor (Galatia 5:14). He finds an express prohibition, however, in *Didache*, or *The Teach-ings of the Twelve Apostles* (c. 100 A.D.), which provides, "You shall not slay the child by abortions. You shall not kill what has been generated." The same passage proscribes killing, adultery, corruption of boys, fornication, stealing, practice of magic and medicine, and desiring a neighbor's wife.[15]

Other theological pronouncements are also less than uniform. Noonan cites second-century writings, including those of Clement of Alexandria and Tertullian, condemning abortion. Cyril Means has argued, however, that Tertullian justified therapeutic abortions.[16] In later centuries, views on abortion began to include an emerging concept of fetal development that centered on the notion of "ensoulment."* The idea that the fetus does not achieve cognizable status until some point in its gestation dates back at least to Aristotle, and ensoulment eventually became the critical ecclesiastical boundary for abortion (as quickening was later to become the secular borderline). According to Riddle, "The early mideval church continued the ancient distinction, as stated by Aristotle, that there was a difference when an antifertility measure was administered," citing for example an Allemanian sacramentarium using forty days as the dividing line and Irish canons (c. 675) to the same effect.[17] He also cites several secular sources, including early Allemanian laws (c. 600 A.D.), distinguishing between early and late pregnancy.

Noonan argues that Christian theologians from the fifth to the fifteenth centuries carried forward the earlier patristic absolute prohibition on abortion throughout pregnancy, but even he notes that Avicenna's eleventh-century *Canon of Medicine*, the standard European medical text until the mid-seventeenth century, described abortion-inducing techniques and endorsed therapeutic abortion.[18] From the fifth century until very recently, one can find theological and philosophical references that regard abortion before "ensoulment" (often regarded as occurring at forty days) in a much different light than later abortions.

In the eleventh and twelfth centuries Roman Catholic opposition to contraception and to abortion became clearer. Riddle explains that the writings of Ivo (bishop of Chartres from 1091 to 1116), Peter Lombard, and Gratian established that "both contraception and abortion were out of order and jeopardized a person's soul." "But what was not at all clear, and was little discussed was the question, 'when is an abortion an abortion?'."[19]

Historical arguments that rest on selected Roman Catholic writings as evidence of prevailing anti-abortion morality, especially those drawn from the Middle Ages, are incomplete. The real-life

---

*A council of eastern bishops, the Council of Ancyra, in 314 A.D. prohibited abortion without regard to ensoulment but provided for a reduced penalty of ten years' penance.

historical picture is much more complex. As the historian Barbara Tuchman has noted, in "the daily condition of medieval life... hardly an act or thought, sexual, mercantile, or military, did not contravene the dictates of the Church." Yet church officials from pope to cardinal to village priest engaged—sometimes quite openly and routinely—in virtually every proscribed practice, including murder, sexual extravagance (from simple promiscuity to incest), commercial corruption, and warfare by mercenaries. Ecclesiastical prohibitions, enforced by excommunication, covered such matters as translating the Bible into English, striking for or merely demanding a bare subsistence wage from secular employers, and even the wasting of wool by spinners. Tuchman has also concluded that in medieval society, "On the whole, babies and young children appear to have been left to survive or die without great concern in the first five or six years."[20]

In any event, the Roman Catholic church has not always categorically treated abortion throughout pregnancy as the moral equivalent of homicide, and the case for therapeutic abortion was sometimes argued. One important sixteenth-century writer, the Spanish Jesuit Tomás Sanchez, describes several cases of justified therapeutic abortion. He includes the case of a rape victim who fears death from her husband's relatives should they discover she is bearing the child of another. Means credits Sanchez "with having proposed the first non-medical grounds for therapeutic abortion."[21] Further, as Noonan himself notes, "The Sacred Penitentiary by the time of Gregory XIII [1572–1585] did not treat as homicide the killing of an embryo under 40 days. Even where the embryo over 40 days was sinfully destroyed, the Penitentiary made less difficulty about dispensations than when an adult human was killed."[22] In 1588 Pope Sixtus V issued the bull *Effraenatum*, which equated abortion with homicide throughout pregnancy and without regard to maternal health. Yet in 1591 Pope Gregory XIV repealed all penalties of *Effraenatum* except those concerning ensouled fetuses. In 1679, however, Innocent XI condemned sixty-five propositions, including Proposition 34, that "it is lawful to procure an abortion before ensoulment of the fetus lest a girl, detected as pregnant, be killed or defamed."[23] Although

89

some writers, including Paolo Zacchia in his influential 1620 treatise *Medico-Legal Questions*, began questioning the theory of ensoulment, that theory remained prevailing dogma until the nineteenth century. A few writers can be found defending it even in the twentieth century. Contributing to the gradual abandonment of the ensoulment theory were nineteenth-century medical advances, including Karl Ernest Baer's discovery in 1827 of the human ovum and the later discovery of the joint role in conception of the spermatozoan and the ovum.

The decline of the ensoulment theory was accompanied by a hardening of the papal position on abortion. In 1869 Pius IX deleted reference to "ensouled fetus" in the excommunication for abortion, a change interpreted as meaning that ensoulment occurred at conception. Several late-nineteenth-century papal pronouncements declared illicit many forms of therapeutic abortion. The new Code of Canon Law in 1917 specifically included "mothers" among those to be excommunicated for procuring abortion. In 1930 Pius XI issued an encyclical condemning abortion for therapeutic, social, and eugenic grounds. And the Second Vatican Council declared in the early 1960s, "Life from its conception is to be guarded with the greatest care. Abortion and infanticide are horrible crimes."[24]

ENGLISH COMMON LAW

The history of secular legal treatment of abortion also is in dispute. References can be found both condemning abortion (though not to the degree of the ecclesiastical authorities) and apparently tolerating it. The secular record suggests that express assertion of a *compelling* government interest in preserving fetal life throughout gestation is a relatively recent development. To be sure, abortion has rarely been regarded in a positive light. But a hard-line anti-abortion policy does not appear to have been prevalent throughout much of the history of the common law. To the contrary, abortion seems to have received uncommonly little, and very late, attention from the law for a matter of the moral gravity that its more extreme modern opponents attribute. And fetal protection has never been a salient objective. The record indicates that at common law, abortion before "quickening" was either not a serious crime or no crime at all.

Early common law records of abortion cases are sparse. Dellapena argues in *Webster* that the common law has condemned abortion since its earliest days, offering as evidence a dozen or so thirteenth-century common law prosecutions for abortion. Conceding that "the terse records do not indicate any punishment," he argues that the "many clear records of 'not guilty' demonstrate that the indictments and appeals were valid under the common law."[25]

Means, on the other hand, argues that two fourteenth-century cases establish a common law "liberty" of voluntary abortion throughout pregnancy. In the first, labeled by Means as the Twinslayer's Case, the defendant was accused of having beaten a woman who was in an advanced stage of pregnancy with twins. One twin died and the other was born alive but died a few days later (after being baptized). Because "the Justices were unwilling to adjudge this thing a felony, the accused was released...." In the second case, which Means named the Abortionist's Case, "the opinion was that [the defendant] shall not be arrested on this indictment since no baptismal name was in the indictment, and also it is difficult to know whether he killed the child or not...."[26]

Means goes on to cite two sixteenth-century treatises to the effect that the Twinslayer's and Abortionist's cases established that abortion, even late in pregnancy, lacked any criminal character at common law. One treatise, *Pleas of the Crown* (vol. 1, 1557), by Sir William Stanford, states that for the crime of homicide, "It is required that the thing killed be *in rerum natura* [in actual existence]. And for this reason if a man killed a child in the womb of its mother: this is not a felony, neither shall he forfeit anything...."[27] The other, *Of the Office of the Justice of the Peace* (4th ed., 1588), by William Lambarde, takes a similar position. Stanford identifies the difficulty of proving that death resulted from the abortionist's conduct as the basis for the decision in the Abortionist's Case.

A later case, *Sims's Case* (1601), suggests that it is murder if the child is born alive and subsequently dies, but not if the child is stillborn (because it cannot be established whether the defendant's conduct caused the death). While consistent with the Abortionist's Case, *Sims's Case* seems contrary to the Twinslayer's Case as far as the liveborn twin is concerned. Means questions the justice's treatment of the liveborn twin example but points out that *Sims's Case* leaves intact the result concerning the stillborn twin.[28]

Other modern legal scholars dispute Means's analysis. For example, Dellapena cites *Sims's Case* as establishing that abortion was a serious crime at common law.[29] Robert M. Byrn argues that the Twinslayer's Case is "authority for nothing except the unwillingness of the court to let the abortionist go unpunished and the justices' puzzlement over how properly to deal with him. Subsequent history suggests that the justices' dilemma was rooted in problems of proof."[30] And Robert A. Destro suggests that the justices believed the defendant's conduct was criminal but were precluded from haling him back into court because he was under arrest in another place on a different charge.[31]

Other early commentators on the common law had a still different view of abortion. Lord Bracton's thirteenth-century treatise *On the Laws and Customs of England* regarded abortion after the fetus was "formed" or "animated" (i.e., quickened) as homicide. Both Stanford and Lambarde say Bracton is simply wrong. They, with another commentator, Michael Dalton, in his *The Countrey Justice, Conteyning the Practice of the Justices of the Peace* (1618), found neither felony nor misdemeanor ("misprision") in abortion at any point in pregnancy.[32]

Sir Edward Coke, on the other hand, stated that abortion after quickening was "a great misprision":

> If a woman be quick with childe, and by a Potion or otherwise killeth it in her wombe; or if a man beat her, whereby the childe dieth in her body, and she is delivered of a dead childe, this is a great misprision, and no murder; but if the childe be born alive, and dieth of the Potion, battery, or other cause, this is murder: for in law it is accounted a reasonable creature,

in rerum natura, when it is born alive.... And so horrible an
offense should not go unpunished. And so was the law holden
in Bractons time.... And herewith agreeth Fleta [a fourteenth-
century commentator]: and herein the law is grounded upon
the law of God, [here Coke quotes Genesis 9:6] If a man
counsell a woman to kill the childe within her wombe, when
it shall be born, and after she is delivered of the childe, she
killeth it; the counsellor is an accessory to the murder, and yet
at the time of the commandment, or counsell, no murder
could be comitted of the childe in utero matris: the reason of
which the case proveth well the other case.[33]

Stephen Kranson and William Hollberg, writing in the 1980s,
suggest that by "great misprision" Coke meant "an offense that
could be equated with some felonies today that are not punishable with death."[34] Dellapena, not surprisingly, regards Coke as
authoritatively recording the criminality of abortion at common
law. Means characterizes Coke's statement as "nonsense," discredited by Stanford; and he points out that the only precedent
cited by Coke—the Twinslayer's and Abortionist's cases and
Stanford himself—contradict Coke's conclusion.[35]

Be that as it may, other eminent common law commentators
were heavily influenced by Coke's view that postquickening
abortion was criminal, though not murder. Serjeant Hawkins, in
his *Treatise of the Pleas of the Crown* (1716), stated:

> And it was anciently holden, That the causing of an Abortion
> by giving a Potion to, or striking, a Woman big with Child,
> was Murder: But at this Day, it is said to be a great Misprision
> only, and not Murder....[36]

By "big with Child" Hawkins presumably meant a pregnancy in
the postquickening stage.

Sir Matthew Hale, in *History of the Pleas of the Crown* (1736),
appears at first glance to attempt to follow Coke, the Abortionist's Case, and the Twinslayer's Case simultaneously:

> If a woman be quick or great with child, if she take, or another
> give her any potion to make an abortion, or if a man strike her,

93

whereby the child within her is kild, it is not murder nor manslaughter by the law of *England*, because it is not yet *in rerum natura*, tho it be a great crime, and by the judicial law of Moses [Exodus 21:22] was punishable with death, nor can it legally be known, whether it were kild or not [citing the Abortionist's Case]. So it is, if after such child were born alive, and baptized, and after die of the stroke given to the mother, this is not homicide [citing the Twinslayer's Case].

But if a man procure a woman with child to destroy her infant, when born, and the child is born, and the woman in pursuance of that procurement kill the infant, this is murder in the mother, and the procurer is accessory to murder if absent, and this whether the child were baptized or not.[37]

According to Means, Hale contradicts Coke's dictum. Means interprets Hale's statement that a postquickening abortion "be a great crime" to mean an *ecclesiastical* rather than a temporal crime. And he contrasts Hale's open endorsement of the Twinslayer's Case with Coke's statement that its rule "was never holden for law." Sir James Fitzjames Stephen's 1883 description of early English crimes supports Means: "Procuring an abortion seems to have been regarded as an ecclesiastical offense only."[38] In any event, Means concedes Coke's criticism of the difficulty-of-proof justification for the judgment with respect to the live-born twin (who after all was demonstrably alive before the abortionist's act) and notes that English courts finally and unambiguously accepted Coke's view in such cases. But he maintains that the result as to the stillborn twin survived until statutory revision and rested ultimately on abortion's inherent lack of secular criminality.[39]

Sir William Blackstone, in his monumental *Commentaries on the Laws of England* (1765–1769), attempted to organize the common law's various pronouncements. His conclusions eventually became accepted as authoritative by the first American courts to face the voluntary abortion issue in the nineteenth century. In volume one, concerning the Rights of Persons, Blackstone describes the legal status of prenatal life. There is something for pro– and anti–abortion rights advocates alike in his discussion.[40] Blackstone simultaneously endorses the sanctity of life; the concept that legally protectable life does not form until sometime after conception; the proposition that while abortion is criminal in certain circumstances, its criminality had become relatively less serious at common law; by implication the proposition that abortion is perfectly lawful in other circumstances; and the notion that the unborn enjoy certain legal rights.

Blackstone concludes that quickening is the dividing line between criminal (misdemeanor) and noncriminal abortion. For certain other purposes, however, the law looks upon the unborn as having legal existence. Thus:

> Life is the immediate gift of God, a right inherent by nature in every individual; and it begins in contemplation of law as soon as an infant is able to stir in the mother's womb. For if a woman is quick with child, and by a potion, or otherwise killeth it in her womb; or if any one beat her, whereby the child dieth in her body, and she is delivered of a dead child; this, though not murder, was by the ancient law homicide of manslaughter [citing Bracton]. But at present it is not looked upon in quite so atrocious a light, though it remains a very heinous misdemeanor [citing Coke].
>
> An infant *in ventre sa mere*, or in the mother's womb, is supposed in law to be born for many purposes. It is capable of having a legacy, of a surrender of a copyhold estate made to it. It may have a guardian assigned to it; and it is enabled to have an estate limited to its use, and to take afterwards by such limitation, as if it were then actually born. And in this point the civil law agrees with ours.[41]

In his fourth volume, concerned with Public Wrongs, Blackstone describes the relationship between abortion and murder:

> Farther; the person killed must be *"a reasonable creature in being, and under the king's peace,"* at the time of the killing. Therefore to kill an alien, a Jew, or an outlaw, who are all under the king's peace or protection is as much murder as to kill the most regular born Englishman; except he be an alien-enemy, in time of war. To kill a child in it's mother's womb, is

now no murder, but a great misprision: but if the child be
born alive, and dieth by reason of the potion or the bruises it
received in the womb, it is murder in such as administered or
gave them [citing Coke and Hawkins].[42]

In view of his citations to Coke and Hawkins, and his statements in the first volume, Blackstone presumably was referring
to a quickened "child in it's mother's womb...."

In sum, it is difficult to embrace the entirety of either side's
interpretation of the common law record. Abortion obviously was
practiced to some extent throughout recorded English history,
though estimates of its incidence are necessarily uncertain. At
least some cases of abortion were prosecuted, but the real wrongdoing in some of those cases involved an assault on the woman.
Nevertheless, respected commentators on the common law over a
three-hundred-year period regarded abortion in at least some circumstances as criminal. On the other hand, the paucity of cases
on the subject, the absence of a recorded case of punishment, the
discounting of criminality from felony to misdemeanor, and the
apparent noncriminality of prequickening abortions all suggest
that even postquickening abortion was not regarded by the common law with the moral opprobrium attributed to it by its modern opponents. The common law's disapproval of abortion seems
even more mild in view of the kinds of misdeeds that English law
held to be capital offenses at one time or another. Besides high
treason, rebellion, homicide, and rape, capital offenses also
included false coining, clipping of gold coin, larceny above twelve
pence, and purse-cutting.[43] Had the common law regarded abortion as the moral equivalent of genocide, surely the record would
say so much more clearly than it does.

It seems most unlikely that the common law was dedicated to
preserving fetal life in anything like modern pro-life terms. One
indication of the common law's unconcern for fetal life, especially
prequickening fetal life, is the maternal reprieve. According to
Means, under "an ancient rule of common law...an expectant
mother under sentence of death was examined by a jury of
matrons. If their verdict was that her foetus was not yet quick, she
was hanged forthwith; if they found that quickening had already

taken place, she was reprieved until after her delivery, and then hanged." Of course, at the time quickening was the most reliable method of detecting pregnancy. Prequickening hanging therefore may have reflected not the common law's disregard for fetal life but skepticism about its existence in a particular case. But, as Coke himself explains, "she shall have the benefit of that [reprieve] but once, though she be again quick with childe...." In other words, the common law was quite prepared to sacrifice the fetus by hanging a woman felon pregnant a second time, even if quick, to prevent abuse of the reprieve.[44]

On the other hand, had voluntary abortion throughout pregnancy been a cherished "liberty" rigorously protected by English common law, it seems unlikely that the record would reflect as much disapproval as it does. The possibility that the abortionist's common law immunity rested on the difficulty of proving cause of fetal death scarcely counts as a positive endorsement of a policy favoring abortion rights.

The overall impression is rather one of haphazard toleration, not consistent approval or disapproval. Because abortion procedures until quite recently were often dangerous to the pregnant woman—consisting of the administration of toxic substances, the infliction of violent blows or other trauma to induce miscarriage, or risky septic surgery—much common law opposition to abortion may well have been in the interests of protecting maternal health. That interest played a large role in the first legislative efforts to restrict abortion in the United States.

The English common law's uneven toleration of abortion was largely displaced in 1803. In that year Parliament enacted an omnibus crime bill, Lord Ellenborough's Act, to toughen England's criminal law. Among the new capital felonies, which included certain kinds of assault and fraud and attempted murder by poison, was the attempt to procure abortion after quickening by the administration of poison. The act also provided for transportation to the penal colonies of offenders convicted of producing abortion by any method before quickening. A subsequent amendment in 1828, Lord Lansdowne's Act, made postquickening abortion by instrument equally criminal with abortion by poison. England thus did not establish a strongly anti-abortion policy until the early nineteenth century. That policy was to endure for almost a century and a half. The pregnancy reprieve, however, was to remain the law until modified by a 1931 statute.[45]

AMERICAN ABORTION POLICY

Colonial America imported the English common law, which largely governed the treatment of abortion until the mid-nineteenth century. Abortion before quickening thus appears not to have been regarded as a crime at common law in early America. Dellapena argues, "Abortion simply was never accepted in American society." But he supports that assertion with only a few isolated colonial prosecutions (some for assaults on pregnant women, and none described as for postquickening abortions) and one 1716 municipal ordinance from New York.[46]

The first pronouncement on voluntary abortion by an American court of last resort, the Supreme Judicial Court of Massachusetts' 1812 opinion in *Commonwealth v. Bangs*, recognized the noncriminal nature of prequickening abortion; but the court's brief opinion left the grounds for the decision unclear. Thirty-three years later, however, the Supreme Judicial Court of Massachusetts clearly held in *Commonwealth v. Parker* that voluntary abortion before quickening was no crime at common law. After reviewing the common law commentators described above, the Massachusetts court concluded that "although the acts set forth are, in a high degree, offensive to good morals and injurious to society, yet they are not punishable at common law" because the state had failed to allege quickening in one count of the indictment and to prove it under another.[47]

Almost all other mid-century courts that considered the question also understood the common law to tolerate prequickening abortions. For example, New Jersey took that view in *State v. Cooper* in 1849. After reviewing the common law authorities, the New Jersey Supreme Court went so far as to conclude:

98

There is in none of them a reference to the mere procuring of an abortion by the destruction of the foetus unquickened, as a crime against the person or against God and religion. *Abortion*, as a crime, is to be found only in modern treatises and in modern statutes.[48]

Other courts following *Cooper* include the Iowa and Alabama supreme courts in two slander cases,* Maine's Supreme Court, and, as late as 1879, the Supreme Court of Kentucky.[49]

The Supreme Court of Pennsylvania, however, reached the opposite conclusion in 1850, in a decision that appears to have been anomalous. In *Mills v. Commonwealth*, the court upheld a conviction under an indictment alleging an attempt to procure an abortion, but not alleging quickening. *Mills* certainly shows judicial disapproval of abortion:

> It is a flagrant crime, at common law, to attempt to procure the miscarriage or abortion of the woman; because it interferes with and violates the mysteries of nature, in that process by which the human race is propagated and continued. It is a crime against nature, which obstructs the fountain of life, and therefore it is to be punished.

While expressly rejecting the quickening doctrine on its own merits, the court did not purport to be stating the general rule:

> [The quickening doctrine] is not, I apprehend, the law in Pennsylvania, and never ought to have been the law anywhere. It is not the murder of a living child, which constitutes the offense, but the destruction of gestation, by wicked means and against nature. The moment the womb is instinct with embryo life, and gestation has begun, the crime may be perpetrated.[50]

Although the *Mills* court's views did not accurately reflect the

---

*In both cases the alleged slander consisted of the accusation that the plaintiff had performed a prequickening abortion. Under the law of slander at the time, recovery depended on whether such a statement accused the plaintiff of an indictable offense. The court in each case concluded that it did not, and therefore denied relief to each plaintiff.

state of the common law, they foretold what was to become America's abortion policy in the ensuing decades. James Mohr's *Abortion in America* describes the evolution of that legislatively defined policy as proceeding in two waves, the first from 1821 to 1841, and the second between 1841 and 1880. Both waves were intertwined with, and in large part the result of, substantial changes in the organization and regulation of the medical profession.

Someone seeking health care in the unregulated era of the early nineteenth century could visit a "regular" physician, who was a graduate of one of the country's few reputable medical schools and a member of an established medical society, or an "irregular," who had little or no formal medical training or had graduated from a private "degree mill." The regulars, viewing the irregulars as a threat to their status and to the public's health, turned to state legislatures for the enactment of comprehensive laws to control the spread of malpractice. Such measures included provisions governing abortion and formed the first wave of regulation.

The first American abortion statute, passed in Connecticut in 1821, is a good example. The original Connecticut law, enacted as part of an omnibus crime bill, amended the provision concerning administration of "any deadly poison, or other noxious or deadly substance" with the intention "thereby to murder," by adding "or thereby to cause or procure the miscarriage of any woman, then being quick with child...." According to Mohr, the law "might best be characterized as a poison control measure." He points out that the provision did not proscribe abortion as abortion, but only one particularly unsafe method:

> It is likely, in other words, that the abortion clause in section 14, the nation's first, was aimed primarily at apothecaries and physicians, who the state could presume should know better than to seek profits by selling preparations that were only marginally effective as abortifacients, but demonstrably dangerous as poisons.[51]

In 1830, however, Connecticut enacted another omnibus bill

which included provisions not only to criminalize postquickening abortion by the use of instruments as well as by poison, but also to reduce the penalty from life to seven to ten years. Thus Connecticut made it a crime to attempt to produce an abortion after quickening by any means. In effect, however, the law merely codified the common law's toleration of prequickening abortion and its substantially more lenient punishment of postquickening abortion than of various forms of homicide.[52] Mohr argues that the Connecticut law could even be viewed as pro-choice because it preserved the common law doctrine notwithstanding England's contemporaneous abandonment of it in Lord Ellenborough's and Lord Lansdowne's Acts.

New York's first legislative dealings with abortion further illustrate the origins of the first wave of abortion legislation. Like Connecticut's law, New York's statute resembled the common law: it prohibited only postquickening abortions and did not operate against the pregnant woman herself. Another provision of the new code prohibited the administration of abortion-inducing substances or the use of instruments to procure an abortion, "unless the same shall have been necessary to preserve the life of such woman, or shall have been advised by two physicians to be necessary for that purpose," thereby codifying the concept of an exception for "therapeutic abortions."[53] Although this section could have been interpreted also to prohibit prequickening abortions, it "lay buried in the code, unenforced."[54]

Cyril Means's detailed analysis of the legislative history of the New York law concludes that the legislators' overall purpose was chiefly to protect women from the hazards of certain medical procedures. That concern was shown, for example, in a proposed but ultimately unenacted provision establishing similar restrictions for other surgical procedures, and an explanatory note that expressed the legislators' concern with "the rashness of many young practitioners in performing the most important surgical operations for the mere purpose of distinguishing themselves." In large part because discovery and adoption of aseptic surgical techniques lay several decades in the future, surgery in the early nineteenth century was often extremely risky.[55]

In addition to their altruistic concern for the public's health and their more self-interested worry about competition from irregulars—intensified by the regulars' own limited skills at the time—many regulars also were opposed to abortion on moral grounds. The regulars' strong opposition to the taking of human life, together with their doubts about the use of quickening as a developmental milestone, formed an additional source of their opposition.

Some statutes enacted during this period were limited to postquickening abortions; others were not. It made little practical difference:

> Yet in practice, indictments could not be brought under these laws before quickening because intent had to be proved and the only way that intent could be proved was to demonstrate that the person who administered the poison could have known beyond any doubt that the woman was pregnant. Thus the omission of explicit reference to quickening in these two early laws probably reflected the fact that the quickening distinction was taken completely for granted rather than any effort to eliminate it.[56]

This first wave of legislative activity, viewed in historical context, does not reflect a clear social judgment that abortion was inherently unacceptable. Each law was part of a larger bill, and enforcement was minimal. Moreover,

> there was no substantial popular outcry for anti-abortion activity; or, conversely, no evidence of public disapproval of the nation's traditional common law attitudes. No legislator took a political stand on abortion; no legislator cast a recorded vote for or against abortion as a question by itself. The popular press neither called for nor remarked upon the passage of the acts; the religious press was equally detached. This would later change, but the criminal status of abortion originated as a doctors' and lawyers' issue, not a popular issue in any sense.[57]

Mohr thus characterizes these measures, which sought to punish the abortionist and not the pregnant woman, as "malpractice indictments in advance," intended primarily to regulate medicine rather than deter women from abortions. Abortion was largely perceived at the time as "a fundamentally marginal practice usually resorted to by women [unmarried, young, and "in trouble"] who deserved pity and protection rather than criminal liability."[58] That protection of fetal life did not underlie these early statutes is further shown by the adoption in some states of the common law rule of pregnancy reprieve.[59]

Conditions changed dramatically in the second wave of legislation, between 1840 and 1880, as abortion moved from the economic and social fringes to the highly visible mainstream. During this period more and more white, married, Protestant, native-born, middle- and upper-class women were having abortions as a form of family planning at a time of sharply declining fertility rates among that segment of the population. To meet this growing demand, a thriving and conspicuous abortion service and product industry developed. Aggressive entrepreneurs, consisting largely of irregulars, established "clinics," peddled abortion-inducing remedies (which included autoabortive instruments, wholly inert pills, mild laxatives, cottonroot, and potentially dangerous compounds containing ergot, savin, or black hellebore), and vigorously advertised their goods and services.[60]

The driving force behind the increasingly stringent anti-abortion legislation enacted during this period, according to Mohr, once again was the regular physicians' concerted campaign to organize, professionalize, and control the practice of medicine in the United States. Just ten years after the formation of the American Medical Association in 1847, Horatio Storer, a young physician seeking to establish his reputation, kicked off his anti-abortion crusade with a report to the association on the inadequacy of current law. Medical societies and publications around the country joined the crusade. The AMA published Storer's anti-abortion essay, *Why Not? A Book for Every Woman*, which Mohr characterizes as "scare propaganda aimed at women," for popular consumption. In 1868 Storer, in collaboration with Franklin Fiske Heard, published the legal treatise *Criminal Abortion: Its Nature, Its Evidence, and Its Law*. The

AMA and local medical societies kept up the anti-abortion campaign throughout the 1870s, having "a direct impact upon the evolution of abortion policy in the United States...."[61]

Two other factors contributed to the growing opposition to abortion. One factor was nativistic and classist fears of "race suicide," prompted by the declining fertility of white, Protestant, native-born Americans. Another was the changing legal, economic, and social status of women. Many states were already reforming their property and divorce laws, the women's suffrage movement was gaining considerable momentum, and women's political consciousness was expanding. Many conservative physicians feared this new challenge to women's traditional role of childbearing and child-rearing. Thus the medical profession's position on abortion may also have been influenced by sexist attitudes about women's proper roles in society, as well as by the profession's campaign against midwives and others to establish hegemony over pregnancy and childbirth.[62] Mohr points out, however, that feminists of the time were much more divided on the abortion issue than they are today. While women's reproductive freedom was and is certainly a central feminist demand, many feminists then regarded abortion as a degrading evil made necessary by men's sexual dominance. They advocated abstinence or contraception as alternatives. Thus some feminists actually aided the anti-abortion cause of the staunchly anti-feminist regulars.

The legislative impact of these forces appeared in two steps during this period. In the first step, from approximately 1840 to 1860, statutory reforms appeared in a number of states; but their practical effect was relatively modest. One important reform was an effort to abrogate the common law immunity for prequickening abortion and thus to adopt a more consistently anti-abortion policy. For example, close on the heels of *Commonwealth v. Parker*, described above, the Massachusetts legislature enacted what Mohr characterizes as the first bill in America to deal separately and exclusively with abortion, which criminalized prequickening abortion.[63] New York and other states also attempted similar reforms. A typical pattern was to make prequickening abortions less serious offenses than postquickening abortions. New York also took the unprecedented step of making the pregnant woman herself criminally liable. Several other states followed suit.

Another measure enacted during this period tried to address one of the more visible products of the proliferation of abortion practice: Massachusetts and several other states attempted to ban abortion advertising. At least some of the motivation for such measures appears to have been the sordidness of abortion's extreme commercialization.

The reform effort from 1840 to 1860 had little real impact. Although opposition to abortion was increasing, it was still relatively moderate. Only a handful of states repealed the pregnant woman's common law immunity for abortion. The few anti-advertising laws were weak. Because of the difficulty of proving pregnancy and intent, the quickening doctrine retained its practical force even in the states that sought to abolish it. And a third of the states had no abortion laws in 1860, leaving the common law in force.

Between 1860 and 1880, however, the regulars' crusade—boosted by the formation of the AMA and the anti-abortion leadership of Horatio Storer—began to shape public opinion and to produce stronger, more effective legislation. For example, the *New York Times* and the *New York Tribune* endorsed restrictions on abortion advertising. The regulars' campaign also gained the support of the anti-obscenity movement, and Anthony Comstock's prosecution of abortionists was especially effective in suppressing abortion advertising. On the other hand, though a few church groups (primarily Congregationalists and Old School Presbyterians) backed the regulars, the Protestant and Catholic press as a whole was largely silent on abortion before the Civil War and not prominently involved in the anti-abortion movement during the next two decades.[64]

Legislative enactments between 1860 and 1880 were numerous and potent. "Some of the laws passed during the period remained literally unchanged through the 1960s; others were altered only in legal phraseology, not in basic philosophy." Many states thus prohibited abortion throughout pregnancy. The quickening doctrine was laid to rest by laws criminalizing the use of instruments or substances in attempted abortion, whether or not the woman was actually pregnant, thereby relieving the prosecution of the burden of proving pregnancy. A number of states, though not all, enacted measures making it a crime for the pregnant woman to request or allow an abortion to be performed on her.[65]

The next decade saw the consolidation of this trend. By the turn of the century the United States had completed a transition from a nation without abortion laws of any kind to one in which abortion was legally proscribed.[66] Most states had acted to prohibit abortion, and the courts' previously tolerant attitude toward abortion had hardened against defendants, in some cases shifting to the defendant the burden of proving therapeutic necessity.

Just as the success of the regulars' anti-abortion crusade reached its apogee, however, their enthusiasm began to wane. By 1900 the regulars had largely achieved their goal of winning control over the practice of medicine in America. The advent of antiseptic techniques and other technological advances substantially enhanced their professional credibility during the late nineteenth century. The growing power of medical societies enabled them to press for outright state licensure, as the irregulars were forced from the marketplace.

The result of these developments was to freeze American abortion policy as of the 1880s for the next eighty to ninety years. While surgical abortion was becoming much safer, the most powerful group behind the anti-abortion movement lost interest in the issue. The regulars no longer needed it; they had gained control over medical practice. But the effectiveness of their anti-abortion efforts (assisted perhaps by the growing availability of contraceptives among the married middle and upper classes), drove much of the practice of abortion—or at least popular perceptions of its incidence—back to the social fringes. Abortion once again became associated with back alleys, the lower classes, and the young and unmarried.

This state of affairs endured until the mid-twentieth century, when social forces began pushing toward liberalizaton of abortion laws. Fears of declining fertility had been displaced by concern about overpopulation. Contraception became more openly endorsed and subsidized by government, and oral contraceptives (the "pill") appeared in the early 1960s. Advances in medical science's ability to prolong life, and to compromise it with treatments such as the drug thalidomide, raised penetrating questions about the distinction between the quality of life and life itself.[67] As Mohr has noted, "Abortion no longer seemed to involve a choice between absolutes—life or not life—but matters of degree—what kind of life under what circumstances."[68] The women's movement largely overcame its nineteenth-century opposition to abortion and asserted a woman's right to full control of her body. And many prominent members of the medical community, spurred by growing evidence of the relative safety of early abortions if performed by competent physicians, compared with the risks of childbirth or illegal abortions, pressed for reform. In a survey by *Modern Medicine* magazine in 1967, 87 percent of American physicians favored relaxing anti-abortion policies, and so did the executive board of the American Public Health Association.[69] By the 1970s the American Medical Association's House of Delegates adopted resolutions emphasizing the "best interests of the patient," "sound clinical judgment," and "informed patient consent."[70]

These forces produced a legislative response in a few states in the late 1960s and early 1970s. At the time most states outlawed abortion except as necessary to save the life of the mother. A few states also allowed abortions if necessary to preserve maternal health. Some states prohibited abortions only after the early states of pregnancy.[71]

One writer has noted, "Abortion has probably been the only aspect of medical practice regulated by criminal statute. As a result, lawyers preparing drafts of revised legislation have tended to work within the context of a criminal code rather than with statutes regulating the medical profession; the Model Penal Code is the prototype of this approach."[72]* The Model Penal

*The Model Penal Code is a proposed uniform criminal code developed by the American Law Institute (ALI), an organization of prominent lawyers, legal scholars, and judges which proposes model statutory laws and prepares compilations of com-

107

Code's 1962 proposed revisions to state abortion laws reflect an early expression of this reform movement. The code proposed to legalize abortion in certain circumstances: if continuing the pregnancy would gravely impair the pregnant woman's mental or physical health; if the child would be born with a grave physical or mental defect; or if the pregnancy resulted from rape, incest, or illicit intercourse with a girl under the age of sixteen. These proposals were to have a major influence on legislation in reforming states.

After 1966 a number of states began liberalizing their abortion laws. By the early 1970s eighteen states had relaxed such laws, some substantially. Not surprisingly, in view of the medical profession's role in the reform movement, the primary focus of legislative change was to expand the scope of permissible therapeutic abortions and consequently physicians' control over access to abortion. By the early 1970s thirteen states allowed abortion in order to avoid harm to the woman's physical or mental health. Because this exception is potentially as elastic as the willingness of physicians to find justification (especially if a subjective, good-faith belief standard is used), many states required consultation or approval by peer physicians (sometimes in the form of a hospital review board) before therapeutic abortions could be performed. Twelve states allowed abortion if the fetus would have been born with a serious mental or physical handicap. And the third principal exception was for the case of rape or incest. A handful of states eliminated all restrictions except to regulate the qualifications of the person performing the abortion, the place where it was performed, and the gestational age by which the pregnancy could be legally terminated.

One concern of liberalizing states was that they not become an "abortion magnet," drawing women seeking abortions from neighboring, less liberal states. Thus many reform laws provided that the woman must have been a resident of the state for a specified

---

mon law principles in the various disciplines of law. Although the ALI is not a government body, and its proposals and compilations have no legal force, it has been highly influential in shaping the law in a number of legal areas. Many states, for example, have adopted various provisions of the Model Penal Code.

time period before she could apply for a therapeutic abortion. The reform movement also took hold across the Atlantic. England substantially liberalized its abortion laws in 1967 by allowing the range of justifications for therapeutic abortion to include almost any aspect of the pregnant woman's circumstances, including the impact on existing children.[73]

Whether this nascent reform movement ever would have gained national acceptance of its own accord will never be known. A modern anti-abortion movement was already in place and had begun to fight legislative reform. But the reform movement was gaining momentum and political influence.

In 1973, however, the course of American abortion policy, American constitutional law, and national politics was dramatically altered by the Supreme Court's decision in *Roe v. Wade*. That case established a federal constitutional right to abortion, and thus made every state law on abortion subject to federal judicial review for compliance with the standards established by the Court in *Roe*. Some observers have suggested that *Roe* led the pro-choice movement to rely largely on the federal judiciary to protect abortion rights, while the case stimulated conservative pro-life activists to a high level of political organization. Perhaps the course of reform eventually would have produced substantial legislative change at the state level, but it seems unlikely that change would have gone nearly as far as *Roe* mandated, and certainly not as quickly.

In any event, since 1973 the federal courts have been squarely in the center of the abortion controversy. Informed consideration of the abortion issue today therefore requires an understanding of the Supreme Court's approach to the issue. That approach has gone through four distinct evolutionary stages in the twenty years since *Roe*. In the first, dominated by *Roe* itself, the Court explicitly recognized a constitutional right to abortion. In the second stage the Court elaborated—some have said expanded— the contours of abortion rights, as challenges were brought to a variety of state laws regulating abortion. In the third stage the Court reversed its expansive trend and began to authorize a greater range of restrictive state regulation of abortion. And in

109

the fourth and most recent stage, a narrow and fragile majority of the Court announced its continuing commitment to *Roe*'s "core holding" and the use of viability as a legal boundary but also substantially revised the constitutional test for previability abortion regulations. These stages are explored in detail in the chapters to follow.

Part Two

. . . .

ROE V. WADE AND THE RECOGNITION OF A CONSTITUTIONAL RIGHT TO ABORTION

5. Constitutional Conflicts

· ·

The abortion issue is caught between sometimes conflicting forces in American political and legal culture. One is society's aspiration to protect individual liberty from the constraints of the majority. Another is faith in and respect for the representative democratic process. And yet another is society's felt need for order, some minimal standards of decency in conduct, and myriad adjustments to social and economic conditions. American constitutional law, including the past twenty years of abortion rights cases, has often been an exercise in balancing and adjusting the tension between those forces.

Plainly, our liberty—including the freedom to make one's own important life choices—is far from absolute. Elected government officials and their appointees directly or indirectly limit our choices in many areas. For example, anyone who has built or bought a house, entered a profession, run a business, or operated a farm has encountered a profusion of direct restrictions on individual action in the form of zoning regulations, licensing requirements and malpractice standards, minimum-wage and maximum-hour laws, health and safety regulations, environmental laws, trade practice regulations, and so on. Government also indirectly, but no less powerfully, affects the choices citizens make through a network of benefit, entitlement, subsidy, and tax programs. Welfare payments increasingly come with strings attached to encourage recipients to seek employment and to preserve family units. And the health-care choices available to Americans are heavily influenced by direct local, state, and federal regulations as well by indirect regulations through benefit programs like Medicare and Medicaid.

On the other hand, many Americans take it as an article of

national faith that some areas of life ought to remain relatively free of government interference. Under our society's constitutional form of government, with its long tradition of judicial review of the constitutionality of legislation, this tension expresses itself in a struggle between the legislative and judicial processes as our more intractable moral, philosophical, and political dilemmas sometimes find uneasy resolution in the courts.

In the area of abortion, this process has produced a complex and shifting structure of judicial limitations on legislative authority to make rules that affect a woman's decision whether to give birth. Whatever one's views on the morality of the abortion/childbirth decision, informed participation in this great debate requires some background in the legal principles and rules that the Supreme Court has developed as it has struggled with this difficult issue. Explaining the Court's abortion cases provides a sample of the various ways legislatures have attempted to limit the abortion decision. More fundamentally, the painstaking efforts of the country's highest judicial authority to reconcile abortion's agonizing dilemmas with the Court's vision of liberty under the Constitution are part of a much larger conversation about America itself. The constitutional struggle over abortion calls into question the relationship between the elected legislative and unelected judicial branches of government; the distribution of power between the central government and the states under our federal system; the balance between individual liberty and the authority of government; and the gnawing problem of who counts as a person entitled to claim the law's protection.

6. The Background to *Roe*

. . . .

Abortion rights raise special constitutional problems. The Supreme Court in *Roe v. Wade* held that the freedom to choose abortion is part of a right to privacy protected by the due process clause of the Fourteenth Amendment. That clause forbids a state from depriving citizens of "liberty" without due process of law. The Court has long recognized that the due process clause not only requires government to provide adequate procedures (such as fair notice and a hearing before a neutral decision-maker) before depriving a citizen of liberty ("procedural" due process), but also prohibits government from invading certain areas of an individual's life, at least not without a very good reason ("substantive" due process). But the Constitution nowhere mentions "privacy," "abortion," "sexuality," "family," or "procreation." The right to abortion therefore has no explicit basis in the text of the Constitution, apart from the very open-ended term "liberty"; and there is no evidence whatsoever that the framers of the Fourteenth Amendment understood "liberty" to include elective abortion.

Abortion rights' lack of a clear foundation in the text or in the framers' intent is one of the most controversial aspects of *Roe*—and the cases leading up to *Roe*—as a matter of constitutional law. Understanding the main points in this larger debate about constitutional interpretation will help in considering the Court's decisions in abortion cases.

In a thoughtful essay in the *Stanford Law Review*, Thomas Grey discusses *Roe* as a matter of constitutional interpretation. He identifies two basic, conflicting theories of constitutional interpretation. Under one theory, which he labels "pure interpretivism," "judges confine themselves to determining whether...

114

laws conflict with norms derived [or inferred] from the written Constitution," and only those norms—as opposed to norms not expressed or implied by the framers. This approach is not to be confused with a literal interpretation of the text of the Constitution, because it does allow identification of underlying purposes and principles: "Normative inferences may be drawn from silences and omissions, from structures and relationships, as well as from explicit commands."[1] *Roe* is the antithesis of pure interpretivism because it cannot be tied to any express or implied value choice of the framers, apart from their adoption of the due process clause.

The 1803 case of *Marbury v. Madison*, the seminal case in which the Court announced its great power to declare invalid laws that conflict with the Constitution, is an example of pure interpretivism. Chief Justice Marshall pronounced for the Court in *Marbury* that it is "emphatically the province and duty of the judicial department to say what the law is." He described several bases for the assertion of such a power. First, he characterized the Constitution as expressing the "original and supreme will" of the people. By expressing that will in specific *written* form, the people intended its express terms to limit government power. Any other interpretation, Marshall reasoned, would render the Constitution an exercise in futility.

Second, Marshall relied on several specific constitutional provisions as a basis for the power of judicial review, including Article III, which places the judicial power of the United States in the courts.[2] Deciding real cases and controversies is the Court's constitutional function, Marshall reasoned, even if those decisions require the Court to rule on the constitutionality of legislation. Further, although not mentioned in *Marbury*, there is historical support for the power of judicial review. The *Federalist Papers*, for example, argued that a countermajoritarian institution—the judiciary—was needed to check the legislature's tendency to concentrate all power in its own hands.[3]

Another important early case, again by Justice Marshall, illustrates how interpretivism relies on inference from the Constitution's text.[4] In *McCulloch v. Maryland*, which questioned the authority of Congress to establish a Bank of the United States,

Marshall developed the concept of implied powers. The federal government is one of limited, enumerated powers, and the Constitution does not specifically authorize the establishment of a federal bank. Marshall nonetheless concluded that the power to do so was implicit in the grant of other, more general powers (for example, over revenue and currency) and Article I's explicit grant of power "To make all Laws which shall be necessary and proper for carrying into Execution, for the foregoing Powers, and all other Powers vested by this Constitution in the Government of the United States...."

Marshall observed that "we must never forget that it is *a consti-tution* we are expounding," and reasoned that the nature of the Constitution requires "that only its great outlines should be marked, its important objects designated, and the minor ingredients which compose those objects be deduced from the nature of the objects themselves." In other words, Justice Marshall viewed the Constitution as laying out general principles of government—or "outlines"—with the details to be filled in by necessary inference. Any other interpretation, he maintained, would render the document "a splendid bauble." True, *McCulloch* involved the implication of government (legislative) *power* and not limitations on that power in the form of judicially enforceable individual rights; but it nevertheless established a method of reading the Constitution's text that includes inference, and the consequence of inferring congressional power in *McCulloch* was to limit the power of the state of Maryland. As Marshall also observed in *McCulloch*, the Constitution was "intended to endure for ages to come, and consequently, to be adapted to the various crises of human affairs."[5]

Thomas Grey calls the other theory of constitutional interpretation "noninterpretivism"—that is, not really based on an interpretation of the Constitution's text. This more expansive view of judicial authority accepts "the courts' additional role as expounder of basic national ideals of individual liberty and fair treatment, even when the content of these ideals is not expressed as a matter of positive law in the written Constitution."[6] Arguments usually offered in support of *Marbury* and

116

judicial review that are *not* based on the Constitution's text are noninterpretive. Those arguments provide both an example of noninterpretive reasoning and an understanding of why it may sometimes be a good idea to allow unelected judges to invalidate the enactments of our elected representatives.

One such argument is that the legislature and the executive feel too much pressure from constituents (typically organized into "interest groups") to decide constitutional questions with the kind of careful deliberation they require. We can see this theme expressed in *Casey*, the Court's most recent abortion decision. Another argument is that the existence of a judicial power to invalidate unconstitutional laws gives a kind of implicit seal of approval to all other laws as complying with our constitutional system of limited governmental powers.[7] Still another argument is that the courts, in the process of deciding constitutional questions, help the country to understand and to develop its national values.[8] This notion also appears in *Casey*.

Some noninterpretive rulings, as Grey explains, are further removed from the Constitution's text and the framers' intent than others. In some cases the Court applies express constitutional provisions to circumstances not intended by the framers. A good example is racial segregation in the public schools. The historical record shows that the framers most likely did not intend in 1868 to outlaw school segregation by adopting the equal protection clause of the Fourteenth Amendment—which at least generally relates to some kinds of racial discrimination— but the Court held such segregation unconstitutional in 1954. In another class of cases, however, "courts have created (or found) independent constitutional rights with almost no textual guidance. Examples are the contemporary right of privacy and the older liberty of contract."[9] *Roe*, as part of the right of privacy, is an extreme example of noninterpretivism.

Although the recognition of rights not clearly based on the text of the Constitution remains controversial, courts have long done it. *Roe v. Wade* can be seen as part of that tradition. And *Roe* is also squarely in the middle of the constitutional problems raised by that tradition. The key problem is that when courts invalidate laws without a clear basis in the text or history of the Constitution for doing so, they appear to be threatening representative democracy without adequate justification. The central tension thus is between judicial protection from legislative encroachment on various strongly held values, such as reproductive freedom, and the converse fear of allowing the democratic process to be thwarted by judges who are unconstrained by the value choices reflected in duly ratified constitutional provisions.

The idea that some values are so fundamental to our understanding of ourselves as a people that legislative enactments contravening them are invalid and therefore not "law" has considerable precedent. The Declaration of Independence, for example, speaks of "inalienable rights" and "self-evident truths."[10] And there also is precedent for the notion that not all such rights and interests are expressly written into the Constitution. For example, Alexander Hamilton wrote in 1774, "The sacred rights of mankind are not to be rummaged for, among old parchments, or musty records. They are written, as with a sun beam, in the whole *volume* of human nature,...and can never be erased or obscured...."[11] Early in our constitutional history this notion took the form of "natural rights" or "natural law," based in part on the social contract theory of John Locke.[12]

In their separate opinions in the 1798 Supreme Court case of *Calder v. Bull*, Justices Chase and Iredell debated whether courts may use natural law principles to invalidate legislative acts. Their exchange describes the conflict raised by natural law theory and applies with full force today to *Roe*. Justice Chase argued in favor of natural law:

> I cannot subscribe to the omnipotence of a state legislature, or that it is absolute and without control; although its authority should not be expressly restrained by the Constitution, or fundamental law of the State.... [There] are acts which the Federal, or State legislature cannot do, without exceeding their authority. There are certain vital principles in our free Republican governments, which will determine and over-rule an apparent and flagrant abuse of legislative power.... An Act of the legislature (for I cannot call it a law) contrary to the

118

great first principles of the social compact, cannot be considered a rightful exercise of legislative authority.[13]

Justice Iredell's opinion voiced the principal objection to invalidation on natural law grounds:

> ...It has been the policy of all the American states, [and] of the people of the United States, [to] define with precision the objects of the legislative power, and to restrain its exercise within the marked and settled boundaries. If any act of Congress, or the Legislature of a state, violates those constitutional provisions, it is unquestionably void.... If, on the other hand, the Legislature of the Union, or the Legislature of any [state], shall pass a law, within the general scope of their constitutional power, the Court cannot pronounce it to be void, merely because it is, in their judgment, contrary to the principles of natural justice. The ideas of natural justice are regulated by no fixed standard: the ablest and the purest men have differed upon the subject; and all that the Court could properly say, in such an event, would be, that the Legislature (possessed of an equal right of opinion) had passed an act which, in the opinion of the judges, was inconsistent with the abstract principles of natural justice.[14]

The objection, in other words, is that Justice Chase's "vital principles" are by no means as "certain" as he suggests. Nor is there necessarily consensus on what it means "to establish justice, to promote the general welfare, to secure the blessings of liberty, and to protect their persons and property from violence."

A modern scholar, John Hart Ely, has suggested that the courts are justified in holding laws invalid without an express constitutional authorization only when the judiciary is acting to correct blockages in the democratic process.[15] In other words, judicial review is seen in this light not as fundamentally antidemocratic but instead as reinforcing representative government. The Court recognized this important constitutional principle as early as *McCulloch*. In holding unconstitutional a Maryland tax on notes of the Bank of the United States, Marshall pointed out that the Bank of the United States was created by the federal government, where the people of all the states are represented, while the Maryland tax was enacted only by the representatives of Maryland's citizens. Allowing the representatives of only one state's citizens to impose a tax on federal agencies would defeat the process of representative government at the national level, Marshall concluded: "When a state taxes the operations of the government of the United States, it acts upon institutions created, not by their own constituents, but by people over whom they claim no control."

In the most famous footnote in constitutional law, Justice Harlan Fiske Stone in 1938 captured this concept when he stated, citing *McCulloch*, that "prejudice against discrete and insular minorities may be a special condition, which tends seriously to curtail the operation of those political processes ordinarily to be relied upon to protect minorities, and which may call for a correspondingly more searching judicial inquiry."[16] A good example of intervention to correct such defects would be judicial invalidation of racially discriminatory measures in voting.[17]

Considering these principles as a whole reveals significant tensions. *Marbury*'s idea that an important source of the power for judicial review flows from the Constitution as a *text* seems at odds with *McCulloch*'s approach of inferring powers—and rights—not expressly provided for in the document. After all, if the text is what matters, what basis is there for going outside it? As Marshall explained in *McCulloch*, however, inference may sometimes be necessary to give the written text real meaning and effect that endure over time—to prevent it from becoming "a splendid bauble." And reinforcing representative democracy—a value choice clearly reflected in the Constitution's text—may require inference from the text.

Marshall's reference to the Constitution as a *text* derives from his observation that the document reflects the will of the *people*. Courts may need to infer rights from the text both to effectuate the original expression of that will in the Constitution itself and to give it meaning in an unblocked political process. Nevertheless, the problem remains of how far courts should go. How can we tell when a judge is legitimately trying to enforce the value choices made by "the people" and reflected in the Constitution's text, and when the judge is illegitimately imposing his or her own value choices in the guise of interpretation? For some observers, the further from the text and history the Court gets—in other words, the more noninterpretivist—the more it looks like the judiciary is simply imposing its own views on everyone. This risk is greatest when the only tie to the text—as was the case in *Roe*—is a broad, open-ended term like "liberty."

The interpretivists' way of telling good inference from bad is to look at history and tradition. If the value being protected by the court has a solid basis in our history and traditions, we can say that the value choice is really the people's and not the Court's—even if that choice was not clearly expressed in the text of the Constitution. A frequent criticism of *Roe v. Wade*, for example, is that the framers—and thus the people—never intended to create abortion rights.

But to rely only on history and tradition can raise several problems. One is that the historical record, at least of the 1787 Constitutional Convention, is sketchy at best. The most complete account of the debates at the convention is James Madison's notes, which were not published until 1840, after his death. One estimate is that his notes, while accurate as far as they go, preserve less than 10 percent of each day's debates.[18] And if the framers' intent matters, what about their "intent" about whether later generations should consider the framers' subjective intent on specific issues? There is good reason to believe they intended to let the document speak for itself. They deliberately chose not to leave a detailed record of the debates; the official journal of the convention, published in 1819, recorded only the delegates' votes. Finally, it is not clear whose intent counts. The product of the delegates' labors that summer of 1787 did not become the Constitution until it was ratified by state conventions. Those conventions generated their own records as well as newspaper, pamphlet, correspondence, and essay coverage, including the collection of essays known as the *Federalist Papers*, written by James Madison, Alexander Hamilton, and John Jay in support of ratification. The adoption of the

Fourteenth Amendment in 1868 generated a large mass of documents, from records of congressional proceedings to records and press coverage of ratification proceedings at the state level. Too rich an historical record can make determining the framers' intent as uncertain as too sparse a record.[19]

Another problem is that the use of history can become what Michael McConnell has characterized as "original intent subverting the principle of the rule of law."[20] This occurs when the Court selects specific historical references that have something in common with the challenged activity but that bear little relation to a coherent principle of constitutional law. For example, in the 1983 case of *Marsh v. Chambers*, the Court reasoned that because the First Congress appointed legislative chaplins, the practice must be an accurate reflection of the framers' intent concerning the establishment clause of the First Amendment (which prohibits Congress from making laws respecting the establishment of religion) and therefore is constitutional today. *Roe*'s critics point to the prevalence of anti-abortion laws when the Fourteenth Amendment was drafted as clear evidence that abortion rights cannot be inferred from that amendment. This approach to history defines traditions in terms of the presence or absence of specific practices—such as legislative chaplins, abortion, adulterous fatherhood—rather than broader principles. The problem with such a narrow approach is that it can fail to identify any enduring, coherent set of principles, connected to constitutional purposes, to guide decisions about contemporary conduct.

This objection to "originalism" argues that the profound changes in American society in the last two hundred years— many unimaginable in 1787 or even in 1868—require a more enriched approach that identifies such principles. Otherwise the Constitution will become at best an anachronistic irrelevancy—a rather tarnished bauble—and at worst an ill-fitting straitjacket that constricts the nation's social, economic, political, and moral development. For example, the Court in *Marsh* failed to account for America's transformation into a culturally diverse and religiously pluralistic society. Another risk is that judges will resort to what the constitutional scholar Philip Kurland has described as "'law office history,' written the way brief writers write briefs, by picking and choosing statements and events favorable to the client's cause."[21] The abortion debate has seen advocacy on both sides masquerading as history, and the justices in *Casey* remain unable to agree on the content or the meaning of the historical record.[22]

PRECURSORS TO *ROE* AND PRIVACY RIGHTS: SUBSTANTIVE DUE
PROCESS IN THE ECONOMIC SPHERE

The Court's path to *Roe*, and its application of natural law theory, has been anything but straightforward. The Court continued to invoke natural law up to the Civil War, and the abolitionist movement gave additional force to natural law theory. Immediately after the Civil War, however, the Court retreated from natural law in its first ruling on the Fourteenth Amendment. The Court in the *Slaughterhouse Cases* rejected an important opportunity to infer that individual liberties were protected by the privileges or immunities clause of the Fourteenth Amendment. The *Slaughterhouse Cases* are significant for two reasons. First, that clause would have provided a sounder historical basis for natural rights claims that the Court did recognize in later cases that preceded *Roe*.* Second, the Court expressed concerns about excessive judicial power in the *Slaughterhouse Cases* that are echoed today in objections to *Roe*. Justice Antonin Scalia's criticisms of *Roe*, for example, have a strong philosophical link to the *Slaughterhouse Cases*.

The Court in the *Slaughterhouse Cases* rejected a challenge by an association of local butchers to Louisiana's granting a monopoly to a private corporation to operate New Orleans abattoirs. The challenge rested on a claim, based primarily on the privileges or immunities clause of the Fourteenth Amendment,

*Although the privileges or immunities clause does have an historical tie to natural law, it is extremely doubtful that the drafters of the Fourteenth Amendment had in mind the kind of natural law that included anything like abortion rights.

123

to the right to pursue one's chosen livelihood. That claim, though rooted in natural law, arguably would be valid under interpretive theory as within the value choices made by the framers of the Fourteenth Amendment. The model for the language of that clause, according to its draftsman Representative John A. Bingham, was the privileges and immunities clause of Article IV of the Constitution—which generally requires a state to extend to nonresidents the same rights it provides its own citizens. Supreme Court Justice Bushrod Washington, sitting as a Circuit Justice, had interpreted Article IV in 1823 in natural law terms as preserving those privileges "which are, in their very nature, fundamental; which belong, of right, to the citizens of all free governments."[23] Those privileges, according to Justice Washington, included the right of a citizen to pass through or to reside in another state "for the purposes of trade, agriculture, professional pursuits, or otherwise." The record suggests that the drafters of the Fourteenth Amendment had Justice Washington's opinion in mind when they wrote the privileges or immunities clause.

But in the *Slaughterhouse Cases* the Supreme Court in effect discounted the historical record of the framers' intent and concluded—based on a strained reading of the text—that the privileges or immunities clause of the Fourteenth Amendment did not provide federal protection of the butchers' right to pursue their livelihood against interference by their own state. That clause, the Court stated, was confined to the privileges of *national* citizenship. By interpreting those privileges as including largely those matters already protected by the Constitution, the Court gave almost no substantive content to the clause at all. And the privileges and immunities clause of Article IV, the Court concluded, protects individuals only from discrimination because of state citizenship by states *other* than their own. The Court's interpretation left state legislatures free to define the rights of their own citizens largely without federal interference. The Court also rejected the butchers' challenge based on equal protection of the laws, confining the operation of that provision to racial discrimination against black Americans. And the due process clause scarcely played a significant role in the case at all.*

The Court supported its decision with warnings of excessive federal judicial (and legislative) power at the expense of state autonomy. The Court's concerns in that regard are at the heart of the interpretive debate about natural rights, and are as relevant to the abortion issue as to the butchers' case. The Court specifically objected to the role that it would be required to assume under the butchers' natural law claim:

> ...Such a construction followed by the reversal of the judgments of the Supreme Court of Louisiana in these cases, would constitute this court a perpetual censor upon all legislation of the States, on the civil rights of their own citizens, with authority to nullify such as it did not approve as consistent with those rights, as they existed at the time of the adoption of this amendment.[24]

The Supreme Court's fears ultimately proved prophetic. The Court flexed its postbellum noninterpretivist muscles in a protracted campaign to limit both state and federal legislative power from the late nineteenth century until the 1930s. During that period the Court aggressively applied natural rights notions of individual "liberty of contract" and "economic substantive due process" to invalidate social and economic legislation (such as laws regulating working conditions and minimum wages). That campaign was driven by the Justices' ideological commitment to laissez-faire economic and social policy. The textual basis for those decisions was principally the due process clauses of the Fifth and Fourteenth Amendments, which the Court has understood to embrace not just requirements of fair legal procedures but also certain kinds of substantive rights.† The Court also

---

*The Court rejected the butchers' claim that the monopoly deprived them of property without due process on the basis that there was no deprivation of property.

†The basic idea is that the due process clauses require both procedural and substantive regularity. For example, suppose Congress enacted a law, without publishing it in any form and punishable by imprisonment, that redheads may not drive cars on interstate highways on Tuesdays. Procedural due process would require some form of fair notice to those who might be affected by the law, such as by publication in the United States Code. Further, before any Tuesday-driving redheads could be penalized for violating the law, due process would require (at a minimum) notice to him or her

employed the equal protection clause to invalidate disfavored legislative classifications.*

The early "substantive due process" cases, which struck down economic and social welfare legislation, in several important respects are the conceptual forebears to *Roe v. Wade.* One striking example, and the case whose name has become an epithet for unrestrained judicial review, is *Lochner v. New York* (1905). *Roe's* critics assert that *Roe* is indistinguishable from *Lochner*—a point hotly debated by the Justices in *Casey*. In *Lochner* a bakery employer was fined under a New York law that prohibited employing bakers more than ten hours a day or sixty hours a week. The Court ruled that the New York law interfered with the "right of contract between the employer and employees, concerning the number of hours in which the latter may labor in the bakery of the employer. The general right to make a contract in relation to his business is part of the liberty of the individual protected by the 14th Amendment of the Federal Constitution."[25]

To a later generation of lawyers, *Lochner* has come to stand for a genre of cases striking down a range of progressive legislative measures that benefited the "have nots" at the expense of the "haves." The variety of reforms that the Court rejected was impressive, ranging from controls on labor negotiation to price fixing to wages and hours of employees.[26] During this time, especially during the early days of the New Deal, the Court also struck down federal laws addressing similar subjects on the ground that they were not within the scope of Congress's constitutional power to regulate interstate commerce, as well as on substantive due process grounds.[27] The Court thus ruled during this period that matters such as child labor, unemployment, sweat shops, coal mining, and agricultural production were

---

of the charges and an opportunity to be heard before a neutral decision-maker. Substantive due process would look at the merits of the law itself, asking whether it was an appropriate subject for exercise of government power and whether the exercise of that power was properly related to a legitimate government purpose.

*The Court's analysis under the equal protection clause would examine how closely the classifications drawn by the legislature fit the legislative purpose. Suppose the legislative purpose in the hypothetical law described in the preceding footnote were the reduction of traffic congestion. Under the equal protection clause, the Court would ask whether singling out redheads was an acceptable approach.

beyond Congress's power to regulate because they were either not commerce or not sufficiently national in character, and that both state and federal reform legislation violated substantive due process rights. The Court did allow some laws to stand, upholding for example regulation of rail rates, women's (but not children's) working hours (but not wages), and impure foods and drugs.[28] As a consequence, state and federal legislatures alike were precluded from addressing several acute social problems, except for a patchwork of areas left open by the Court.

The Court's reasoning during this era was strained and formalistic. Thus, manufacturing, mining, and agricultural production were not commerce. Wage and hour laws, intended to free employees from the ravages of sweatshop conditions and their lack of real bargaining power as isolated individuals, violated the *employees'* liberty. Underlying at least some of the Court's rulings in this period was an ideological antipathy to measures that redistributed wealth or bargaining power.[29] *Roe*'s critics similarly have accused the Court of mandating, *Lochner* style, an ideology of extreme individualistic libertarianism, in personal as opposed to economic matters, that was never chosen by the people.

The Court's *Lochner*-style conception of social and economic conditions, while shared by other conservative observers and policymakers of the early twentieth century, eventually came to be badly out of touch with the times. The Court appeared to believe that its rulings would restore some halcyon natural economic and social order that had been disrupted by positive government intervention. But the Great Depression shook the country's faith in laissez-faire, "invisible hand" policies.[30] The old order suddenly no longer worked, and government did not seem quite so evil.

Of course, entrenched interests continued to contest the new measures, placing mounting pressure on the Court which came to a head in the infamous Roosevelt "Court-packing" plan of 1937. Widely viewed as an outright assault on the independence of the judiciary, the plan was overwhelmingly defeated in Congress.[31] In that same year, however, the Court clearly reversed its direction in both the substantive due process and the commerce clause cases—an about-face dubbed "a switch in time which saved nine." Although there is evidence that Justice Roberts, who provided the crucial fifth vote in the Court's 1937 switch, changed his mind based on the merits and not out of fear of the Court-packing plan, the Court obviously was feeling the heat of public opposition.[32] *Roe* again presents the difficult question of when, if ever, the Court should overrule its own precedent in response to hostile public opinion. The Court directly addressed that issue in *Casey* in light of the Court's 1937 experience.

Since 1937 the Court's substantive due process cases have asked only whether there is any conceivable reason for the law—unless the law burdens a fundamental right, in which case the review is much stricter. Unless the law is wholly arbitrary, it will be upheld against a substantive due process challenge.[33] The Court's 1937 rejection of a claim based on freedom of contract reveals the extent of the Court's ideological shift:

> What is freedom? The Constitution does not speak of freedom of contract. It speaks of liberty and prohibits the deprivation of liberty without due process of law.... But the liberty safeguarded is the liberty in a social organization which requires the protection of law against the evils which menace the health, safety, morals and welfare of the people. Liberty under the constitution is thus necessarily subject to the *restraints* of due process, and the regulation which is reasonable in relation to its subject and is adopted in the interests of the community is due process.[34]

In fact, since 1937 the Court has rejected every substantive due process challenge to prospective economic or social welfare legislation—unless the law implicates some interest that the Court considers a fundamental right.

A similar shift has occurred under the commerce clause. Since 1937 the Court has upheld exercises of the commerce clause power to regulate matters as local as the production and consumption on a single farm of several hundred bushels of wheat, racial discrimination in a motel and a barbecue restaurant, loan sharking, arson, and the development of hiking trails.[35] This approach to the commerce clause will become important if the federal Freedom of Choice Act becomes law, for the power Congress purports to exercise in enacting it is the commerce power.

One other development, in addition to the privacy cases discussed next, is relevant to the evolution of constitutional law that led to *Roe*. The most obvious textual source of individual constitutional rights is the Bill of Rights.* The Court held in 1833 that the Bill of Rights applied only to the federal government and not to the states.[36] In the twentieth century, however, the Court ruled that the Fourteenth Amendment "incorporated" provisions of the Bill of Rights to apply to the states.

The debate about "incorporation" further illustrates the difference between interpretivism and noninterpretivism, and the outcome of that debate ultimately formed one of the bricks in *Roe's* foundation. On one extreme of the incorporation debate was Justice Hugo Black, the arch-interpretivist. He argued that statements by the drafters of the Fourteenth Amendment established that they specifically intended to incorporate all of the first eight amendments through the privileges or immunities clause. In his view, those privileges or immunities are to be defined by, and limited to, the first eight amendments.[37] On the other side were Justice Frankfurter and the younger Justice Harlan.[38] They reasoned that the due process clause of the Fourteenth Amendment embodies evolving, natural law principles of "liberty," justice, and fundamental fairness. To them the Bill of Rights would not set a ceiling on the rights the Court might recognize.

The Court ultimately compromised between these two positions by selectively incorporating most provisions of the Bill of Rights through the due process clause of the Fourteenth Amendment. In the 1937 case of *Palko v. Connecticut* the Court stated that incorporation would be guided by "principle[s] of justice so

---

*The Bill of Rights includes the First Amendment's freedoms of speech, press, assembly, and religion; the Fourth Amendment's protection from unreasonable searches and seizures; the Fifth Amendment's right to just compensation for property taken by government and freedom from compelled self-incrimination and double jeopardy; the Sixth Amendment's right to counsel and to a speedy, public trial before a jury, and to compulsory process to obtain witnesses; and the Eighth Amendment's protection against cruel and unusual punishments.

129

rooted in the tradition and conscience of our people as to be ranked as fundamental" and therefore "implicit in the concept of ordered liberty...."[39] Thirty-six years later, in *Roe v. Wade*, the Court referred to the *Palko* standard as the defining principle behind the implied right of privacy: "Only personal rights that can be deemed 'fundamental' or 'implicit in our concept of ordered liberty,'...are included in this guarantee of personal privacy."[40]

MARRIAGE, PROCREATION, AND FAMILY: PRE-ROE RECOGNITION OF AN INTEREST IN AND A RIGHT TO PRIVACY

As the Court abandoned economic substantive due process, it began to recognize implied rights oriented around freedom of speech and religion, family autonomy in child-rearing and education, and procedural fairness.[41] *Roe v. Wade*, an outgrowth of this trend, is based on an implied right of privacy, which the Court found in "the Fourteenth Amendment's concept of personal liberty and restrictions upon state action."[42] The Court has held that the federal government is limited to the same extent by the due process clause of the Fifth Amendment.

As a general matter, the concept of a right to privacy arises in a variety of legal contexts and involves a range of interests. The common law of torts, for example, protects both freedom from intrusion into personal matters and freedom from disclosure of information about a person's private life. The Supreme Court has considered both aspects of privacy in constitutional law as well. *Whalen v. Roe*, for example, involved a privacy-based (primarily in the disclosure sense) challenge to a state's computerized collection of names and addresses of prescription drug users. The concept of privacy also finds constitutional expression in the Fourth Amendment's protection against unreasonable searches and seizures, and the First Amendment has been interpreted to protect some measure of privacy rights in speech and association. In his famous dissent to the Supreme Court's refusal to strike down wiretapping as a violation of the Fourth Amendment in *Olmstead v. United States*, Justice Louis Brandeis declared the "right to be let alone—the most comprehensive of rights and the right most valued by civilized men."[43] And, as mentioned earlier, privacy also involves broader concerns of personal autonomy and self-determination. *Roe v. Wade* is largely concerned with privacy in this latter sense.

Two cases are frequently cited by the Supreme Court as laying the foundation for the constitutional right to privacy that was later applied in *Roe*: *Meyer v. Nebraska* (1923) and *Pierce v. Society of the Sisters* (1925). In *Meyer* the Court invalidated a state law that prohibited grade schools from teaching any language other than English. In *Pierce* the Court struck down a state law requiring schoolchildren to attend public rather than private schools. In both cases the Court relied in part on the laws' infringement on the parents' liberty to direct the upbringing of their children and on the conclusion that children are not creations of the state but have their own autonomous existence. Of course, these cases were decided during the heyday of economic substantive due process. Indeed, in *Meyer* the Court also relied on a German teacher's interest in pursuing his livelihood; and in *Pierce* the Court relied in part on the private schools' interest in conducting their businesses.* Nevertheless, these two cases have come to be regarded as recognizing some measure of a right to private decision-making in family matters as implicit in the Fourteenth Amendment's concept of liberty.

The next important conceptual development came in *Skinner v. Oklahoma* (1942). In that case the Court invalidated under the equal protection clause a statute authorizing the sterilization of persons convicted and sentenced two or more times for a felony of "moral turpitude." That statutory term included grand larceny but excluded embezzlement (no matter how much money the convicted person embezzled or how many times he or she did so). Because the statute involved "one of the basic

---

*In *Prince v. Massachusetts,* after the Court's 1937 rejection of economic substantive due process, the Court upheld an application of child labor laws to prohibit sale on a public street of Jehovah's Witnesses literature by a minor accompanied by her adult guardian. The Court concluded that the guardian's claims both of religious freedom and "parental right" did not preclude the guardian's conviction for unlawfully providing literature to the minor for sale.

rights of man...[in that] marriage and procreation [are] fundamental to the very existence and survival of the race," the Court
examined closely the relationship between the statute's means
and ends.[44] The artificiality of the line between larceny and
embezzlement, in view of the importance of the interest at
stake, led the Court to strike the statute.

Although the Court in *Skinner* did not speak in terms of a
right to "privacy," the Court's analysis established three important related constitutional principles. First, certain "fundamental
rights" under the equal protection and due process guarantees
require special judicial defense against legislative encroachment.[45] Second, the Court will closely examine both the ends
and means of a law burdening such rights. Thus government
may invade fundamental rights, if at all, only for compelling reasons, and only in a way that goes no further than necessary.
Third, interests in procreation are "fundamental" and therefore
entitled to especially close judicial scrutiny.[46]

The constitutional right to privacy as it concerns matters of
marriage and procreation received its first articulation in Justice
Harlan's dissent in *Poe v. Ullman* (1961). The majority of the
Justices in *Poe* did not regard the case as appropriate for judicial
review. Justice Harlan, however, would have concluded that the
Connecticut statutes prohibiting the use of contraceptive
devices, and the giving of medical advice concerning their use,
violated the substantive due process right to privacy of married
persons by intruding on the "most intimate details of the marital relation."[47]

The Court first expressly recognized a constitutional right to
privacy in marital and procreational matters in the 1965 case of
Griswold v. Connecticut. In *Griswold* the Court held unconstitutional the same Connecticut statutes at issue in *Poe v. Ullman*
because they violated married persons' fundamental right to privacy. Justice Douglas's opinion for the Court in *Griswold* tried to
avoid association with the discredited noninterpretive theory of
Lochner-style substantive due process. He reasoned that certain
express guarantees of the Bill of Rights (such as the First
Amendment's free speech rights, the Fourth Amendment's pro-

tection against unreasonable searches and seizures, and the Fifth Amendment's protection against coerced confessions) give off "penumbras" and "emanations" that protect zones of privacy. And *Pierce v. Society of the Sisters* and *Meyer v. Nebraska*, Justice Douglas said, reflect the Court's recognition of a special value in the liberty to make personal decisions about family matters without government regulation. Because the Connecticut statutes regulated the intimate marital relationship without a sufficiently strong reason, authorized government to inquire into such matters, and created the unseemly possibility that husbands and wives would be required to testify against each other about the most intimate details of their marriage and that police officers might even search the marital bedroom for evidence, the Court held the statutes unconstitutional.

In his concurring opinion, Justice Goldberg (joined by Chief Justice Warren and Justice Brennan) agreed that the "concept of liberty protects those personal rights that are fundamental, and is not confined to the specific terms of the Bill of Rights."[48] For support in the Constitution's text, Justice Goldberg invoked the Ninth Amendment, which provides: "The enumeration in the Constitution, of certain rights, shall not be construed to deny or disparage others retained by the people." Despite its sweeping language, the Ninth Amendment has not been given much force by the Court—though the Court did invoke it in *Casey*. One objection is that the amendment seems to beg the question of what rights are "retained by the people"—bringing the courts squarely back to the natural rights problem.

As Justice Stewart observed in his concurring opinion in *Roe v. Wade*, Justice Douglas's *Griswold* opinion is best understood as part of the long line of substantive due process cases (despite Justice Douglas's creative efforts to avoid the term) that has survived the Court's 1937 switch in the limited context of matters concerning marriage, family life, and procreation.[49] Since *Griswold* the Court has decided several cases involving family and procreation, apart from the abortion cases, and it has generally guarded privacy interests related to contraception and conventional marital relations. In *Loving v. Virginia* the Court struck down a

133

Virginia statute that prohibited mixed-race marriages in part because of its unwarranted interference with the choice of one's spouse. And in *Moore v. City of East Cleveland* the Court invalidated a city housing density ordinance limiting occupancy of a dwelling unit to members of a single family, which in effect made it a crime for a grandmother to have living in her house two grandsons who were cousins rather than brothers. In *Eisenstadt v. Baird* the Court held unconstitutional a statute that prohibited distribution of contraceptives to unmarried persons for the prevention of pregnancy. Instead of relying on the due process clause of the Fourteenth Amendment as applied in *Griswold*, however, the Court in *Eisenstadt* concluded that the statute's distinction between married and unmarried persons was insufficiently related to any legitimate purpose and thus violated the equal protection clause. And in *Carey v. Population Services* the Court invalidated a law prohibiting the sale of contraceptives to persons under sixteen years of age and to anyone by someone other than a licensed pharmacist. The Court held that the restriction to sales by pharmacists unconstitutionally burdened the "right of decision in matters of childbearing."[50]

Recently a more conservative Court has declined to extend the scope of interests that can claim protection as liberties under the due process clause. The Court has limited those interests to child-rearing and education, conventional family relationships, procreation, heterosexual marriage, and contraception, and has refused to protect less conventional privacy interests, such as homosexual relations and out-of-wedlock parenthood.* The underlying principle thus has become less of a general right to personal autonomy in matters of family and sexuality and more of a list of particular rights defined by the specific practice in question. For example, in *Bowers v. Hardwick* the Court refused to recognize private homosexual conduct between consenting adults as included in those fundamental liberties "deeply rooted in this Nation's history and

---

*The Court has, however, recognized that intimate associations apart from traditional family relationships, such as those in some kinds of private organizations, might be protected by the right to privacy. One case discussing this point is *Board of Directors of Rotary International v. Rotary Club of Duarte*.

tradition" or "implicit in the concept of ordered liberty."[51] In dissent, Justice Blackmun objected that the majority opinion had too narrowly described the nature of the interest at stake:

> This case is no more about "a fundamental right to engage in homosexual sodomy," as the Court purports to declare, than Stanley v. Georgia,...was about a fundamental right to watch obscene movies, or Katz v. United States...was about a fundamental right to place interstate bets from a telephone booth. Rather, this case is about "the most comprehensive of rights and the right most valued by civilized men," namely, "the right to be left alone."[52]

In *Michael H. v. Gerald D.* a divided Court upheld a California ruling denying a man the opportunity to establish his paternity of a child born to the wife of another man. Justice Scalia's opinion, joined by Chief Justice Rehnquist, would define liberty interests protected under the due process clauses as including only those capable of support in the most specifically defined historical tradition. Justice Scalia described the issue narrowly as whether society traditionally had recognized the rights of an adulterous natural father instead of unwed parenthood or parental rights generally.[53]

The split on the Court in *Michael H.* over how to define protected liberty interests also applies to abortion. If the relevant "history and tradition" that defines the liberty at stake is limited specifically to abortion, *Roe* is more difficult to defend. If instead the relevant tradition is a broader interest in personal autonomy and self-determination, *Roe* stands on somewhat stronger ground. This question was sharply debated in *Casey*.

In sum, the constitutional origins of *Roe v. Wade* in one sense can be traced all the way back to the early days of the Republic, when the notions of natural rights and judicial review first entered constitutional law. And the constitutional problems raised by *Roe* are part of the larger debate over constitutional interpretation that has been simmering, and occasionally boiling over, ever since. The Court has swung like a pendulum between an expansive and more limited conception of its power of judicial review, and the grounds the Court has found appropriate for the exercise of that power have shifted as well over time. The Court's treatment of abortion rights has illustrated this pattern of waxing and waning.

Before turning to *Roe*, two other cases should be briefly mentioned, for *Roe v. Wade* was not the Court's first consideration of the constitutionality of an abortion law. Two years before deciding *Roe*, the Court in *United States v. Vuitch* upheld a District of Columbia statute that made it a crime to "procure or produce" an abortion unless necessary to save the mother's life or health. The trial court in *Vuitch* had held the statute unconstitutionally vague because it presumed the physician guilty upon proof of an abortion, and because it placed the burden on the physician of proving that the abortion was necessary for the mother's life or health. The trial court also found that the word "health" was vague. A criminal law that is vague deprives persons of due process because it fails to inform them of the specifically prohibited conduct so that they might conform their behavior to the law's requirements. Vague laws also create the risk of arbitrary or discriminatory enforcement.

Although the trial court also discussed (and the parties argued) the issue of a possible conflict with the right to privacy under *Griswold*, the Supreme Court read the trial court opinion as based on the vagueness issue and thus did not consider the privacy question. The Court upheld the statute against the vagueness challenge, construing it to place the burden on the prosecution of alleging and proving that the abortion was not therapeutic. The Court thereby postponed grappling with the central question of a fundamental right to abortion.

The other case is *People v. Belous*, a 1969 decision by the Supreme Court of California. Although the United States Supreme Court is not bound by state court interpretations of the federal Constitution, the California court's *Belous* opinion nevertheless was influential. The *Belous* court reversed a conviction under California's old anti-abortion law (before the 1967 reform) on vagueness grounds. But the court also recognized the force of the pregnant woman's interest in her own health and

136

reproductive freedom as against the state's interest in protecting the unborn child. Those interests, and the privacy claim passed over in *Vuitch*, were met head-on by the United States Supreme Court in *Roe v. Wade*.

7. *Roe v. Wade* and *Doe v. Bolton*

. . . .

The case of *Roe v. Wade*, like many other landmark civil liberties cases, was originally conceived in the minds of lawyers intent on effecting social change through the courts. The lawyers in this instance were Linda Coffee and Sarah Weddington, both fresh out of law school in Texas, active in the women's movement, and committed to the idea that the key to freedom for women was control of their own reproductive processes—including control through abortion. Concluding that legislative reform of Texas's abortion laws would come too late—if it ever came at all, considering women's lack of political power at the time— Weddington and Coffee made the audacious decision to take on the state of Texas in the federal courts.

In December 1969 Linda Coffee was twenty-six years old, Sarah Weddington was twenty-three. They had been two of a handful of women to enter the University of Texas Law School in 1965. Weddington graduated early in the top quarter of her class, in 1967, only to discover that the male-dominated legal establishment of Texas was resisting women's entry into the profession. She therefore continued her work with her former law professor on the American Bar Association's new Code of Professional Responsibility. She also had helped to organize a problem-pregnancy counseling and referral service in Austin. The Austin group performed the legally risky service of referring clients to places where legal abortion was available—usually Mexico, but occasionally England or Europe, or to American physicians willing to risk prosecution. Coffee, on graduating, obtained a prestigious position clerking for a federal judge on the Fifth Circuit Court of Appeals; but despite her admirable record, the only job she could find after her clerkship was with a small corporate firm. When Weddington contacted her former classmate about working on the abortion issue, both were ready to challenge the constitutionality of Texas's nineteenth-century abortion laws.

Both women were committed, bright, ambitious, and in need of a plaintiff. They had begun speaking publicly on the abortion issue, had put the word out among their colleagues in various women's groups, and had considered and rejected several possible plaintiffs. Coffee originally planned to use a Dallas couple— "young, married two years, both professionals with advanced degrees, churchgoing Methodists, active and involved in community life, and most important, they had an excellent [medical] reason for using abortion as a method of backup birth control."[1] But the existence of a possible medical justification for an abortion diminished the scope of the couple's challenge on constitutional grounds. As Coffee was about to file a lawsuit, in December 1969, she found her client—a pregnant young woman who wanted an abortion.

NORMA MC GORVEY

When she first met Coffee and Weddington, Norma McGorvey was twenty-one, the divorced mother of a five-year-old girl (then in the custody of Norma's mother and stepfather in Arkansas), only tenuously employed in Dallas as a waitress, sleeping wherever a friend had a spare bed or sofa, and several months' pregnant. She told the lawyers she had been raped while working as a ticket seller in a carnival in Georgia. Apparently both lawyers were skeptical about McGorvey's account of the rape, and they concluded that her constitutional claim would be stronger if it were left out of the case. For one thing, Georgia's prohibition against abortion by 1969 contained an exception for rape (although the Texas law did not).

According to Marian Faux's account of *Roe:*

After hearing so much about McGorvey's background, Weddington and Coffee became concerned that she might not be such a good plaintiff after all. Her life thus far—a high school dropout, married at sixteen, a daughter she did not have custody of, walking out on a visit with her daughter to join a carnival, her present hand-to-mouth existence—was a major problem.[2]

Although many lawyers might agree with those strategic concerns about McGorvey's circumstances, in some respects those circumstances made her a most appropriate plaintiff. McGorvey was a perfect example of the kind of woman on whom restrictive abortion laws have the greatest impact: young, low income, working, separated or divorced, and poorly educated. And McGorvey's sense of despair, helplessness, and isolation evoke the painful images described in the pre-*Roe* narratives of women.

In any event, McGorvey, Coffee, and Weddington decided to proceed with the lawsuit and to keep McGorvey's identity confidential. The lawyers were true to their word: "For ten years, until Norma herself broke the silence, no one, not even other lawyers who would work on the case, knew who Jane Roe was."[3] The lawyers and their client also had to confront the likelihood that the judicial system would not move fast enough to allow McGorvey to obtain a legal abortion in Texas. McGorvey decided to have the child—at around four months she was probably too late for a safe abortion anyway, considering the state of medical technology at the time—and to remain the plaintiff. The three women proceeded to launch themselves into the forefront of the abortion reform movement and to turn the gradual process of state-by-state legislative change into an overnight judicial revolution. Weddington ultimately argued the case to the United States Supreme Court.

Roe v. Wade actually involved three named plaintiffs. "Jane Roe" (Norma McGorvey) brought a class action on her own behalf and on behalf of all women similarly situated. The Dallas married couple, "John and Mary Doe," also were named as plaintiffs. Mary Doe was not pregnant at the time she filed suit, but she alleged that should she become pregnant she would want to terminate her pregnancy by abortion. The third plaintiff was Dr. James Hubert Hallford, who intervened in the case to challenge the constitutionality of charges

140

pending against him for violation of the Texas abortion statute.

ROE V. WADE

January 23, 1973, was a newsworthy day indeed. Banner head-lines in the *New York Times* announced two historic events: the death of Lyndon Johnson and "High Court Rules Abortions Legal the First Three Months." The Texas statute challenged in *Roe v. Wade*, which dated back to the 1850s, made it a crime to "procure" or to attempt an abortion, except "by medical advice for the purpose of saving the life of the mother."[4] The statute was similar to laws subsequently enacted in many other states and the District of Columbia.

The Court's 7-2 opinion was written by Associate Justice Harry Andrew Blackmun, then in his mid-sixties, the Court's ninety-eighth Justice. Blackmun, formerly a judge on the Eighth Circuit Court of Appeals, had been nominated by Richard Nixon and confirmed in 1970 to replace Abe Fortas. He was a boyhood acquaintance of Chief Justice Warren Burger, and the press had fun calling them (inaccurately) the "Minnesota Twins." Before stepping onto the federal bench Blackmun was house counsel for the Mayo Clinic, where he frequently advised physicians and worked to protect doctors' professional autonomy.

Justice Blackmun's opinion for the Court first addressed the plaintiffs' right to seek judicial review of the Texas law. By the time Jane Roe's case reached the Supreme Court, "she and all other members of her class [were] no longer subject to any 1970 pregnancy."[5] Ordinarily, an actual controversy must exist through-out a federal case. When circumstances change to remove the controversy, the case is said to be "moot." The problem in *Roe v. Wade* was that the wheels of justice usually take longer to turn than the normal nine-month cycle of human gestation. Litiga-tion involving pregnancy therefore would hardly ever reach the appellate stage if termination of pregnancy rendered the case moot. Because Jane Roe's case was "capable of repetition, yet evading review,"—that is, the problem could keep recurring without surviving the lengthy trip to the Supreme Court—the Court concluded it was not moot.

The Court dismissed the cases of John and Mary Doe and Dr. Hallford. Applying the rule that federal courts ordinarily will not interfere with ongoing criminal prosecutions in state court, the Court ruled that Dr. Hallford had to raise his constitutional claims, if anywhere, as defenses in the Texas criminal proceedings against him. And the Does' claim, the Court ruled, was too speculative and hypothetical to present a real controversy.

Turning to the merits of the *Roe* case, Justice Blackmun reviewed the history of abortion laws and found that restrictive criminal abortion laws such as the Texas statute were not common in America until the latter half of the nineteenth century. He also found that ancient Greek and Roman law afforded little or no protection to the unborn. Blackmun further observed that the common law of England did not regard prequickening abortion as a crime (or at least as a felony), reflecting the philosophical and theological concept of ensoulment. Blackmun concluded that it was "doubtful that abortion was ever firmly established as a common-law crime even with respect to the destruction of a quick fetus."[6]

As we have seen, the law in effect in the United States until the mid-nineteenth century largely mirrored English common law. Effective prohibition of abortion did not emerge until after the Civil War. Justice Blackmun concluded for the Court, "It is thus apparent that at the common law, at the time of the adoption of our Constitution, and throughout the major portion of the 19th century, abortion was viewed with less disfavor than under most American statutes currently in effect. Phrasing it another way, a woman enjoyed a substantially broader right to terminate a pregnancy than she does in most States today."[7] Blackmun's history is largely accurate; but whether that history supports a constitutional right to abortion is far less clear.

The Court saw *Roe* and the abortion issue as presenting a conflict among competing individual and state interests. State interests included (1) protection of pregnant women from unsafe medical procedures, and (2) preservation of prenatal life.

On the first interest the Court observed that mortality rates for women undergoing abortions early in the pregnancy are as low or lower than the rates for normal childbirth. The Court concluded that "the prevalence of high mortality rates at illegal 'abortion mills' strengthens, rather than weakens, the State's interest in regulating the conditions under which abortions are performed." Second, the Court reasoned that recognition of a legitimate state interest in fetal life did not depend on resolution of the difficult philosophical and theological question of when life begins. Instead, some "recognition may be given to the less rigid claim that as long as at least *potential life* is involved, the State may assert interests beyond the protection of the pregnant woman alone."[8]

After briefly reviewing the evolution of the right to privacy, the Court simply, indeed almost casually, announced: "This right to privacy, whether it be founded in the Fourteenth Amendment's concept of personal liberty and restrictions upon state action, as we feel it is, or, as the District Court determined, in the Ninth Amendment's reservation of rights to the people, is broad enough to encompass a woman's decision whether or not to terminate her pregnancy." In defining the woman's privacy interest to include abortion, the Court considered the harm that the state would impose by denying her the choice:

> Specific and direct harm medically diagnosable even in early pregnancy may be involved. Maternity, or additional offspring, may force upon the woman a distressful life and future. Psychological harm may be imminent. Mental and physical health may be taxed by child care. There is also the distress, for all concerned, associated with the unwanted child, and there is the problem of bringing a child into a family already unable, psychologically and otherwise, to care for it. In other cases, as in this one, the additional stigma of unwed motherhood may be involved.[9]

As mentioned earlier, the Court's Fourteenth Amendment cases require that laws restricting "fundamental rights" such as the right to privacy must be justified by "compelling state interests" and must be "narrowly drawn" to serve those interests. The state's interest in safeguarding maternal health, maintaining medical standards, and protecting potential life, the Court reasoned, becomes sufficiently compelling at some point in pregnancy to sustain regulation of the factors that govern the abortion decision. As the Court analyzed the case, the question therefore became balancing opposing legitimate individual and state interests.

Before weighing those interests, however, the Court first had to determine whether a conceptus is a "person" for purposes of the Fourteenth Amendment. If so, the constitutional guarantees of due process and equal protection of the laws would have defeated *Roe's* claim. Usage of the term "person" elsewhere in the Constitution, as well as the generally more liberal abortion practices of the early nineteenth century, persuaded the Court that "the word 'person,' as used in the Fourteenth Amendment, does not include the unborn."[10] As Justice Stevens pointed out in his separate opinion sixteen years later in *Webster v. Reproductive Health Services*, "No member of this Court has ever questioned the holding in *Roe*...that a fetus is not a 'person' within the meaning of the Fourteenth Amendment. Even the dissenters in *Roe* [and the anti-*Roe* Justices in *Webster*] implicitly endorsed this holding by arguing that state legislatures should decide whether to prohibit or to authorize abortions."[11]

Thus the Court declined Texas's invitation to determine, apart from the Fourteenth Amendment's use of the word "person," when life begins. Recognizing that the respective disciplines of medicine, philosophy, and theology had been unable to reach consensus, the Court concluded that "the judiciary, at this point in the development of man's knowledge, is not in a position to speculate as to the answer." And the Court rejected the idea that, "by adopting one theory of life, Texas may override the rights of the pregnant woman that are at stake."[12]

The Court's ultimate resolution of the conflict between the pregnant woman's privacy rights and the state's interests in maternal health, proper medical standards, and potential life took shape in *Roe's* trimester framework. That analysis has been the point of departure (and a source of increasingly divisive debate) in every abortion case from *Roe* to *Webster*. (*Webster* signaled the demise of the trimester framework, and it was ultimately repudiated by a divided Court in *Casey*.)

The Court's conclusion in *Roe* is worth quoting in full:

> With respect to the State's important and legitimate interest in the health of the mother, the "compelling" point, in the light of present medical knowledge, is at approximately the end of the first trimester. This is so because of the now established medical fact...that until the end of the first trimester mortality in abortion may be less than mortality in normal childbirth. It follows that, from and after this point, a State may regulate the abortion procedure to the extent that the regulation reasonably relates to the preservation and protection of maternal health.... This means, on the other hand, that for the period of pregnancy prior to this "compelling" point, the attending physician, in consultation with his patient, is free to determine, without regulation by the State, that, in his medical judgment, the patient's pregnancy should be terminated. If that decision is reached, the judgment may be effectuated by an abortion free of interference by the State. With respect to the State's important and legitimate interest in potential life, the "compelling" point is at viability. This is so because the fetus then presumably has the capability of meaningful life outside the mother's womb. State regulation protective of fetal life after viability thus has both logical and biological justifications. If the State is interested in protecting fetal life after viability, it may go so far as to proscribe abortion during that period, except when it is necessary to preserve the life or health of the mother.[13]

Justice Stewart's concurring opinion reasoned that the right recognized in *Roe* necessarily followed from *Griswold*. Chief Justice Burger also joined the Court's opinion, adding that the broad statutes in *Roe* and *Doe v. Bolton* (discussed below) left women at the mercy of prosecutorial discretion. He indicated he might allow a broader scope of state regulation but was nevertheless willing to join the Court's opinion. In later cases Chief Justice Burger would retreat from his endorsement of *Roe*.

Justice Douglas's concurring opinion described the underlying right in broad terms of personal autonomy and self-determination. He described the interests protected by the Fourteenth Amendment's concept of liberty: "First is the autonomous control over the development and expression of one's intellect, interests, tastes, and personality.... Second is freedom of choice in the basic decisions of one's life respecting marriage, divorce, procreation, contraception, and the education and upbringing of children.... Third is the freedom to care for one's health and person, freedom from bodily restraint or compulsion, freedom to walk, stroll, or loaf."[14] His objection to the Texas statute was that it cast the balance between the state's interests and that of the pregnant woman wholly in favor of the state. As mentioned above, and as is evident in *Casey*, the Court does not view privacy rights in such broad terms today.

Justices White and Rehnquist dissented. Justice White viewed the Court's decision as "an improvident and extravagant exercise of the power of judicial review," which declared—without any support in the language or the history of the Constitution—that the Constitution "values the convenience, whim, or caprice of the pregnant woman more than the life or potential life of the fetus...."[15] While expressing respect for Justice Blackmun's legal and historical scholarship, Justice Rehnquist nevertheless criticized the Court for resorting to "judicial legislation," reminiscent of *Lochner*'s economic substantive due process era, in breaking pregnancy into three phases and outlining the permissible regulation the state may impose on each one. He disagreed that the notion of "privacy" had any application to the abortion decision, which he characterized as a mere "transaction" between the pregnant woman and the physician.[16]

146

DOE V. BOLTON

Doe v. Bolton, a companion case to *Roe v. Wade*, was decided the same day. The Georgia statute at issue in *Doe* was an example of late 1960s reform legislation. By deciding cases involving both nineteenth-century and modern statutes, the Court demonstrated the broad scope of constitutional abortion rights.

The Georgia statute criminalized abortion except when the physician's best clinical judgment found it necessary because (1) continuation of pregnancy would endanger the mother's life "or seriously and permanently endanger her health"; (2) "the fetus could likely be born with a grave, permanent and irremediable mental or physical defect"; or (3) the pregnancy resulted from forcible or statutory rape. Like many other reform laws, the Georgia statute also established a number of preconditions before an abortion legally could be performed. These conditions included the following: (1) residency of the woman in Georgia; (2) written concurrence by at least two other Georgia-licensed physicians; (3) performance of the procedure in an accredited hospital; (4) advance approval by a committee of at least three members of the hospital staff; (5) certification in a rape case; and (6) maintenance and confidentiality of records. The law also provided that the courts could determine the abortion's legality upon petition of a law officer or close relative of the unborn child, and allowed hospitals and staff to refuse to admit or to treat abortion patients.[17]

The district court in *Doe* held unconstitutional the limitation on the availability of abortions to the three situations specified, the rape certification, and the provision for a medical test. The remaining portions of the statute, including the provision that an abortion must be necessary in the physician's best clinical judgment (in light of all circumstances), came before the Supreme Court. The Court rejected the argument that unqualified reference to the physician's best clinical judgment rendered the statute unconstitutionally vague, because "medical judgment may be exercised in the light of all factors—physical, emotional, psychological, familial, and the woman's age—relevant to the well-

147

being of the patient." Reflecting his view of abortion as largely a medical issue between physician and patient, Justice Blackmun concluded that such "room" for medical discretion "operates for the benefit, not the disadvantage, of the pregnant woman."[18]

The Court held the procedural requirements unconstitutional, however. It invalidated the requirement that abortions, unlike many other surgical procedures, are to be performed only in accredited hospitals on the grounds that there is no medical reason to single out abortion from other surgical procedures. The Court also struck down the hospital committee approval requirement, which was not applied to any other medical procedure, because it unnecessarily burdened a pregnant woman's rights and because the Court believed that a woman's medical needs are best determined by her own physician. Finally, the Court ruled unconstitutional the two-physician concurrence requirement, which also was applied only to abortions, because it made for unnecessary and added delay. The Georgia residency requirement, the Court held, violated the rights of nonresidents, guaranteed by the privileges and immunities clause of Article IV of the Constitution, to enter another state to seek medical services. The concurring and dissenting opinions in *Roe v. Wade* also applied to *Doe v. Bolton.*

8. Criticisms of *Roe*

. . . .

Any case as controversial as *Roe v. Wade* is bound to generate a large body of commentary. It is impossible to do more here than briefly consider some major criticisms of *Roe* and some responses to them. The several opinions in *Webster* and *Casey* also offer their observations on *Roe*, particularly the trimester framework.

THE CONCEPTUS AS A "PERSON"

Although the Court has given it little attention, the "person-hood" issue is at the heart of the abortion rights dilemma. It also is the most pivotal question. The pro–abortion rights position depends on a negative answer, or no answer at all, to the question whether an unborn child is a "person" in any meaningful sense. And the anti-abortion position's moral force depends on the assumption that the conceptus is a human life. Despite this issue's importance, there is a large element of question-begging and -dodging on both sides.

To the Court in Roe, this issue raised two related questions. One is whether the conceptus is a "person" as that term is used in the Fourteenth Amendment. The other is whether Texas may define when human "life" is entitled to claim the protection of state law. As described above, the Court regarded the first question as answerable from conventional interpretive sources: history, semantics, context, and contemporary usage. It found that the conceptus is not a "person" under the Fourteenth Amendment. The Court's response to the second question was partly epistemological and partly determined by the outcome of the Court's balancing process. The absence of medical, philosophical, or religious consensus on the question of when life begins, the Court reasoned, supported the Court's denial to Texas of the power to impose an answer at the expense of women's reproductive freedom.

The Court's approach may raise more questions than it answers. First, the Court's reading of constitutional text and history on this question of personhood seems accurate as far as it goes. As one of *Roe*'s critics recently conceded, "There is not a shred of historical evidence, of which I am aware, that would suggest that the framers [of the Fourteenth Amendment] thought of fetuses as persons against whom the state could not act except with due process of law."[1] But it is difficult to see why the inquiry should end there. The Court fails to explain why the text and history should be read more strictly on the "person" question than on the question of recognizing abortion rights. On the issue of a right to privacy, *Roe* reflects the very essence of the "living Constitution" approach; it is the most extreme form of noninterpretivism. No one seriously argues that the framers of the Fourteenth Amendment thought they were creating a constitutional right to abortion. It also is most unlikely that they had in mind anything like the modern notion of privacy. But throughout the twentieth century the Court has consistently assumed that the amendment embodies a broader principle of individual liberty than what the framers had in mind in either 1787 or 1868—a principle shaped by changing social conditions and values.

The Court's analysis of the "person" question thus begs the question whether the meaning not only of "liberty" but also of "persons" can evolve. Anti-abortion forces offer advances in medical science, particularly embryology, fetology, and genetics, as evidence that human life begins at conception. They also point to recent developments elsewhere in the law—such as the recognition of a tort claim for wrongful fetal death—as showing the law's growing acknowledgment of the fetus as a person. And several pro-life briefs in *Webster* rely heavily on natural law theory to support their assertion that the fetus is to be regarded as a "person" under the Fourteenth Amendment. The irony there is

150

that anti–abortion rights forces usually advocate a strictly interpretivist approach and reject natural law in criticizing *Roe's*
recognition of a right to privacy.

One response to the anti-abortion argument that life begins at
conception is that a fertilized egg represents only the *potential*
for developing into a baby; most fertilized eggs spontaneously
abort. If it is murder to destroy a fertilized egg, then the
destruction of sperm cells or unfertilized eggs would also seem
to be murder, as they too are only the potentiality of life. Yet
while some people may believe that male masturbation or intercourse (even intercourse leading to conception)—which destroys
millions of sperm cells at each ejaculation—is immoral, few
would maintain that either is homicide. Too, there are such
obvious and enormous differences among various stages of
human development that distinct legal status seems to many
people to be appropriate. After all, a blastocyst hardly resembles
a fully developed fetus.

Nevertheless, there is something undeniably human and indi-
vidually unique—at least in genetic terms—about the conceptus
(at least once it reaches the blastocyst stage). And it is unquestionably "alive" in many potent ways that individual gametes are
not. What's more, it may be argued that the conceptus is much
more of a human being than is a corporation, which the Court
has concluded is a "person" under the Fourteenth Amendment.
The anti-abortion argument is thus more powerful than its
opponents admit—indeed, as we shall shortly see, it is more
powerful than many of its *proponents* admit as well. It is not surprising that a common pro–abortion rights response is to avoid
the problem entirely. *Roe* reasoned that since no one really
knows when "life begins," literally pro-"life" arguments are inadmissible. The abortion decision must be left to the pregnant
woman or the issue at least must be resolved by balancing the
moral claims to liberty of a visible "person" against the abstrac-
tion of "state interests" in "potential life." Of course, the
Court's wariness of a debate that usually resorts to religiously
inspired, dogmatic absolutes is understandable. And the pro-life
movement's association with the fundamentalist religious right

makes even moderates suspicious that arguments about fetal personhood are really disguised attempts to impose a minority's religious views on everyone else.

But those objections are insufficient. It is possible to argue, without relying on controversial religious doctrine to any greater extent than we do in addressing other claims to justice, that the conceptus is entitled to the same intrinsic moral standing and hence legal protection as postnatal people. A concise articulation of this position is Sidney Callahan's essay "Context of the Abortion Debate." Callahan invokes values of equality, justice, and nonviolence that, in other contexts (such as racial and gender equality), liberal and "socially conscious" people would endorse. To her,

> The coherent moral justification undergirding these diverse struggles is an assertion that *the less powerful members of the human community must not be denied their equal intrinsic moral worth, nor be sacrificed to the interests of stronger and more powerful parties.* The abortion debate is one more domain in which persons must challenge those in the society who defend expediency, inequality, and violently destructive solutions to human problems. Moral consciousness and conscience must reverse what some feminists have called the western patriarchal logic of domination and control—a misuse of power aided and abetted by technologies that dehumanize both user and victim.[2]

For Callahan the issue "can no longer be discounted as a matter of conflicting religious beliefs." As she points out, many people holding diverse religious beliefs nevertheless agree that racial and gender discrimination (or capital punishment) are morally wrong.

Callahan's anti-abortion argument rests on two propositions: "[1] accepting the basic democratic claim that all members of the human community are equal in intrinsic worth, and [2] then discerning that the human community must include all members of the human species—both born and unborn."[3] She includes the unborn in the human community based on liberal arguments about moral equivalency that, in other contexts, most pro-choice advocates probably would accept.* In short she contends that the conceptus is undeniably human and alive, and that the only reasons for denying its moral equivalency with other humans are morally unacceptable.

Callahan challenges the assumption that the only persons who are entitled to the law's minimal protections are "entities necessarily possessing sentience, self-consciousness, rational self-determination, and rational moral agency." One sees this assumption, for example, in arguments like Carl Sagan's intellectual functioning test for personhood, described earlier. Callahan explains:

> If we look at the whole human race throughout time, we see that fully developed, rationally functioning persons who are moral agents are not necessarily in the numerical majority. We can more realistically picture a core grouping of fully performing persons as being surrounded by countless numbers of human lives which shade off in various gradations from full personhood. There are infants and children, the senile, the enfeebled, the retarded, the mentally deranged, those temporarily ill, drugged or in comas, others who are deprived, depraved, or radically stunted in rational and moral development. All of these, along with infants, neonates, fetuses, and embryos certainly are not persons in the fullest sense. Obviously, by nature of their condition, the multitudes of non-performing persons cannot effectively challenge, choose, or determine the way they will be treated.[4]

In other words, the principal differences between the conceptus and other members of the human species are its developmental and functional limitations and its dependency on others for its survival. But those attributes are shared to a greater or lesser extent by many other postnatal persons whose moral claim to the law's basic protection is not open to question. If anything, in a morally mature community one's dependence would *strengthen*, not diminish, one's moral claim to the law's protec-

---

*Callahan's "genetic community" argument presumably would apply to the blastocyst, morula, and zygote as well as the fetus and embryo; and presumably she would oppose implantation-blocking agents such as RU-486.

tion. When its extreme vulnerability is considered together with its most complete innocence, the conceptus's moral claim ought by these lights to be the strongest of all. A similar argument applies to distinctions based on the conceptus's appearance. Denying the intrinsic moral worth of a category of human beings, and thus denying them the law's basic protections, simply because they "look different" from members of the category in power violates widely held social and constitutional norms. Indeed, the textual expression of those norms—the equal protection clause—is much clearer than the textual basis for abortion rights.

Consider a commonplace example: A person undergoing surgery under general anesthetic is temporarily not capable of rational thought, volitional action, or even (much) consciousness, and depends entirely on the care of others for his or her survival and well-being. Assuming that the surgery is nonelective, the patient really did not have much of a choice about entering such a vulnerable and helpless condition. Few persons would entertain the argument that such circumstances rendered the patient a nonperson during his or her disability, and removed the patient from the law's most basic protection. No one would have a privilege to end the patient's life on the justification of the patient's temporary disability. Indeed, the patient's very dependence would be a reason for the law to impose *higher* demands on the care-givers.

Unlike the conceptus, of course, the patient in this example is not biologically linked to his or her care-givers. Some pro-choice advocates have pointed out that the law usually does not impose a duty to save, care for, or rescue a stranger—even if the stranger's life is in peril and the cost of rescue is negligible. The biologically intimate demands and risks to the woman, they argue, make the continuation of pregnancy an obligation that the law may not legitimately impose. That argument concludes that abortion restrictions are therefore unconstitutional, even if the fetus is considered a person.[5] As Ronald Dworkin has observed, however, abortion involves not just a failure to care but an affirmative taking of life (if the fetus is regarded as a person). Moreover, parents

154

are not strangers to their offspring, and the law does impose an obligation on parents to care for their children.[6]

This distinction between an anesthetized patient and pregnancy illustrates that Callahan's argument seeks to set apart the personhood issue from the competing interests of the fetus and the pregnant woman. In other words, one's basic moral status as a person usually does not depend on one's situation or relation to others, but instead is inherent and noncontingent by virtue of membership in the human gene pool and thus is inalienable. Callahan demands that we first come to grips with the problem of fetal membership in the human community *before* we consider the woman's competing claims.

Because the only differences in level and kind of functioning (and, one might add, in appearance) between pre- and postnatal "persons" are ones of degree,* Callahan argues there is no moral justification for the grossest kind of basic human rights violation—singling out a category of wholly innocent life and subjecting its survival to the unconstrained discretion of another person. Callahan adds that *Roe* allows an arbitrariness "that is morally offensive to those who believe in equal justice for all": In one ward of the hospital a woman is allowed to direct the physician to kill her healthy fetus, while in another part health-care workers strive heroically to save the lives of fetuses or premature neonates "not much different in achieved functionality from those fetuses being freely aborted."[7]

Callahan concludes by warning that the creation of categories of "nonpersons" threatens everyone's rights. At one time or another we may all find ourselves in a position of dependency and relative powerlessness:

> In a world in which the strong abuse their greater power and human ambivalence abounds, the human rights of all those who will ever be vulnerable or dependent stand or fall

*Given time, most fetuses will achieve the missing functional capabilities. While difficult moral issues also arise at the opposite end of the human life cycle—for example, in the case of individuals in a persistent vegetative state—the temporary nature of fetal "disability" may allow consideration of the fetus's moral and legal status separately from the problem of terminal disability.

155

together. Basic human rights in an egalitarian morality must be inalienable and not subject to the arbitrary decisions or desires of those who can dominate through strength, social resources, or other forms of privilege and power. If women can either confer or withhold fetal right by private choice, then logically a woman's own rights are endangered when she is no longer wanted. In fact, women were all too recently legally defined, like the fetus today, as subordinate appendages to their husband-owners, considered part of a one-flesh dyad which the husband controlled at will. Morally establishing the intrinsic equal worth of women (or non-white races), despite their biological differences and lesser social power, has been a revolutionary moral struggle in the U.S.—a struggle not yet fully won in practice.[8]

The other side in the personhood debate has been argued by, among others, Ronald Dworkin. He first points out that abortion rights opponents often argue that because courts are ill equipped to resolve the personhood question, such matters are better left to the representative political process. Dworkin offers two replies. The first, that state-by-state legislation could be dominated by the anti-abortion lobby and would not necessarily take account of individual women's needs, is more a pragmatic than a legal argument.

Dworkin's second reply to the "let-the-states-decide" position is a legal one. He argues:

> The key question in the debate over *Roe v. Wade* is not a metaphysical question about the concept of personhood or a theological question about whether a fetus has a soul, but a legal question about the correct interpretation of the Constitution which in our political system *must* be settled one way or the other judicially, by the Supreme Court, rather than politically. It is the question whether the fetus is a *constitutional* person, that is, a person whose rights and interests must be ranked equally important with those of other people in the scheme of rights the Constitution establishes.[9]

For Dworkin, then, the question is not one of personhood but rather one of "*constitutional* personhood"—that is, determining the constitutional rights of the conceptus in the context of deciding "who *else* has rights a state must or may also recognize."[10] That question, he concludes, is a matter of constitutional law for the courts to decide.

Dworkin acknowledges that if a conceptus is a constitutional person, "then *Roe v. Wade* is plainly wrong, as the Court's opinion in that case conceded." In that event the equal protection clause not only would *authorize* a state to extend the same protection to fetal life that it provides all other persons, it might well *require* a state to do so. The anti-abortion advocates' argument in favor of fetal personhood thus is at odds with another value (and political expedient) they often invoke: that the question of abortion rights ought to be left to state legislatures. As Dworkin points out, recognizing a fetus as a constitutional person would preclude states from liberalizing abortion laws. He explains:

> The equal protection clause requires states to extend the protection of their laws against murder and assault equally to all persons, and if fetuses were constitutional persons, any state legislation that discriminated against them in that respect, by permitting abortion, would be "suspect," under equal protection principles, and the Supreme Court would have an obligation to review such legislation to determine whether the state's justification was sufficiently "compelling."[11]

Such compelling justifications would probably arise, if at all, only in the relatively few cases involving rape, incest, or therapeutic abortion.

But Dworkin argues on several grounds that an unborn child is not a constitutional person. One is the historical contention, which is subject to the criticism of interpretive inconsistency. His other point is more consistent with the kinds of arguments usually offered in defense of *Roe*. He asserts that the conceptus's unique circumstances justify denying it constitutional status:

> The state can take action that affects it, in order to protect or advance its interests, only through its mother, and only through means that would necessarily restrict her freedom in

157

ways no man or other woman's freedom could constitutionally be limited: by dictating her diet and other personal and intimate behavior, for example. Apart from anti-abortion statutes, there are few signs in our law of the kind of regulation of pregnancy that would be appropriate if the fetus were a constitutional person, and the Supreme Court has never suggested any constitutional requirement of such protection.[12]

Dworkin thus defines the conceptus's personhood by balancing the woman's interests, instead of approaching those issues separately, as Callahan would do. In other words, Dworkin implicitly accepts the proposition that one's claim to the law's most basic protections can be contingent on the interests of another. And Dworkin buttresses his conclusion with an argument directly at odds with Callahan's position: "a human being has no moral right to life until it has developed self-consciousness as a being whose life extends over time."[13]

The suggestion that personhood is a question of constitutional law has been sharply criticized. John Noonan argues that such a suggestion implicitly assumes that an unborn child's very existence is simply a legal construct, that is, that "personhood depends on recognition by law."[14] He points out that an important aspect of American slavery was the dehumanizing effect of the legal definition of a class of human beings as "property." The Supreme Court's affirmation of that legal definition in its infamous decision in *Dred Scott v. Sandford* is widely reviled, including by many abortion rights advocates. Also, *Meyer v. Nebraska* and *Pierce v. Society of the Sisters,* on which the Court relied in *Roe,* recognize that people are *not* creatures of the state and thus dependent on its legal recognition of their existence, but instead have independent, autonomous existences.

ROE AS THE JUDICIAL CREATION OF A NEW RIGHT

Roe is frequently criticized as the kind of judicial usurpation of the political process that characterized the *Lochner* era. In other words, the interpretivist objection is that the Court is illegiti-

158

mately constraining representative democracy based on nothing other than the Justices' individual beliefs. Whatever the motivations of its proponents, this argument is about constitutional interpretation and not the morality of abortion.

One of the most outspoken advocates of this position is Robert Bork.* He observes:

> The years of the Burger and Rehnquist Courts also saw the "right of privacy" invented by the Warren Court mature into a judicial power to dictate moral codes of sexual conduct and procreation for the entire nation. The Court adopted an extreme individualistic philosophy in these cases, seeming to assert that society, acting through government, had very little legitimate interest in such matters.[15]

For Bork, *Roe* is an extreme example of pure judicial invention. The "crux of the opinion" in *Roe* is Justice Blackmun's "simple assertion," quoted above, that the right of privacy includes the right to abortion:

> That is it. That is the crux of the opinion. The Court did not even feel obliged to settle the question of where the right of privacy or the subsidiary right to abort is to be attached to the Constitution's text. The opinion seems to regard that as a technicality that really does not matter, and indeed it does not, since the right does not come out of the Constitution but is forced into it. The opinion does not once say what principle defines the new right so that we might know both why it covers a liberty to abort and what else it might cover in the future.[16]

Bork's interpretivism stems from "the seeming anomaly of judicial supremacy in a democratic society."[17] Under what he somewhat loosely labels the Madisonian resolution of that tension, the judiciary protects from "majority tyranny" certain individual freedoms. But "minority tyranny" by the judiciary itself

---

*Ironically, Bork's nomination to the Supreme Court was defeated through the same representative political process that he believes should determine matters like a woman's right to abortion, in part because of his views on that very subject.

can be avoided only by requiring that the Court adhere to what the constitutional scholar Herbert Wechsler has called "neutral principles." Such principles "rest on reasons with respect to all issues in a case, reasons that in their generality and their neutrality transcend any immediate result that is involved."[18] To ensure that the Court has not overstepped those limits, Bork insists that

> the Court's power is legitimate only if it has, and can demonstrate in reasoned opinions that it has, a valid theory, derived from the Constitution, of the respective spheres of majority and minority freedom. If it does not have such a theory but merely imposes its own value choices, or worse if it pretends to have a theory but actually follows its own predilections, the Court violates the postulates of the Madisonian model that alone justifies its power. It then necessarily abets the tyranny either of the majority or of the minority.[19]

The problem for Bork is that "where constitutional materials—[the text and the history, and their fair implications]—do not clearly specify the value to be preferred, there is no principled way to prefer any claimed human value to any other."[20] In other words, unless we are prepared to allow unelected, life-tenured judges the essentially legislative power to decide every aspect of our lives, the only way to constrain their power is to insist that it be exercised only according to the dictates of interpretivism. Otherwise courts are as free to create a fundamental right to play tennis, to pollute the environment, or to operate child-labor sweatshops as to terminate a pregnancy.

Other constitutional scholars have challenged Bork's position. Grey, for example, explains that the task of applying generally accepted social norms (such as personal autonomy) to specific cases (such as abortion) is characteristically judicial, not a species of legislation. He adds that a long line of cases holds that the due process clause of the Fourteenth Amendment protects a number of personal liberties from government intrusion.

Grey contends that the noninterpretivist approach generally meets Bork's criteria of legitimacy—"original understanding, judi-

cial precedent, subsequent history, and internal consistency...."
First, the concept of natural law "was widely shared and deeply
felt" by the generation that framed the Constitution. Second,
natural law theory continued to develop throughout the nineteenth century and formed the philosophical backdrop to the
framing of the Fourteenth Amendment. Third, as the Court
emerged from its protection of laissez-faire economic policy, it began to recognize "new civil libertarian constitutional rights whose
protection was deemed 'essential to the concept of ordered liberty'—for example, rights against state governments of freedom
of speech and religion, rights to 'fundamentally fair' proceedings,
and rights to familial autonomy in childrearing and education."
Today's privacy rights, while based more on notions of autonomy
than social contract, are "the modern offspring, in a direct and
traceable line of legitimate descent, of the natural-rights tradition
that is so deeply embedded in our constitutional origins."[21]

Viewed this way, noninterpretivism itself is a well-established
constitutional tradition. Its roots are older than the Constitution
itself. The idea that the Court may protect only those rights
specifically listed in the Constitution, which underlies the *Roe*-
as-judicial-invention objection, therefore seems revolutionary
today. As Laurence Tribe has pointed out, this objection could
require overruling the Supreme Court's incorporation of most of
the provisions of the Bill of Rights as applying against the states.
States thus would be free, for example, to censor free speech;
prohibit or mandate religious practices; search homes without a
warrant; coerce confessions; subject criminal defendants to double jeopardy and to trial without jury, counsel, or the right to
confront one's accusers; and administer cruel and unusual punishments. A strictly interpretivist approach also could require the
abandonment of federal judicial protection of other important
rights, including the right to vote in a state election; the freedom of association; the right to equal protection of federal laws
(in other words, the federal government could, for example,
operate a racially segregated school system); the presumption of
innocence and the requirement that the prosecution prove its
case beyond a reasonable doubt; and the right to marry. Finally,

if the framers' subjective intent with respect to specific historical practices is to control, there could be no federal constitutional remedy for intentional racial discrimination in public schools or other public places (at least assuming that the facilities were roughly equivalent).[22]

THE RIGHT TO CHOOSE AN ABORTION AS A FUNDAMENTAL RIGHT

Another criticism of *Roe* is that even if one concedes *Roe's* non-interpretivist approach to discovering fundamental rights, abortion is not one of them. There is no tradition in this country of protecting or valuing a woman's decision to have an abortion. To the contrary, this argument runs, one can find a powerful tradition of protecting and preserving life, which *Roe* starkly opposes.

Some historians reply that if the decision is properly understood in its long-term historical context, it is not a radical departure from the past. They argue that *Roe* is consistent with the historical tradition of allowing abortion until a developmental milestone is reached (formerly quickening, now viability). America's deviation from that position was caused by transitory interests of regular physicians and the shift in the sociological statistics of abortion in America. These historians argue that those forces are unlikely ever to recur in tandem.[23]

There are at least two problems with this reply. First, the historical record is at best inconclusive. Women before the mid-nineteenth century did enjoy greater freedom from legal restraint on abortion. But Anglo-American culture has never *endorsed* abortion as it plainly has other traditions and values, such as marriage or child-rearing. Instead, secular society at times has tolerated abortion and at other times has condemned and prohibited the practice. Second, the argument strains the concept of "tradition"—in a country barely two hundred years old—by trying to dismiss as an historical anomaly legal conditions that prevailed for almost a century. That strain becomes even more evident when one considers that the movement toward a much more restrictive abortion policy in America was

162

well under way when the Fourteenth Amendment was adopted.

Other supporters of *Roe* argue more persuasively (if one accepts their noninterpretivist approach) that it rests on a broader understanding of the woman's liberty interest than its critics contend. The relevant liberty is not the specific practice of abortion, as critics would assert, but the woman's own self-determination and autonomy over the supremely important and personal matters of procreation, family, her physical integrity, and her future life. Proponents of this view, as did Justice Blackmun in *Roe*, point to the dramatic physical changes in a woman's body during pregnancy; the risks and burdens of childbirth; the profound psychological, economic, and social impact of motherhood; the disparate impact of abortion prohibitions on the poor; and the horrors of illegal and self-induced abortions. In addition, "Recent history and current events have shown that governments can and will fashion abortion regimes that seek to coerce reproductive choice as official state policy. The nightmarish policies of criminalized abortion in Nazi Germany and the Soviet Union [and in Rumania] on the one hand and forced abortion in China on the other, are chilling reminders that women must be afforded the ability to make fundamental reproductive decisions free of government interference."[24] Denial of a fundamental right of reproductive choice raises the specter of coerced sterilization, forced abortion, and perhaps even involuntary implantation of embryos fertilized in vitro.

Laws prohibiting abortion are obviously directed only at women, and therefore arguably give rise to equal protection concerns. Whether the Supreme Court would find an equal protection violation in such circumstances is doubtful. The Court generally looks more closely at laws classifying by gender than at economic or social welfare legislation (but less closely than at laws classifying by race).[25] But the Court has stated, none too convincingly, that "it does not follow that every legislative classification concerning pregnancy is a sex-based classification" that violates the equal protection clause.[26] In view of the Court's ruling in *Bray* that efforts to prevent women from choosing abortion do not amount to sex discrimination, an equal protection challenge on such grounds appears unlikely to succeed.

In any event, abortion rights advocates argue that the Court ought to construe either the due process or equal protection clause to accommodate changing social values and circumstances.[27] The progress of American women toward full citizenship has accelerated dramatically over the past few decades, and full constitutional protection of their right to liberty must take into account the unequal demands that pregnancy and childbirth place on them and the ways in which laws can deprive women of real choice about undertaking such burdens. Solicitor General Charles Fried argued to the Court in *Webster* that proscribing abortions would not deprive women of real choice because they still could elect contraception or abstinence (or presumably sterilization). One response to this is that contraception is hardly foolproof (estimates are that most women who have abortions did use contraception), and abstinence or sterilization for the three or four decades of fertility in a woman's life are scarcely practical alternatives.[28]

One pointed rejoinder to the foregoing arguments derives from the representation-reinforcement theory of judicial review. As explained earlier, under that theory the courts are justified in interfering with the process of representative democracy—beyond specific textual authorization to do so, such as under the First Amendment—when necessary to correct defects in that process. The constitutional scholar John Hart Ely has argued that the heightened judicial scrutiny of state abortion laws mandated by *Roe v. Wade* is not warranted by the representation-reinforcement principle. He first observes:

> Let us not underestimate what is at stake: Having an unwanted child can go a long way toward ruining a woman's life. And at bottom, *Roe* signals the Court's judgment that this result cannot be justified by any good that anti-abortion legislation accomplishes. This surely is an understandable conclusion—indeed it is one with which I agree—but ordinarily the Court claims no mandate to second-guess legislative balances, at least not when the Constitution has designated neither of the values in conflict as entitled to special protection.[29]

164

Ely concedes that women in many circumstances are entitled to special judicial protection. "Compared with men, very few women sit in our legislatures, a fact I believe should bear some relevance—even without an Equal Rights Amendment—to the appropriate standard of review for legislation that favors men over women." The problem with the abortion rights claim, however, is that "*no* fetuses sit in our legislatures." Ely explains that the two competing interests—women and conceptuses—have struggled continually in the legislative arena. *Roe*'s objection was that the woman's interest has always lost, but Ely reminds us that every political contest has its winners and losers.[30] The Court's task is to determine whether the outcomes result from constitutionally suspect blockages in the political process.

Invoking Justice Stone's concept of "discrete and insular minorities," Ely argues that sometimes the Court ought to

> throw *its* weight on the side of a minority demanding in court more than it was able to achieve politically. But even assuming this suggestion can be given principled content, it was clearly intended and should be reserved for those interests which, *as compared to the interests to which they have been subordinated* constitute minorities incapable of protecting themselves. Compared with men, women may constitute such a "minority"; compared with the unborn, they do not. I'm not sure I'd know a discrete and insular minority if I saw one, but confronted with a multiple choice question requiring me to designate (a) women or (b) fetuses, I'd expect no credit for the former answer.[31]

Ely concludes: "What is frightening about *Roe* is that this super-protected right," in addition to lacking any basis in the value choices reflected in the Constitution's text or history, is not "explainable in terms of the unusual political impotence of the group judicially protected vis-à-vis the interest that legislatively prevailed over it."[32]

165

THE STATE'S INTEREST AS COMPELLING

Even conceding that a woman has a fundamental right to make her own choices about reproduction, and that the right includes abortion, it has been argued that the state's interest in preserving fetal life is sufficiently compelling throughout pregnancy (not just after viability) to override the woman's right. A premise of this argument often is that life begins at conception. Under the Supreme Court's fundamental rights analysis, recognition of a right does not ensure absolute protection. Rather, it means that the Court will require government to demonstrate (1) that its interest is legitimate and of such importance (in other words, "compelling") that the individual's rights must be overcome, and (2) that government has chosen means that are no more burdensome on the right than necessary to accomplish its purpose.*

Responses to this argument address both the "compelling interest" and the "narrowly tailored" aspects. First is the counterargument that states generally have not sought to protect all potential human life. State abortion laws, like the Texas law in *Roe*, have usually made some exceptions, such as for victims of rape or incest and in cases of endangerment to maternal health. It is difficult to see either how the circumstances of conception diminish the conceptus's moral claim to life, or how to strike a moral balance between the mother's claim to life and the conceptus's. Some statutes did not make it a crime for the woman to obtain an abortion but focused instead on the abortionist's conduct. And pre-*Roe* enforcement patterns were inconsistent and incoherent, raising charges of economic discrimination. The point is that the state's claim to a compelling interest is undermined by irrational distinctions, inconsistent enforcement, and unequal burdens placed on disadvantaged groups.

Those who raise the compelling interest argument also have a

---

*The Court's upholding of laws prohibiting nonobscene child pornography is an example of a compelling state interest (protection of children from the harms of being made the subjects of pornography) that overcomes a constitutional right of free expression (which otherwise would include nonobscene pornography). The cases are *New York v. Ferber* and *Osborne v. Ohio*.

difficult historical record to contend with. Just as the record docs not clearly indicate that society has long cherished and protected abortion rights, neither does it show a consistent commitment to the protection of fetal life. Until only very recently, protecting potential life was not the primary purpose behind most abortion legislation. Abortion was legal in America when the Constitution was framed. Nineteenth-century laws were enacted initially to protect women from the grave hazards of the primitive medical procedures of the day. As discussed earlier, some historians have argued that the more restrictive abortion laws passed later in the nineteenth century were addressed primarily to concerns

> that are either now medically outmoded or recognized as discriminatory: restrictive views about women's sexuality and proper societal role; health concerns concerning surgical procedure; nativist fears about declining birthrates among white Protestant women who were practicing birth control and having abortions at a time when immigrant populations were rising; and an effort by the medical profession to secure its hegemony over reproductive medical procedures by preventing mid-wives who would induce abortion from practicing.[33]

SUMMING UP

It is small wonder that *Roe v. Wade* has been a source of intense legal, no less than political and moral, debate. There is simply no single trump argument which forces one side or the other to concede that reason compels defeat. Powerful arguments about the inalienability of individual moral worth, which in other contexts would be embraced by civil libertarians, challenge the Supreme Court's disposition of the personhood problem. And our national experience has demonstrated the dreadful consequences of allowing a class of human beings' claim to humanity itself to be defined away by the legal dictates of another, more powerful class. On the other hand, women's claim to liberty, in the context of the unique demands that pregnancy makes on them, argues strongly in favor of abortion rights. And denial of such rights both in the United States and abroad has produced conditions that any fair-minded person would have to admit seem oppressive.

It also is apparent that the debate over *Roe* is about much more than the enormous issue of abortion. It is more fundamentally about the mechanism by which our Republic will decide such questions. By recognizing a privacy right to abortion, the Supreme Court in *Roe* in effect extended the realm of value choices that will be decided in the courts. Some constitutional scholars find the Court's assertion of such an undemocratic power unjustified. Other constitutional scholars find it equally disturbing to deny the Court such authority.

The constitutional debate did not end with *Roe*; in a sense it only began there. Although *Roe* established the basic right to abortion, and went even further to pronounce what some observers say looks very much like a legislative code, the issue was far from resolved. Between 1973 and the 1989 decision in *Webster* the Court proceeded to elaborate—some observers (including members of the Supreme Court) would say expand— the content of that right as constitutional challenges were brought against a series of legislative measures that had the purpose or effect of restricting abortion. Not all measures, however, were struck down. For example, the Court has upheld restrictions on abortion funding, reporting requirements, and parental consent laws that meet certain requirements. The pre-*Webster* cases are reviewed next.

Part Three

. . . .

ELABORATING A CONSTITUTIONAL RIGHT TO ABORTION: THE POST-*ROE*, PRE-*WEBSTER* CASES

9. A Search for Balance

. . . .

In *Roe* the Supreme Court established the following trimester structure for evaluating the constitutionality of abortion laws. Obviously *Roe* emphasized the role of unconstrained medical judgment in the abortion decision.

1. Until the end of the first trimester "the abortion decision and its effectuation must be left to the medical judgment of the pregnant woman's attending physician."

2. After the first trimester the state may regulate abortions "in ways that are reasonably related to maternal health."

3. After "viability"—the point at which the fetus "presumably has the capability of meaningful life outside the mother's womb"—"the State in promoting its interest in the potentiality of human life may, if it chooses, regulate, and even proscribe, abortion except where it is necessary in appropriate medical judgment, for the preservation of the life or health of the mother."[1]

Between *Roe* and *Webster* the Court reviewed a variety of abortion restrictions, which can be grouped roughly into three categories. The first covers regulation of the medical aspects of the abortion procedure itself. Such measures govern the definition of viability, abortion facilities and methods, and record-keeping requirements. The second category covers measures that directly control the abortion decision, such as informed-consent procedures, waiting periods, and notice to parents and spouses and consent requirements. The third category includes state and federal laws governing public funding of abortions. As the Court has addressed these legislative initiatives (many of which have been thinly veiled efforts to restrict the availability of abortions), a growing number of Justices have begun to question the framework established in *Roe*.

170

As we have seen, the Court seeks to balance the woman's privacy interest against the government's asserted interest. This kind of balancing, while common in constitutional law, is inherently uncertain because it does not dictate the weight the Court must give the opposing interests. As a result, the strength of a so-called fundamental right will depend on which government interests the Court regards as overriding and how closely the Court will require the legislatures' chosen means to fit their purposes. The Court's post-*Roe*, pre-*Webster* cases generally subjected abortion laws to fairly rigorous review, though some decisions upheld substantial restrictions (particularly in the case of minors).

10. Regulating the Medical Aspects of Abortion

. . . .

Before *Webster* the Court generally struck down laws that it viewed as interfering with the physician's medical judgment on previability abortion. The Court also held unconstitutional laws that appeared to single out abortion for burdensome requirements. The Court's test under *Roe* was whether previability regulations are genuinely related to protecting maternal health.

VIABILITY

The Supreme Court has reviewed laws governing the definition of viability, procedures for determining viability, and the consequences of that determination. Recall that in *Roe* the Court held that nontherapeutic abortion could be prohibited after viability. The statutory definition of viability therefore typically forms the critical boundary between lawful and unlawful abortion. Before *Webster* the Court emphasized that "the determination of whether a particular fetus is viable is, and must be, a matter for the judgment of the responsible attending physician,"[1] and that regulations must not interfere with the physician's obligation to protect the patient's welfare.

The Court has sustained statutory definitions of viability that allow for independent medical judgment. For example, in *Planned Parenthood of Central Missouri v. Danforth* the Court upheld Missouri's definition of viability as: "that stage of fetal development when the life of the unborn child may be continued indefinitely outside the womb by natural or artificial life-support systems."[2]

172

The Missouri definition, the Court concluded, was sufficiently flexible to allow reliance on the physician's judgment, skill, and technical ability, and therefore met the Roe standard.

By contrast the Court has stricken laws that intrude on that judgment. "Because [viability] may differ with each pregnancy, neither the legislature nor the courts may proclaim one of the elements entering into the ascertainment of viability—be it weeks or gestation or fetal weight or any other single factor—as the determinant of when the state has a compelling interest in the life or health of the fetus."[3] The Court therefore held unconstitutional, in *Colautti v. Franklin*, a Pennsylvania statute that combined an overly broad definition of viability with vague restrictions on the standard of care and abortion techniques.

The Pennsylvania statute defined "viable" to mean "the capability of a fetus to live outside the mother's womb albeit with artificial aid." That definition, the Court reasoned, failed to distinguish between mere "momentary survival" and indefinite survival as under the Missouri law. The statute also imposed penalties on the physician for performing an abortion when there is "sufficient reason to believe that the fetus may be viable." Upon determining that the fetus is viable, or "may be viable," the Pennsylvania statute required the physician to exercise the same professional care to preserve the fetus's life and health as if the fetus were intended to be born alive. The Court concluded that such provisions, instead of referring to the doctor's best clinical judgment, based criminal liability on "confusing and ambiguous criteria" such as "may be viable."[4]

HOSPITALIZATION

In *Doe v. Bolton* the Court had held unconstitutional a requirement that all abortions (including those in the first trimester) be performed in an accredited hospital. The Court reasoned that such a categorical requirement interfered with medical judgment and unnecessarily increased costs in many cases. The Court reaffirmed that judgment ten years later in *City of Akron v. Akron*

173

Center for Reproductive Health, when it held unconstitutional a hospitalization requirement for all second-trimester abortions. The Court reached that decision under the *Roe* standard that second-trimester regulations must bear a reasonable relationship to protection of maternal health. By more than doubling the cost of the procedure and imposing additional travel burdens for women living in remote areas, Akron's requirement "imposed a heavy, and unnecessary, burden on women's access to a relatively inexpensive, otherwise accessible, and safe abortion procedure."[5]

The Court's conclusions in *Doe* and *City of Akron* are supported by the greatly increased safety of second-trimester abortions. The American Public Health Association has, since *Roe*, abandoned its recommendation that second-trimester abortions be performed in hospitals. And the American College of Osbtetricians and Gynecologists has revised its position to recommend that abortions may be performed safely in an outpatient clinic until the fourteenth week of pregnancy and in a free-standing surgical facility until the eighteenth week.[6]

The Court has, however, upheld laws requiring second-trimester abortions to be performed in facilities that meet the standards of outpatient surgical facilities. Although such requirements can significantly increase the cost of abortion, the Court has regarded them as rationally related to the state's interest in protecting maternal health.[7]

ABORTION METHODS

So far the Court has rejected, as an undue interference with the physician's medical judgment, state laws that seek to prescribe precise methods for second-trimester abortions. But the Court has upheld ancillary requirements, such as record keeping and pathology reports, that it considers not unduly burdensome and reasonably related to the state's interest in health.

For example, the Pennsylvania law held unconstitutional in *Colautti v. Franklin* required, for fetuses that "may be viable," that physicians "use the abortion method that would provide the best opportunity for the fetus to be aborted alive so long as a different technique would not be necessary in order to preserve the life or health of the mother." At that time saline amnio-infusion, which is almost always fatal to the fetus, was the physician's method of choice in the second trimester. Other methods that increase the chances of fetal survival—such as hystero-tomy—involve serious disadvantages for the woman. The statute's constitutional defect lay in its muddled interference in medical judgment. The law was unclear whether (and under what conditions) the physician was required to compromise the woman's welfare against better chances of fetal survival.[8]

The Court also has held unconstitutional more clear-cut inter-ference with the physician's choice of previability abortion method. For example, Missouri attempted to prohibit saline amniocentesis after the first trimester. The Court in *Planned Parenthood of Central Missouri v. Danforth* rejected Missouri's contention that this prohibition was reasonably related to the preservation of maternal health.[9] Quite to the contrary, saline amniocentesis was at the time the procedure of choice nation-wide and was much safer than continuation of the pregnancy. The Court concluded that this forced choice of less safe meth-ods was an unreasonable and arbitrary regulation designed to inhibit the vast majority of second-trimester abortions. The Court further held unconstitutional a provision, enforced by threat of a manslaughter charge, requiring physicians to use their skill to save the life of the fetus regardless of when in the preg-nancy the abortion is performed.*

The Court takes a different view of laws regulating postviabil-ity abortion methods. After viability under *Roe* the state may seek to protect fetal life consistently with protection of the preg-nant woman's health. Some states have thus required a second physician to attend at postviability abortions to care for any

---

*The Court has also held unconstitutional an ordinance requiring that physicians performing abortions "insure that the remains of the unborn child are disposed of in a humane and sanitary manner." The Court held the term "humane and sanitary" unconstitutionally vague, reasoning that it could be read as requiring "some sort of a 'decent burial' of an embryo at the earliest stage of formation." *City of Akron v. Akron Center for Reproductive Health.*

175

child born alive. The Court has upheld such measures as long as they do not compromise maternal health.

Missouri's statute required a second physician at postviability abortions for this reason, and the Court upheld it. The statute also required both physicians to take all reasonable steps—that did not increase the risk to the woman—to preserve the child's life and health. Missouri further forbade use of abortion procedures fatal to the fetus in medically necessary postviability abortions, unless alternative procedures would pose a greater risk to the woman's health. There was no opinion joined by a majority of Justices upholding the law in *Planned Parenthood of Kansas City, Missouri v. Ashcroft.* Justice Powell and Chief Justice Burger concluded that, given the ability of the second physician to tend to the fetus while the primary physician looks after the woman, the statute reasonably furthered the state's compelling interest in preserving the life and health of the fetus—despite the significant increase in cost and the relatively unlikely chance that the fetus could be saved in any event.[10]

But the Court has invalidated second-physician requirements that it viewed as threatening the woman's health. A Pennsylvania law, for example, imposed two requirements. First, a second physician was required to take all "reasonable steps necessary, in his [or her] judgment, to preserve the child's life and health." Second, the law mandated use of the abortion procedure that would provide the greatest opportunity for the fetus to be aborted alive unless that "method would present a *significantly* greater medical risk" to the woman's life or health.[11] Because the statute dictated a "trade-off" between the woman's health and fetal survival, and did not ensure that the woman's health would be the primary physician's paramount concern, the Court in *Thornburgh v. American College of Obstetricians and Gynecologists* held the standard-of-care provision unconstitutional. And, unlike the Missouri statute, Pennsylvania's second-physician requirement lacked an exception for endangerment of the woman's health caused by delay in the arrival of the second physician.

176

RECORD-KEEPING, REPORTING, AND TISSUE-TESTING REQUIREMENTS

Record-keeping and reporting requirements involve both health and confidentiality. The state plainly has an interest in monitoring the frequency and outcome of abortion procedures. On the other hand, women have a strong interest in not having their private decision become public knowledge, especially in view of the incidence of harassment. The Court has held unconstitutional laws that go beyond the state's interest in promoting maternal or public health and that threaten the woman's confidentiality.

The constitutional boundary once again appears between the Missouri law upheld in *Planned Parenthood of Central Missouri v. Danforth* and the Pennsylvania law struck down in *Thornburgh v. American College of Obstetricians and Gynecologists.* Missouri simply required preservation of confidential records for seven years after each abortion (even those performed in the first trimester). The Court viewed this requirement as reasonably related to maternal health.

Unlike the Missouri reporting law, the "scope of the information required [by Pennsylvania] and its availability to the public belie[d] any assertions by the commonwealth that it is advancing any legitimate [health-related] interest."[12] Pennsylvania required the following information to be reported: the basis for the physician's determination that the child is not viable; identification of the performing and referring physician; the woman's political subdivision and state of residence, age, race, marital status, and number of prior pregnancies; the date of her last menstrual period and the fetus's probable gestational age; the basis for any determination of medical emergency and nonviability; and method of payment. Although the woman's name ostensibly had to be kept confidential, Pennsylvania law required that reports be available for public inspection and copying within fifteen days of receipt. The Court reasoned that, because "identification is the obvious purpose of these extreme reporting requirements," the statute unconstitutionally deterred the "intensely private" decision to terminate pregnancy. Under *Roe* that right "may be exercised without public scrutiny and in defiance of the contrary opinion of the sovereign or other third parties."[13]

The Court also upheld a law requiring all surgically removed tissue, including by abortion, to be examined by a pathologist.[14] Pathological examinations can warn of potentially dangerous conditions, and filing a copy of the report with the state health department allows for statistical study of complications arising out of abortions. The estimated additional cost for abortion was less than twenty dollars. The Court therefore concluded that the regulation was reasonably related to accepted medical practice and imposed only a slight burden.

11. Direct Regulation of the Woman's Decision

. . . .

Most abortion laws have some impact on the woman's decision. But some regulations target the decision-making process directly, short of an outright ban on abortion, in one of three ways. One approach dictates the information that the woman must be given before she can have an abortion. A second method, usually accompanying the first, requires the woman to wait a specified period—presumably so she can consider her decision in light of the state-mandated information. The third approach seeks to include a third party in the decision-making process. Thus some laws require notice to or consent of a spouse or parent.

Before *Webster* the Court tried to draw the line at measures that interfered with an adult woman's decision or placed a third party in a position to veto her decision. The Court upheld laws that include parents in a minor's decision-making process, but has required procedures that allow the minor to bypass her parents when appropriate. After *Webster*, however, the Court began upholding increasingly burdensome requirements; and in *Casey* the Court allowed the state actually to interfere directly and intentionally with the woman's decision, provided it did not do so too aggressively.

INFORMED CONSENT

All medical procedures are subject to some form of regulation to ensure that the treatment is voluntary. Ordinary tort law requires doctors to obtain a patient's informed consent before treating

179

the patient. A physician who fails to obtain *any* consent, unless the patient is unconscious and in a medical emergency, commits a battery even if all goes well with the treatment. And a doctor who fails to inform the patient adequately about a procedure's dangers and alternatives risks malpractice liability. Tort law's consent requirements seek to protect the patient's autonomy— his or her control over certain kinds of physical invasions.

Some states have developed special requirements for informed consent to the abortion procedure. Before *Casey* the Court struck down informed-consent statutes that burdened or influenced the abortion decision, but it upheld laws that merely tried to ensure that the doctor obtained informed consent. For example, the Court upheld laws requiring written certification of the woman's informed consent to ensure that it actually was freely given, even if the state did not impose such a requirement on other medical procedures.[1]

The pre-*Casey* Court also struck down laws apparently intended not to inform the woman's decision but to persuade her to withhold it by imposing a rigidly defined list of information to be given to women in all cases (no matter what a particular woman's needs). For example, the Court held unconstitutional an Akron, Ohio, ordinance requiring that the woman be told, before having an abortion, a list of patently deterrent and arguably misleading statements. Those statements included that "the unborn child is a human life from the moment of conception"; a detailed description of the fetus; that the fetus may be viable after twenty-two weeks; that abortion is a "major surgical procedure" involving serious physical and psychological risks; and that numerous public and private organizations are available to assist in placing the child for adoption. The Court concluded that Akron's ordinance went way beyond informed consent, violated *Roe v. Wade*'s ruling that government may not mandate a particular theory of when life begins, rested on speculation about fetal development and pain sensitivity, and on the whole was designed to pressure a woman to withhold her consent.[2]

Pennsylvania's informed-consent law met the same fate, and for the same reasons, in *Thornburgh v. American College of*

Obstetricians and Gynecologists. In addition to requiring doctors to inform women of abortion's risks, the Pennsylvania statute also required abortion patients to be told of the availability of prenatal care, childbirth, and neonatal care benefits; the father's liability for child support; agencies offering alternatives to abortion; that Pennsylvania urges women to contact such agencies before making a final decision about abortion; and the "probable anatomical and physiological characteristics of the unborn child at two-week gestational increments from fertilization to full term, including any relevant information on the possibility of the unborn child's survival."[3] The Court also invalidated Pennsylvania's twenty-four-hour waiting period on the grounds that it added unnecessary delay.

THE SPOUSE'S CONSENT AND NOTICE

In previability cases, spouse's consent and notice requirements have never survived constitutional scrutiny. The Court has ruled that the state may not delegate a veto power to the husband that the state itself could not constitutionally exercise. The Court has further reasoned that a spouse's veto would not promote the state's interest in preserving marital harmony. In the event of a disagreement, the view of one partner must prevail; and because the woman is the one most immediately affected by pregnancy, her interests have constitutional priority.[4]

PARENTAL CONSENT AND NOTICE

Parental-consent laws bring into conflict three elements: the Court's traditional deference to the state in protecting minors' best interests; a recognition of parents' privacy interest in directing their children's upbringing that dates back to *Meyer* and *Pierce*; and the individual privacy interest recognized in *Roe*. The Court has concluded that a *competent* minor's privacy interests under *Roe* outweigh the state's general interest in protecting her

181

welfare and parental authority. A state-mandated absolute parental veto, the Court has reasoned, would not preserve parental authority if the pregnancy had already so fractured the family structure as to place the parent and minor in conflict.[5]

Justice Powell's thinking on this issue in *Bellotti v. Baird* set the standard for the Court's review of parental-consent laws. He first noted that minors' constitutional rights are more limited than those of adults for three reasons: "[1] the peculiar vulnerability of children; [2] their inability to make critical decisions in an informed, mature manner; and [3] the importance of the parental role in child rearing." The Court's task therefore is to balance minors' interest in autonomy against their special circumstances, particularly "in the making of important, affirmative choices with potentially serious consequences."[6] In other contexts, such as the possession of pornography, the Court has allowed the state to impose restrictions with respect to minors that it has held unconstitutional when applied to adults. Justice Powell also noted that many states require parental consent before a minor may marry.

Justice Powell observed, however, that abortion poses special problems. Unlike the marriage decision, the abortion decision cannot simply be postponed. The burdens of pregnancy and childbirth are no less severe for minors than for adults; in some respects they are more so. Whether abortion is in a minor's best interests varies widely from one case to another, and the minor might not always be capable of making that decision.

Because some parents, out of strongly held anti-abortion beliefs, might seek to obstruct both abortion and access to court, Justice Powell concluded that every minor must have an opportunity to seek judicial approval without first notifying or consulting her parents. He went on to describe the criteria for "judicial bypass" procedures, which eventually became the point of departure for later cases involving both consent and notice: The minor must be allowed to show, in a confidential and speedy proceeding, either (1) that she is sufficiently mature to make the abortion decision on her own, or (2) that an abortion would be in her overall best interests if she is found to be incapable of such a decision.[7]

More recently, in post-*Webster* cases, the Court has upheld more burdensome parental-notice requirements.[8] In *Hodgson v. Minnesota* the Court upheld a Minnesota statute requiring that both parents be notified (even if divorced, separated, or otherwise estranged) forty-eight hours before an abortion could be performed on a minor, provided that the state also allowed an adequate judicial bypass of the notice requirement.[9] In *Ohio v. Akron Center for Reproductive Health* the Court upheld a single-parent notification requirement which included a judicial bypass procedure containing relatively onerous requirements— including technical pleading requirements and a heightened standard of proof.[10]

12. The Public Funding of Abortion

· ·

The Supreme Court has consistently refused to recognize a constitutional right to government funding for abortion. In short the Court has reasoned that denial of government funding does not itself constitute a state-imposed burden on abortion. The Court thus has upheld both state and federal funding restrictions against challenges brought under *Roe v. Wade*. In those cases the Court has distinguished between government *encouragement* and governmental *prohibition* of an activity. Government may, consistent with the Constitution, spend money to encourage carrying the pregnancy to term while denying funds to the exercise of the alternative choice—abortion—even if that choice is constitutionally protected.[1] The Court applied that analysis in *Harris v. McRae* to uphold the 1980 version of the Hyde Amendment, which denies federal funding for all abortions except the very few that are necessary to save the woman's life, or in cases of rape or incest promptly reported to the authorities.[2] The law thus denies benefits for one procedure (abortion) to women who otherwise would be eligible for Medicaid, while providing funding for childbirth. The Court concluded that *Roe* protects only the choice and does not entitle a woman to funding.[3]

The abortion funding cases are worth considering in a critical light for several reasons. First, they illustrate an important aspect of the Court's approach to individual constitutional rights—the idea of negative rights—which has an impact beyond the area of abortion rights. Second, the Court's analysis in *Harris* seems so logical that an appraisal of the argument requires consideration

184

of at least some criticisms. Third, the negative rights idea played an important role in the 1990 case of *Rust v. Sullivan*, where the Court upheld regulations prohibiting abortion counseling and referral in federally funded family planning clinics. *Rust* is troublesome in several respects, which are better appreciated in the light of criticism of *Harris*.

Harris is consistent with the Court's refusal in other cases to recognize a constitutional claim to minimum subsistence or to equal educational opportunity. The idea underlying those cases is that of negative rights.[4] That approach views the Constitution as protecting individuals from only a limited range of active, tangible intrusions by government. For example, the First Amendment under the negative rights approach protects individual speakers from active government censorship, but it does not require government to help disadvantaged speakers be heard.

The Court in *Harris* thus concluded that *Roe* "did not translate into a constitutional obligation...to subsidize abortions." The Court explained that

> although government may not place obstacles in the path of a woman's exercise of her freedom of choice, it need not remove those not of its own creation. Indigency falls in the latter category. The financial constraints that restrict an indigent woman's ability to enjoy the full range of constitutionally protected freedom of choice are the product not of governmental restrictions on access to abortions, but rather of her indigency.[5]

There are several problems with the Court's analysis. First, the Court's assertion that the state has done nothing to interfere with a woman's choice is open to question. Congress enacted a statute that excludes from publicly funded medical care a medical procedure that the Court has expressly held is entitled to constitutional protection. Surely poor women who are in effect bribed to choose childbirth over abortion reasonably feel that the state has "done something" tangible and substantial to them.[6]

Second, *Harris* in a sense begs the real question. The conclusion that poverty, not the Hyde Amendment, restricts a woman's choice is simply another way of saying that the government

185

bears no constitutional responsibility for her circumstances. *Harris* fails to consider the relationship created by Medicaid between the woman and her government in the matter of her health-care financing, and the obligations that might follow from that relationship.

Third, considering the vast inequality of that relationship, the Court's view of state responsibility seems cramped and artificial. In other contexts the law routinely intervenes to prevent *private* parties from exploiting such vulnerabilities and to protect important public policies. For example, in recognizing that a deal between parties of grossly unequal bargaining power may not reflect a real choice, courts will decline to enforce unconscionable contracts. In shifting the costs of accidents to persons who can better bear and spread them, and to deter wrongful and harmful conduct, courts sometimes will not enforce disclaimers of implied warranties or liability waivers. In such cases courts properly reject the argument that the more powerful party is not responsible for the weaker party's vulnerability. Instead the relation between the parties gives rise to minimal obligations of good faith, fair dealing, and due care.[7]

If anything, this argument seems even stronger when applied to the unequal power relationship between Medicaid recipients and the state. They are scarcely strangers to each other. The Court ought to be especially sensitive to the threat of overreaching when one of the parties is the state and the interest at stake is a constitutional right.

One objection to this criticism of *Harrris* is that it seems to regard the indigent pregnant woman as the only vulnerable party, and to ignore the conceptus's greater helplessness. But once the issue becomes balancing the pregnant woman's interests against the state's interest in fetal life, we are back to the debate in *Roe*. Criticism of *Harris* does not necessarily imply an endorsement of *Roe*. *Roe* is open to serious question. The objection here is to *Harris*'s conclusion that, given the existence of abortion rights under *Roe*, the Hyde Amendment does nothing to affect the abortion rights of Medicaid-dependent women. If the real issue is abortion itself, it is difficult to see why indigent women's claims to reproductive freedom should weigh less in the constitutional balance than other women's.

In sum, the Court concluded that Medicaid recipients' utter dependence on government for their health care is constitutionally irrelevant.[8] That conclusion is unconvincing. In a real sense, government does inhibit the choice of abortion when it funds medical care in a way that leads to a poor woman not exercising that choice. To be sure, the Court usually defers to legislative judgments about how to spend society's money. But the plaintiff in *Harris* did not assert a right to state-subsidized health care generally. The state had already decided to offer such benefits. The issue instead was whether the state could deny benefits for a medical procedure that involves a constitutional right. The Court in *Harris* ignored the powerful ways in which government affects the lives of individuals, especially the poor and the vulnerable. After all, the Court has recognized a special responsibility to safeguard the rights of those citizens who are unable to command political support but no less worthy of protection.[9] Perhaps *Harris* is best understood as resting more on the Court's respect for a legislative decision not to fund a practice which some voters find morally abhorrent than on the Court's doubtful conclusions about the statute's impact on women's choice.

13. On the Threshold of Change

· ·

Between 1973 and 1989 the Court largely protected abortion rights against creative state efforts to limit them. Although abortion rights proponents did not always win—especially in the areas of abortion funding, record keeping, outpatient clinic standards, and some third-trimester restrictions—they usually prevailed. They lost on the general question whether parental consent or notification requirements violated *Roe*, but they succeeded in obtaining rigorous judicial bypass guidelines for such laws. In general the Court protected the physician's medical judgment and the doctor-patient relationship from state intrusion; and the Court vigorously guarded those interests in the first trimester.

The Court's ruling on the abortion funding issue, however, has had a significant impact on abortion rights. Its practical effect has been to render the procedure unavailable, or available only by overcoming substantial difficulty, for many low-income women. For those poor women who do scrape together the money for an abortion, the resulting delay increases the medical risks.

Throughout this period the Court's composition gradually changed, in part as the result of a concerted campaign by anti-abortion forces to include more Justices overtly hostile to *Roe*. The Court thus grew divided over abortion, and its commitment to *Roe* became less and less certain. The Court finally reached a turning point in 1989 in *Webster* when it became clear that the era of rights elaboration had ended and the process of rights retrenchment had begun. At that point the question became not how far the Court would go to protect abortion rights, but how far it would go to dismantle them.

Part Four

. . . .

NARROWING ABORTION RIGHTS: *WEBSTER V. REPRODUCTIVE HEALTH SERVICES* AND OTHER PRE-*CASEY* CASES

14. The *Webster* Case

. . . .

Webster v. Reproductive Health Services was a pivotal decision in the Court's consideration of the abortion issue. The Court received a record number of briefs, most of which argued for or against overruling *Roe*. The Court did not go quite that far, but for the first time since *Roe* it did allow the state to regulate abortion in the second trimester to protect fetal life rather than maternal health. Although there was no opinion joined by five Justices on the key issue, a majority in effect voted against *Roe*'s trimester framework.

While *Webster* indicated a change in direction, the Court's destination was unclear. Several Justices, lacking enough votes to overrule *Roe* outright, seemed prepared to chip away at it piece by piece. In so doing the Court failed to provide a clear replacement standard for testing the constitutionality of abortion regulations. Chief Justice Rehnquist's opinion did, however, help pave the way for *Casey*'s redefinition of *Roe*. Although the "undue burden" standard applied in *Casey* had been suggested in earlier separate opinions by Justice O'Connor, it was *Webster* that cast the long shadow over *Roe* out of which *Casey* emerged.

Webster considered three provisions of a particular Missouri statute, each of which touched on matters previously addressed by the Court. First, a statutory preamble provided that life begins at conception (defined as fertilization) and expressed the state's interest in protecting the unborn. Second, the statute prohibited abortion not necessary to save the woman's life if performed by public employees or in public facilities. Third, the statute required the physician to determine viability for all abortions performed on women twenty weeks or more pregnant, providing that the physician "shall perform such medical tests as are necessary to

190

make a finding of the gestational age, weight, and lung maturity of the unborn child."[1] The controversy over *Roe's* trimester framework centered on the third provision's apparent regulation of medical judgment in the second trimester.

A majority of the Justices (Rehnquist, White, Kennedy, O'Connor, and Scalia) joined an opinion written by Chief Justice Rehnquist dealing with the first two provisions. Only Justices White and Kennedy joined the Chief Justice's opinion on the viability-testing provision and on the broader question whether the Missouri law conflicted with *Roe*.

PREAMBLE

The Court concluded that the preamble could be read simply as expressing a pro-life value judgment and not imposing any real limitations on abortion. The Court therefore left the issue of the preamble's practical effect, if any, for later determination by the Supreme Court of Missouri. *Webster* interpreted the United States Supreme Court's earlier cases as holding only that states could not save an actual *restriction* on abortion that otherwise would be invalid under *Roe* by adopting a particular theory of when life begins. The Missouri preamble, the Court concluded, itself imposed no restrictions.[2]

PUBLIC FACILITIES

The Court upheld the prohibition on the use of public facilities or employees to perform abortions not necessary to save the mother's life. That result followed easily from *Harris v. McRae*. The Court reaffirmed the principle that constitutional rights do not create funding entitlements. The state therefore has no constitutional obligation to commit resources to make abortions available to women.

The Missouri statute, however, threatened to go further. As Justice O'Connor pointed out in her concurring opinion, the sweeping statutory definition of "public facilities" could be read as prohibiting abortions even in private clinics located on land leased from the state or using publicly owned utilities. If so, the provision might have crossed the *Harris v. McRae* boundary into actual prohibition. The challenge in *Webster,* however, was to the statute "on its face," as opposed to any particular application of the statute. In such cases, subject to exceptions not relevant here, the person challenging the law generally must prove that "no set of circumstances exists under which the Act would be valid."[3] Because the statute plainly had straightforward, constitutional applications—such as to state-employed doctors in state hospitals—the Court upheld it.

VIABILITY: THE PLURALITY OPINION

The Court's treatment of the viability provision was the crucial aspect of the case. The Justices disagreed over both the proper interpretation to be given the provision and the constitutional significance of the varying interpretations. Thus no opinion for the Court was joined by a majority of the Justices on that provision.

The statute requires that before performing an abortion on a woman twenty or more weeks pregnant, the doctor "shall first determine if the unborn child is viable using and exercising that degree of care, skill, and proficiency commonly exercised by the ordinarily skillful, careful, and prudent physician engaged in similar practice under the same or similar circumstances." The statute goes on to provide: "In making this determination of viability, the physician shall perform or cause to be performed such medical examinations and tests as are necessary to make a finding of the gestational age, weight, and lung maturity of the unborn child and shall enter such findings in the medical record of the mother."[4] In view of the apparently mandatory nature of the statute's language—"the physician *shall perform*"—the court of appeals had interpreted the statute as *requiring* doctors to perform certain tests to find gestational age, fetal weight, and lung maturity.

192

According to the brief of the American Medical Association, a requirement in all cases that physicians perform tests at twenty weeks "interferes with the physician's ability to follow sound medical practices and impermissibly burdens the pregnant woman's fundamental right to make medical decisions in consultation with her physician." First, as the trial court found, the only test to determine fetal lung maturity is amniocentesis. The AMA stated in its brief that "amniocentesis is a procedure that would be useless and contrary to accepted medical practice for the purpose of determining fetal lung maturity until about 34 weeks of gestation," and would impose additional health risks for the woman. Second, determination of fetal weight *in utero*, which is accomplished by sonogram, is "often not necessary or even useful in determining viability." Third, gestational age is usually determined by report of last menstrual period, and sometimes by ultrasound techniques. Ultrasound, however, "provides only a range of ages and may incorrectly date a pregnancy by as much as three weeks." The AMA concluded that "viability is a complicated medical determination to be made by an individual physician in light of the circumstances of an individual pregnancy. There is no set of tests that is always necessary or even indicated."[5]

Chief Justice Rehnquist's extraordinary treatment of this issue was joined by Justices White and Kennedy (Justices O'Connor and Scalia joined in the result but not in the opinion). He interpreted the provision as establishing a *presumption* of viability at twenty weeks, which the physician must overcome by performing tests indicating that the fetus is not viable.[6] Despite the statute's plainly mandatory language, Rehnquist further interpreted it to require only those tests that are "useful" or "feasible" to making subsidiary findings of viability. Construed in this way, the statute does not require a physician to perform any particular test to make the specified findings of gestational age, weight, and lung maturity in *all* circumstances. In effect the Chief Justice transformed a clear statutory command into a mere suggestion.

Now, this is the kind of contortion one might expect to see in an argument by a lawyer trying hard to *avoid* a conflict with

Roe's prohibition on state interference with medical judgment about viability. Remember that the Court had earlier invalidated laws dictating which factors a physician must consider in determining viability. The curious thing, however, in addition to Rehnquist's disregard of the statute's plain language, is that he nevertheless concluded that the statute attempted to regulate the medical determination of viability and increased the cost of abortion services—contrary to *Colautti v. Franklin, Planned Parenthood of Central Missouri v. Danforth,* and *City of Akron v. Akron Center for Reproductive Health, Inc.* In other words, after effectively rewriting the statute in a way that seemed designed to avoid a conflict with the Court's earlier cases, the Chief Justice decided that a conflict existed after all.

According to Rehnquist, the problem lay not with the Missouri statute but with the "rigid trimester analysis of the course of pregnancy enunciated in *Roe*...which is unsound in principle and unworkable in practice." He proposed the concept that later allowed the Court to stop short of completely overruling *Roe* in *Casey*: that *Roe's* recognition of a right to abortion could be detached from *Roe's* trimester framework. He therefore concentrated his criticism on that framework. He described it as quasi-legislative, giving rise to an intricate code of judicially developed regulations. He complained that the trimester framework improperly constituted the Court as a board of medical review. He also criticized the framework for wrongly ignoring the state's compelling interest in previability life and removing the abortion issue from the political process where it more appropriately belongs.[7]

Chief Justice Rehnquist's alternative to the trimester framework, if applied to abortion regulations generally, would effectively overrule *Roe* itself. He thus apparently sought to accomplish indirectly and incrementally what he lacked the votes to do directly and fully. He evaluated the Missouri statute under the same deferential standard of judicial review that the Court applies to general social and economic legislation that does not infringe any fundamental right. That, of course, is where the law stood before *Roe*. All laws must, and virtually all laws inevitably do, pass that review. Rehnquist concluded that the Missouri statute was "reasonably designed to ensure that abortions are not performed where the fetus is viable—an end which all concede is legitimate—and that is sufficient to sustain its constitutionality."[8] Notwithstanding his explicit rejection of *Roe*'s trimester framework (and *Roe*'s accompanying strict standard of judicial review), Rehnquist nonetheless stated that the case gives "no occasion" to overrule *Roe*. He limited *Roe* to invalidating only laws that actually prohibit abortions not necessary to save the woman's life.

VIABILITY: JUSTICE O'CONNOR'S OPINION

Justice O'Connor, in a separate concurring opinion, agreed with Chief Justice Rehnquist's interpretation of the statute and that the statute is constitutional. She disagreed, however, that the statute required reconsideration of *Roe*'s trimester framework. She analyzed the statute under her "undue burden" test, a revised form of which the plurality eventually adopted in *Casey*.

She first observed that the Court had never prohibited the state from promoting its interest in potential life when viability is possible. Second, she understood the statute merely to require that, when not medically imprudent, certain tests be performed that are useful in determining viability. This requirement, she argued, unlike the second-trimester hospitalization requirement struck down in *Akron*, does not impose an undue burden on the pregnant woman.[9] Furthermore, the statute is aimed at determining viability, the point at which the state's interest becomes compelling under *Roe*. In view of her conclusion that the Missouri law did not call for reexamination of any part of *Roe*, Justice O'Connor criticized the Chief Justice for reaching out unnecessarily to reconsider *Roe* (or at least *Roe*'s trimester framework).

Justice O'Connor's opinion also has its inconsistencies. Although she chided Chief Justice Rehnquist for revisiting *Roe*, her application of the "undue burden" standard is itself a revision of *Roe*. In earlier opinions she had offered that standard— which simply asks whether a law imposes an undue burden on the right to previability abortion—as an alternative to *Roe's* trimester framework. Her earlier criticisms of that framework resemble Rehnquist's. And she joined an opinion in *Casey* that regarded adoption of the undue burden test as overruling *Roe's* trimester framework.

VIABILITY: JUSTICE SCALIA'S DISSENT

Justice Scalia's opinion is the most straightforward. He rejected both Justice O'Connor's position that the statute did not conflict at all with *Roe*, and Chief Justice Rehnquist's proposal that *Roe's* trimester framework could be jettisoned without overruling the case. He reasoned that the statute "sometimes requires a physician to perform tests that he would not otherwise have performed to determine whether a fetus is viable. It is therefore a legislative imposition on the judgment of the physician, and one that increases the costs of an abortion."[10] The statute thus conflicts with the principles established in, for example, *Planned Parenthood of Central Missouri v. Danforth.*

Justice Scalia therefore agreed with the *Webster* dissenters that Rehnquist's opinion effectively would overrule *Roe*. Scalia "think[s] that should be done, but would do it more explicitly."[11] He further disagreed with Justice O'Connor's view that the Court should decide its cases on the narrowest possible ground, because he believes (as does Rehnquist) that *Roe* improperly usurps the democratic process and therefore cries out to be overruled.

THE DISSENTERS

Justices Blackmun, Marshall, Brennan, and Stevens dissented. Justice Blackmun's opinion was joined by Justices Brennan and Marshall. Blackmun concluded that the preamble sought to "expand indefinitely the scope of its abortion regulations by creating interests in fetal life that are limited solely by reference to the decisional law of this court."[12] He further found that the preamble unconstitutionally would preclude the use of certain contraceptive devices, such as the IUD and the "morning-after" pill, which operate by disrupting implantation of a fertilized ovum in the uterus. And he found the "public facilities" provision unconstitutional as well, on the same basis raised by Justice O'Connor. He pointed out that in 1985, 97 percent of all hospital abortions of sixteen weeks or later in Missouri were performed at the Truman Medical Center (a private institution staffed primarily by private physicians), which is located on ground leased from the state.

Blackmun considered Rehnquist's interpretation of the viability provision insupportable in view of the statutory language. He accused the Chief Justice of sidestepping the main issue—the validity of Roe's recognition of an implied right to abortion—by contriving a conflict with Roe's trimester framework. Like O'Connor, however, Blackmun found no basis for reconsidering Roe in deciding the constitutionality of the statute. He regarded the statute as lacking any rational basis for furthering the state's interest in protecting fetal life, because the statute required certain tests regardless of their usefulness in determining viability.

Blackmun went on to respond to Rehnquist's criticisms of Roe. First, to the argument that Roe's trimester framework cannot be found in the terms of the Constitution, Blackmun replied that many constitutional law doctrines consist of judge-made standards that have no express textual basis in the Constitution. Those standards instead reflect judicial efforts to accommodate the often competing interests involved in principles that the constitutional text does embody. Examples range from equal protection doctrine to the Court's test for obscenity under the First Amendment.

Second, Blackmun argued that the Roe framework is no more complex than other areas of constitutional law. Examples include the Court's doctrines concerning separation of church and state, or search and seizure. In any event, as Blackmun observed, Rehnquist would never accept Roe even without its trimester framework.

Third, Blackmun rejected Rehnquist's assertion that the state's

197

interest in fetal life is compelling throughout pregnancy. Quoting from Justice Stevens's dissenting opinion, Blackmun argued that the state's interest obviously "increases progressively and dramatically as the organism's capacity to feel pain, to experience pleasure, to survive, and to react to its surroundings increases day by day." In other words, the state's interest in fetal life five minutes before birth is perceptibly stronger than its interest two seconds after fertilization of the ovum.

Finally, Blackmun observed that Rehnquist's standard—asking whether the law reasonably furthers the state's interest in protecting fetal life from conception—would overrule *Roe*. Even the Texas statute struck down in *Roe*, which prohibited all abortions except those necessary to save the mother's life, would be constitutional under that standard. After all, if the state's interest in fetal life at eight weeks' gestation is equivalent to its interest at thirty weeks, then Texas's prohibition would seem entirely reasonable.[13]

Justice Blackmun did not respond directly to the Chief Justice's criticism that *Roe* exceeded the limits of the judicial power by creating a statutelike structure. Constitutional doctrine, like the common law, usually develops on a case-by-case basis, in the process of deciding actual controversies between litigants. For example, *Brown v. Board of Education* prohibited intentional racial segregation in public schools. But it was only after later cases that *Brown*'s prohibition was extended to other public institutions, such as public transportation. *Roe* went further by providing a relatively detailed framework to govern future cases. There are at least two responses that might be made to this criticism of *Roe*'s "excess." First, *Roe*'s framework provided needed guidance to future cases. Second, after sixteen years of litigation there had been plenty of case-by-case development anyway.

Justice Stevens, in a separate dissenting opinion, agreed that Rehnquist's interpretation of the Missouri statute was untenable and that the statute was unconstitutionally irrational quite apart from *Roe*. He criticized the preamble as contrary to *Griswold*'s protection of the right to use contraceptives (on the same basis as that argued by Justice Blackmun). He also characterized the preamble as a legislative endorsement—without any secular basis and therefore in violation of the establishment clause of the First Amendment—of a particular religious belief held by certain Christian sects concerning when life begins.

15. 1989 Term Post-*Webster* Cases

· ·

The Court upheld two state parental-notice laws during its 1989 term. Those cases reveal deep divisions on the Court concerning abortion. Rather than come to grips with the ultimate issue of abortion rights, however, a growing number of Justices seemed inclined to dismantle *Roe* piecemeal by reducing judicial scrutiny of certain kinds of abortion restrictions.

That process is apparent in *Hodgson v. Minnesota*. In that case Justices Kennedy, White, Scalia, and Chief Justice Rehnquist disregarded uncontested findings of fact about the harmful impact of a Minnesota requirement for the notification of both parents. Reciting generalities about the importance of the state's interest in protecting and fostering the parent-child relationship, those Justices deferred to the state legislature's judgment on the wisdom and workability of such laws. Although the other Justices came to different conclusions and applied different tests, they at least were willing to consider evidence of the law's real-world impact and the realities of today's family life. By considering the law in light of the incidence of divorce, separation, dysfunctional families, and abusive parents, those Justices would subject the legislature's judgment to closer review. Only Justices Marshall, Brennan, and Blackmun, however, would have applied the strict judicial scrutiny the Court usually applies to laws infringing fundamental rights.

This disagreement over the level of judicial review goes to the heart of what it means to have a constitutional right. As a practical matter, constitutional rights are only as effective as the courts' willingness to scrutinize legislative decisions affecting those rights. The approach of the Justices joining Justice Kennedy in *Hodgson* thus in effect undermines abortion rights.

HODGSON V. MINNESOTA

In *Hodgson v. Minnesota* a badly divided Court held unconstitutional Minnesota's requirement that *both* parents be provided forty-eight hours' notice before an abortion may be performed on a minor. The statute made no exception for a divorced parent, a noncustodial parent, or a biological father who never lived with the pregnant woman's mother. The Court ruled, however, that the statute was saved by its judicial bypass provision.

The Court was able to form a majority only on these conclusions: (1) that the forty-eight-hour waiting period constitutionally furthered the state's interest, but (2) that the two-parent notification requirement did not do so. A *different* majority of Justices joined in the decision that the judicial bypass procedure saved the Minnesota statute.

The statutory exceptions to the notification requirement were limited to cases in which only one parent was living, the second could not be located after reasonably diligent effort, emergency treatment was necessary to save the pregnant minor's life, both parents had already given written consent, or the minor was the victim of sexual or physical abuse. The abuse exception was available only if the proper authorities had been notified, who would then investigate and contact the parents. The statute also provided, however, that in the event the two-parent notification requirement was struck down by a court, a judicial bypass provision would become effective. That provision satisfied the Court's judicial bypass criteria.

The district court in *Hodgson* made extensive findings of fact concerning the statute's purpose and effect, which were largely undisputed on appeal. On the whole the district court found overwhelming evidence that the law failed to advance the state's interest in promoting the pregnant minor's welfare or enhancing family integrity. Instead it caused considerable harm to the minor and her family. The trial court found that the statute was intended primarily to protect minors' well-being by encouraging them to discuss their pregnancy with their parents, but it also was designed to deter minors from choosing abortion. The court

201

also found that only half the minors in Minnesota live with both parents and a third live with one parent. The two-parent requirement had especially harmful effects on both the custodial parent and the pregnant minor when parents were divorced or separated. The two-parent requirement also had detrimental effects in two-parent families, especially when domestic violence was a serious problem. The abuse exception was not a practical alternative for most minors because of the authorities' involvement and the parental contact. Almost all bypass petitions were granted. "The judges who adjudicated 90% of the petitions testified; none of them found any positive effects of the law."[1]

The Court (Justices Stevens, O'Connor, Brennan, Blackmun, and Marshall) held that requiring *both* parents to be notified, whether or not both are involved in the minor's upbringing, "does not reasonably further any legitimate state interest." Any state interest in ensuring that the minor's decision to terminate her pregnancy is knowing, intelligent, and deliberate could be met by a single-parent notification requirement, even if the family is intact with both parents at home. And the two-parent notification requirement, the trial record showed, was harmful to the thousands of dysfunctional families it affected. The Court rejected the state's apparent effort to force both parents to be involved in the minor's abortion decision. "A state interest in standardizing its children and adults, making the 'private realm of family life' conform to some state-designated ideal, is not a legitimate state interest at all." The Court concluded that "the combined force of the separate interest of one parent and the minor's privacy interest must outweigh the separate interest of the absent parent."[2]

Justice Stevens, in an opinion joined only by Justice O'Connor, stated that the forty-eight-hour waiting period "would reasonably further the legitimate state interest in ensuring that the minor's decision is knowing and intelligent."[3] He distinguished the twenty-four-hour waiting period held unconstitutional in *City of Akron v. Akron Center for Reproductive Health* on the basis that the state had no legitimate interest in forcing a mature woman to delay carrying out her informed decision, while the state does

202

have an interest in protecting a minor from her own immaturity.

Standing on its own, therefore, Minnesota's two-parent notification requirement would have been unconstitutional. A different majority of the Court upheld the statute, however—even though those five justices could not agree on the reason. Justice O'Connor concluded that the judicial bypass provision remedied her constitutional objection to the two-parent notification requirement. Justices Kennedy, Scalia, White, and Chief Justice Rehnquist would have upheld the two-parent notification requirement with or without the bypass. As a result, the Minnesota requirement of two-parent notification and a forty-eight-hour waiting period, coupled with the right to a court order authorizing an abortion without parental notification, was upheld.

OHIO V. AKRON CENTER FOR REPRODUCTIVE HEALTH

Ohio v. Akron Center for Reproductive Health was the second 1989-term abortion case. The Court upheld an Ohio single-parent notification statute that contained a complex judicial bypass provision. Justice Kennedy's approach in *Hodgson*—that the Court ought not to be involved in questions of individual misconduct, parental failures, and social ills—now found its way into a majority opinion of the Court.[4] His opinion for the Court retreats substantially from the Court's pre-*Webster* practice of evaluating the practical impact of state procedures on a woman's choice and requiring the state to demonstrate how its significant interests are furthered by onerous laws. The Court's approach in *Akron Center* thus reflects the kind of deference the Court exhibits when reviewing economic legislation (such as occupational health and safety regulations). This deference contrasts sharply to the scrutiny usually applied to laws affecting fundamental individual rights.

The Ohio statute required, subject to certain exceptions, twenty-four-hour notice to one parent (or guardian) before a physician could perform an abortion on a minor.* The most

---

*The statute also provided that notice to the minor's grandparent, adult sibling, or stepparent would suffice if such person filed an affidavit with the court that the

important exception concerned the judicial bypass provisions, which were technical and complex. The minor must file a form with the juvenile court stating that: (1) she is pregnant; (2) she desires to have an abortion; (3) she desires to do so without notifying one of her parents; (4) she is sufficiently mature and informed to make an intelligent decision whether to have an abortion without notifying one of her parents, *or* one of her parents has engaged in a pattern of physical, emotional, or sexual abuse against her, *or* notice is not in her best interests; and (5) she has or has not retained an attorney.* The minor is required to sign the form and, even if she is represented by counsel, to provide the name of one of her parents.

The minor must prove her maturity, pattern of abuse, or best interest by clear and convincing evidence. This is a stringent standard of proof.[5] The Ohio Supreme Court in *Akron Center* had defined "clear and convincing" evidence as "that measure or degree of proof that will produce in the mind of the trier of facts a firm belief or conviction as to the allegations sought to be established."[6]

The Court held that the Ohio statute satisfied the *Bellotti* criteria. The statute contained the standard provisions concerning the minor's maturity or best interests. Unlike other bypass provisions, however, the Ohio law provided only for confidentiality, not anonymity. The Court concluded that the confidentiality requirements were sufficient. Finally, the Court held that the procedure was sufficiently timely, even though the statute's five-day time period for decision could stretch out to twenty-two days in certain circumstances if business instead of calendar days were used.†

---

minor feared physical, sexual, or severe emotional abuse from a parent. Further, if the physician were unable to give notice after reasonable effort, the physician could perform the abortion after forty-eight hours' "constructive notice" by ordinary and certified mail. Finally, the physician could perform an abortion if one parent had consented in writing.

*If the minor had not retained counsel, the court must appoint a guardian for purposes of the litigation and counsel to represent her.

†In reaching this conclusion the Court: refused to assume that Ohio would construe the statute to create a constitutional difficulty; pointed out that in attacking a statute "on its face" (as opposed to in any particular application) the challengers must show

The law's challengers argued that the clear-and-convincing-evidence requirement was too demanding. The practical effect of elevating the standard of proof to "clear and convincing" was to tilt the court's decision against the minor's request to bypass notifying her parents. That is why the Court has held in other contexts that the Constitution *requires* clear and convincing evidence before *government* may deprive an individual of certain important interests.[7] *Akron Center* is unusual in that the standard is being applied by the state *against* the assertion of an individual's rights. The Court reasoned that it was proper to raise the minor's standard of proof since in most cases she would be the only party, with no one else present to challenge her testimony.

Another objection to the law was that it required minors to run a procedural obstacle course to obtain a judicial bypass, a course that set traps for unwary and uncounseled minors, especially those facing the stress of an unwanted pregnancy.* Notwithstanding this objection, the Court gave Ohio the benefit of the doubt that it would treat the minor's request for a bypass with understanding and flexibility and allow the minor to amend her pleading.

In a separate opinion Justice Scalia continued to object to the underlying right. Because the Court upheld the law, he joined the Court's opinion. But he also said in no uncertain terms that he believes "the Constitution contains no right to an abortion."[8]

Justices Blackmun, Brennan, and Marshall dissented, largely because they concluded that the Ohio statute deliberately and unjustifiably placed a pattern of obstacles in the path of a minor seeking an abortion. Unlike the majority, the dissenters consid-

---

that there are no circumstances in which it could be applied constitutionally (not just that there are remotely possible potentially unconstitutional applications); and hinted that a worst-case delay of twenty-two days might be constitutional in any event.

*The first form referred to the minor's maturity and the second referred to her best interests, while the third referred to maturity, best interests, or pattern of abuse. The problem was that the law required a minor to pick the proper form to match her argument. A minor who selected the "maturity" form would be precluded from arguing that abortion would be in her best interests, and a minor who selected the "best interests" form would be barred from arguing that she was sufficiently mature to make the decision herself.

ered the impact on the minor of the entire process, in addition to considering each provision of the Ohio law. The dissenters criticized the majority for failing to require the state to justify setting a "pleading trap" for the minor, who is bound to be confused and upset at such a difficult moment in her life. Justice Marshall also was concerned about the adverse effects of the clear-and-convincing-evidence requirement on sexually or otherwise physically abused minors. He reasoned that a judicial bypass proceeding is traumatic enough without the added stress of a heightened standard of proof. The chief effects of this standard would be to turn the judge into an adversarial inquisitor about a quite painful subject, and possibly to force the minor to carry the pregnancy to term or confront the abusive parent or parents.

16. *Rust v. Sullivan*

· ·

The Court's 1991 decision in *Rust v. Sullivan,* upholding the so-called "gag rule" for federally funded family planning clinics, was one of the more controversial cases affecting abortion rights in recent years.[1] The decision provoked an outpouring of protest; and Congress passed several bills to overturn the rule, each of which was successfully vetoed by President Bush. Both *Rust* and the gag rule are disturbing quite apart from one's position on abortion and on *Roe v. Wade.* Even some abortion opponents were deeply troubled by the rule's intrusion into the doctor-patient relationship and the Court's willingness to tolerate it.[2]

The regulations upheld in *Rust* prohibited family planning clinics that receive federal Title X funds from discussing abortion as an option with their clients. This is so even if the client requests abortion information, and even if the provider believes such information to be in the woman's best medical interests. Instead health-care providers were required to refer pregnant clients to "appropriate prenatal and/or social services...." For seventeen years the administration had interpreted Title X of the Public Health Service Act to allow "nondirective" counseling or referrals—intended only to inform, not to persuade or influence—on all choices of action in response to pregnancy, including prenatal care and delivery, infant care, foster care, adoption, and abortion. In February 1988, however, the secretary of health and human services issued the regulations upheld in *Rust.* Under those regulations, if a client requests abortion information the provider may respond that "the project does not consider abortion an appropriate method of family planning and therefore does not counsel or refer for abortion."[3]

In an opinion by Chief Justice Rehnquist, the Supreme Court

207

rejected both a free-speech and an abortion rights challenge to the regulations. In the Court's view the administration had simply defined the Title X program as limited to family planning and reproductive health exclusive of abortion. Thus, the Court reasoned, the regulations involve "not a case of the Government 'suppressing a dangerous idea,' but of a prohibition on a project grantee or its employees from engaging in activities outside of its scope." The Court observed that providers remain free to speak on abortion outside the scope of Title X projects. In rejecting the First Amendment claim, Chief Justice Rehnquist also reasoned that the regulations "do not significantly impinge upon the doctor-patient relationship" because "the program does not provide post-conception medical care, and therefore *a doctor's silence with regard to abortion cannot reasonably be thought to mislead a client into thinking that the doctor does not consider abortion an appropriate option for her.*"[4]

On the abortion issue the Court invoked *Harris v. McRae* to conclude that the Constitution does not obligate the government to fund abortion counseling any more than it requires the government to fund abortion itself. The Court noted that informed-consent laws stricken in earlier cases required *all* doctors to give the prescribed litany of abortion information. The regulations in *Rust,* by contrast, applied only to Title X projects and did not affect the information women received from doctors outside that program. The Court concluded that the regulations do not infringe a woman's reproductive freedom because "the difficulty that a woman encounters when a Title X project does not provide abortion counseling or referral leaves her in no different position than she would have been if the government had not enacted Title X." The Court reasoned further that "a doctor's ability to provide, and a woman's right to receive, information concerning abortion and abortion-related services outside the context of the Title X project remains unfettered."[5]

Justices Blackmun, Marshall, and Stevens dissented on the constitutional issues.* Justice Blackmun viewed the regulations as

---

*Justice O'Connor did not express an opinion on the constitutionality of the regu-

interfering with both First Amendment and abortion rights. The regulations, he reasoned, suppress pertinent information, "inject a restrictive ideological message unrelated to considerations of maternal health," and effectively "deny women the ability voluntarily to decide their procreative destiny."[6] This is because some Title X patients would come away with the erroneous impression that they had been medically advised to carry their pregnancy to term (despite their needs and despite the relative safety of the abortion alternative for many of them) or because others would be delayed from seeking an abortion when medically safest (and constitutionally protected) as a consequence of the regulations' requirement that they be referred for prenatal care.

The Court's analysis in *Rust*, like that in *Harris*, provides important insights into the Court's view of the relationship between government, its programs, and citizens' lives. *Rust's* significance lies in the Court's conclusion that the gag rule does not affect constitutional rights at all. When the Court rules that government actions—even actions as far-reaching as the gag rule—have no impact on constitutional rights, it avoids testing the government's choices under constitutional standards. The Court in *Rust* therefore never asked whether the gag rule was closely related to an important government interest.

The Court seemed to regard *Rust* as an easier case than *Harris* in several respects. First, as mentioned, the Court reasoned that if government is not constitutionally required to fund abortion itself, it can scarcely be obligated to fund speech about abortion. Second, the Court pointed out that government is free to spend its money promoting its chosen policies without being obligated to pay for alternative viewpoints. As Chief Justice Rehnquist observed, "When Congress established a National Endowment for Democracy to encourage other countries to adopt democratic principles,...it was not constitutionally required to encourage competing lines of political philosophy such as Communism and Fascism."[7]

In one important respect, however, *Rust* takes *Harris* to a new

---

lations. Justice Stevens dissented from the Court's conclusion that the 1988 regulations were authorized by Title X.

level. *Rust*'s conclusion that the gag rule does not affect women's choices about abortion in a constitutionally meaningful way is even more doubtful than the Court's similar conclusion in *Harris* with respect to the Hyde Amendment. Title X is the largest single source of federal funding of family planning services, with an estimated target population of 14.5 million women at risk for unintended pregnancy. The gag rule will unquestionably have an enormous impact, especially on the health care received by low-income women. Approximately one-third of them are adolescents and 90 percent of all women served have incomes below 150 percent of the poverty level.[8] For many women, their first visit to the Title X grantee is for pregnancy testing, not for contraception. Federal funds account for approximately half the money received by Title X clinics.

As a practical matter, women are *not* in the same position they would have occupied had there been no Title X. The effect of the gag rule is to distort the communication between women and their doctors by providing ideologically slanted medical information for Title X clients to rely upon. By dictating the content of health-care providers' information, the regulations actively impact patients' lives. Title X clients, like anyone, necessarily depend on their health-care providers to give them candid and complete advice in the providers' best judgment—including referral for appropriate treatment. That expectation is reinforced by physicians' ethical and legal obligations to do so. When a woman's physician remains silent about abortion, or recites the administration's prescribed message, she may well be misled "into thinking that the doctor does not consider abortion an appropriate option for her." As Justice Blackmun observed in dissent:

> The undeniable message conveyed by this forced speech...is that abortion is nearly always an improper medical option. Although her physician's words, in fact, are strictly controlled by the Government and wholly unrelated to her particular medical situation, the Title X client will reasonably construe them as professional advice to forgo her right to obtain an abortion. As would most rational patients, many of these women will follow that perceived advice and carry their preg-

210

nancy to term, despite their needs to the contrary and despite the safety of the abortion procedure for the vast majority of them. Others, delayed by the Regulations' mandatory prenatal referral, will be prevented from acquiring abortions during the period in which the process is medically sound and constitutionally protected.[9]

Viewed in this light, the Chief Justice's analogy to the National Endowment for Democracy is flawed. The problem with *Rust* is not that the government's advocacy of childbirth and adoption creates an obligation to fund speech about abortion. Rather, the government's provision of medical services ought to include an obligation to do so in a way that does not mislead women into forgoing constitutional rights and their own medical needs. Given the extent of the Title X program and the nature of the patient-physician relationship, the Court seems to be simply wrong in concluding that the gag rule does not have that effect.

211

17. *Webster* and the Overruling of *Roe*

. . . .

Webster and the other pre-*Casey* cases left the status of abortion rights in an uncertain state. It was evident that the Court had changed direction on abortion rights and had entered a period of retrenchment. But questions remained: how far backward had the Court moved, and would the Court overrule *Roe* in the proper case?

WEBSTER AS PRECEDENT

The answer to the first question was by no means clear. Because it takes five Justices to join an opinion that binds the Court in later cases as to its reasoning and not just its result, none of the opinions in *Webster* has the binding force of precedent. *Roe v. Wade*, including its trimester framework, therefore was not expressly overruled by the Court. Nevertheless, a majority of Justices for the first time upheld a statute that interferes substantially with the doctor-patient relationship during the second trimester for reasons unrelated to maternal health. That result plainly runs contrary to *Roe*'s trimester framework and is in sharp contrast to the Court's approach to abortion rights (apart from the exceptions noted above) over the sixteen years between *Roe v. Wade* and *Webster*.

The law thus plainly had changed. In particular, as Justice Scalia candidly observed, *Webster*'s result is at odds with *Colautti v. Franklin, Planned Parenthood of Central Missouri v. Danforth,* and *City of Akron v. Akron Center for Reproductive*

Health. The post-*Webster*, pre-*Casey* cases also reflect a substantial weakening of the Court's scrutiny of laws restricting the availability of abortions (at least for minors) and access to abortion information (at least for women dependent on government-subsidized family planning). Thus the scope of abortion rights was diminished. But because the Justices were so divided over the reasons for sustaining the Missouri law, the constitutional standard to be applied in later cases remained unclear.

OVERRULING ROE: COUNTING VOTES

After *Webster* it appeared entirely possible that a majority of Justices were prepared to overrule *Roe*. At the time of *Webster* only four of the original members of the *Roe* majority remained on the Court—Justices Blackmun, Brennan, Marshall, and Stevens. The two dissenters in *Roe*—White and Rehnquist—were still on the Court and remained as opposed as ever to *Roe* on the larger question of a woman's constitutional right to abortion. Justice Scalia (who replaced Rehnquist as Associate Justice when he became Chief Justice in 1984, replacing Warren Burger) said in no uncertain terms in his *Webster* concurrence that he would vote to overrule *Roe*.

That left Justices Kennedy (who replaced Justice Powell in 1988) and O'Connor (who replaced Justice Stewart in 1981). Justice Kennedy's position on the question of overruling *Roe* was not as explicit as Scalia's, but he appeared inclined at least to read *Roe* narrowly, if not to overrule it. He joined the Chief Justice's opinion with respect to the viability provision in *Webster*, which was Justice Kennedy's first abortion case on the Supreme Court. And his opinion for the Court in *City of Akron v. Akron Center for Reproductive Health* generally reflects a narrow view of abortion rights. In any event, the 1989 and 1990 terms cases showed the Court chipping away at *Roe* piece by piece by upholding an increasing number of restrictions on abortion, and diluting the right to abortion by applying a weak standard of judicial review.

213

Before Justice Brennan left the Court in 1990, the Court thus appeared to be evenly split on the larger issue of a constitutional right to abortion; and the future of the abortion debate rested largely in the hands of Justice O'Connor, the first woman appointed to the Court. She had made plain her dissatisfaction with *Roe*'s trimester framework and with much of the Court's abortion doctrine, and she had endorsed the position that the state's interest in protecting fetal life is compelling and exists throughout pregnancy.[1] In her concurring opinion in *Webster*, although she did not regard the case as the proper occasion for reconsidering *Roe*, she made the portentous statement, "When the constitutional invalidity of a State's abortion statute actually turns on the constitutional validity of *Roe v. Wade*, there will be time enough to reexamine *Roe*. And to do so carefully."[2] She had never, however, explicitly rejected the proposition that the Constitution extends some protection to a woman's right to choose whether to terminate her pregnancy. Instead her approach had been to ask whether the state regulation imposed an "undue burden" on that right. Before the two-parent notification requirement came before the Court in *Hodgson v. Minnesota*, she had not met a restriction that she found to be an "undue burden," regardless of when in the pregnancy it was imposed, including the requirement that abortions must be performed only in hospitals, second-physician requirements, and parental-consent provisions.[3] And she was willing to tolerate the two-parent notification requirement in *Hodgson* if accompanied by an adequate judicial bypass procedure. In *City of Akron v. Akron Center for Reproductive Health* Justice O'Connor described an "undue burden" as involving an "absolute obstacle" or a "severe limitation," such as the total ban in *Roe*, the prohibition on saline amniocentesis in *Planned Parenthood of Central Missouri v. Danforth* (which effectively prohibited most abortions at the time), and perhaps the parental-veto provision in *Danforth*. Both *Roe v. Wade* and *Planned Parenthood of Central Missouri v. Danforth*, of course, were decided before Justice O'Connor joined the Court.

Upon Justice Brennan's retirement, attention focused on his

replacement, Justice David Souter. This quiet man steadfastly refused to state his position on *Roe v. Wade* during his confirmation hearings, though he did say he was sensitive to the plight of women facing unwanted pregnancy; and his uncontroversial professional life had left his views virtually unknown. He joined the Court's opinion in *Rust v. Sullivan*. When Justice Marshall was replaced in 1991 by Justice Clarence Thomas, however, *Roe's* fate seemed sealed. Although Thomas also tried during his confirmation hearings to dodge questions about his views on abortion, his much more outspoken public life included several indications of his disapproval of abortion rights.

At the beginning of the Court's 1991 term it thus appeared likely that a majority of Justices on the Court were waiting for the proper case in which to overrule *Roe v. Wade*. It also seemed inevitable that the Court would soon get its chance. *Rust* did not present the Court with a good opportunity to reconsider *Roe* because to reach that issue would have required the Court to conclude that the 1988 regulations infringed reproductive choice. The Court avoided that difficulty in *Rust* by concluding that any adverse impact on reproductive choice derived from the client's poverty, not from government action.

Several other likely cases were working their way through the federal courts, however, some more quickly than others and some presenting a more direct challenge. For example, in 1990 the United States District Court for the Territory of Guam enjoined Guam's near-total ban on abortion, finding that it flew directly in the face of *Roe v. Wade*. And a federal court in Louisiana enjoined a similar Louisiana law.[4] Another case, further along in the federal judicial process but involving state laws burdening rather than expressly prohibiting abortion, was *Planned Parenthood of Southeastern Pennsylvania v. Casey*.

OVERRULING *ROE*: POSSIBLE GROUNDS

While the Court seemed poised to overrule *Roe*, less clear was how far the trend might go toward cutting back rights. As explained earlier, *Roe* rests on a right of privacy that the Court in *Griswold v. Connecticut* saw implicit in the Constitution. An important issue in reconsidering *Roe*, which was debated in *Webster*, is whether the Court should overrule not just *Roe* on abortion rights but also *Griswold v. Connecticut* on the more basic question of an implied right to privacy. The questions occur in a series, as they had originally arisen in the evolution of *Roe* itself. First, if the Constitution implicitly protects a constellation of interests related to individual liberty, isn't privacy necessarily included? Second, if privacy—in the sense of autonomy and self-determination—is constitutionally protected, isn't the liberty to make one's own decisions about matters of intimacy, marriage, and procreation free from state interference necessarily included? And third, if those interests inhere in the concept of liberty, don't they necessarily extend to abortion?

Assuming the Court were to overrule *Roe*, the answers to these questions depend on the grounds for doing so. Criticisms of *Roe* suggest several possibilities. One of the broadest grounds would be a repudiation of substantive due process or, broader still, the noninterpretivist inference of unenumerated rights. It is highly unlikely that the Court would take such a far-reaching step. The Court rarely rules explicitly on an overall theory of constitutional interpretation. Indeed, it is rare for the Court even expressly to abandon a particular substantive doctrine. The Court's rejection in *Brown v. Board of Education* of the "separate but equal" doctrine was a judicial rarity; even then the opinion was limited to public education.

The Court would not need to take such a drastic step to overrule *Roe*. Assuming that it confined itself to reconsidering the right of privacy, the Court could take at least two possible general routes. The more sweeping of the two would conclude that, while the Constitution may protect some rights not expressly provided for, privacy is not among them. This approach would overrule *Griswold*, which among some constitutional scholars is as controversial as *Roe*. Some of the rights the Court has inferred have a stronger basis in the Constitution's text and history than do privacy rights. In other words, the Court might attempt to draw the line at different levels of noninterpretivism. Although this approach might, for example, preserve the application of the Bill of Rights to the states and equal protection doctrine to the federal government, it also would allow substantial state control over matters of sexuality.

Another, narrower route would leave *Griswold* intact while revisiting *Roe*. This analysis would recognize a right to privacy in matters of marriage and procreation but would question whether that right protected abortion. The Court could follow this route in one of three ways. First, it might rule that abortion is not a fundamental right. An analogous example is the Court's ruling in *Bowers v. Hardwick* that the right of privacy does not include the right to engage in homosexual relations with a consenting adult. The Court has refused to recognize private homosexual conduct between consenting adults as a fundamental liberty "deeply rooted in this Nation's history and tradition" or "implicit in the concept of ordered liberty." The Court could reach a similar conclusion with respect to abortion, reasoning that, while the nation's tolerance for abortion may have changed over time, the practice has never been cherished and protected by the nation's traditional values. The historical record arguably could be read as supporting such an interpretation.

A second way in which the Court could attempt to dismantle *Roe* while preserving the underlying privacy right would be still narrower. The Court could hold that, even if the fundamental right to privacy includes abortion, that right may be overcome by a sufficiently compelling government interest served by a tightly drawn statute. An analogous example is child pornography, which all the Justices have agreed raises a compelling state interest in protecting children; it justifies government action that otherwise would violate First Amendment rights.[5] In the abortion context the Court could rule that because the state's interest in protecting fetal life is compelling throughout pregnancy, the state is therefore justified in prohibiting abortion—at least unless the pregnant woman's life is threatened by the pregnancy. This rationale presumably would allow (and perhaps require) the state also to make exception for pregnancies of involuntary or especially troublesome origins, such as rape or incest.

A third way to overrule *Roe* without overruling *Griswold* as well was discussed earlier. The Court could overrule *Roe*'s conclusion that a fetus is not a person for the purposes of the Fourteenth Amendment. If a fetus is a person, it is entitled to the equal protection of the laws—including the state's murder laws. Unless the Court were prepared to take the highly unlikely step of recognizing individual gametes as persons as well, recognition of fetal personhood would not require overruling of *Griswold* (at least with respect to contraceptive devices that do not operate by blocking implantation).

OVERRULING *ROE*: IMPLICATIONS

Overruling *Roe* would have the immediate result of returning the determination of abortion policy to the states, or to Congress in the event of national legislation. Unless the federal Freedom of Choice Act becomes law, it seems likely that in at least some states the law would revert to pre-*Roe* terms. A reform movement was under way when *Roe* was decided, but the law in almost every state was substantially more restrictive than it has been under *Roe*. While there would be technical legal questions to be determined in each state—such as the continuing validity of pre-*Roe* laws (especially in states where such laws were enjoined in the wake of *Roe*)—many women eventually would be confronted with all the hazards and burdens of illegal abortion. Conversely there would probably be far fewer legal abortions, and very likely somewhat fewer abortions altogether.

Whether more restrictive abortion laws in some states is a development to be welcomed or lamented is a function of one's position on the overall abortion debate. However one feels about that ultimate question, it is important to realize that there would be larger constitutional implications to overruling *Roe*. Just as *Roe* changed more than just the status of abortion law in the United States, so too would overruling *Roe* affect more than the choices of pregnant women and the fate of unwanted fetuses.

Among the various approaches to overruling *Roe* while preserving *Griswold,* there are practical differences. The personhood approach may well preclude the state from allowing any abortions, except perhaps as necessary to save the pregnant woman's life. Deciding that a fundamental right can be overcome by a compelling state interest also would limit states, but in the other direction. It might require, rather than permit, the state to allow abortions in the case of rape or incest. Under the no-fundamental-right approach, the state would have the greatest latitude to structure its abortion laws as it saw fit. This essentially was the constitutional status of abortion before *Roe*: abortion rights were determined legislatively as a matter of policy rather than judicially as a matter of constitutional law. The scant requirement of minimal rationality would be the only judicial constraint if abortion is not a fundamental right and the law is not held to discriminate on an impermissible basis such as race or gender.

There are important conceptual differences among these three positions as well. In some respects the personhood and compelling-interest arguments are conceptually similar and more doctrinally coherent than the no-right position. They are similar because they both turn on recognition of legal status for the fetus. They are more coherent because both, at least in principle, could recognize that reproductive choice is an essential aspect of individual autonomy, especially for women. They do not take the insupportable position that abortion is not about privacy at all and is instead, as then-Justice Rehnquist put it in his *Roe* dissent, a mere "transaction." In other words, these two approaches do not seek to confine privacy rights to a laundry list of a few historically recognized practices. Instead both approaches view privacy as including individual autonomy; but they require that privacy rights yield to the fetus's equally compelling claim to life—at least when there is no principled basis for distinguishing between the claims of the fetus and the woman.

The no-right position is more difficult to reconcile with *Griswold.* It would call upon the Court to articulate a privacy principle that includes contraception but not abortion. An intelligible distinction between the two is hard to see. To be sure, abortion involves the deliberate termination of fetal life. But that distinction speaks more to the existence of a compelling interest in fetal life than to the scope of privacy rights. If *Roe* is wrong because the fundamental right to privacy does not extend to abortion, then one must ask whether the right of privacy means anything at all. If *Griswold* was about protecting certain spheres of an individual's life that are exceptionally personal, private, and linked to one's self-determination and individual sovereignty, then it is difficult to see why abortion does not also qualify.

A similar conflict surfaced in *Bowers v. Hardwick*. In that case the majority took the position that the right to privacy was confined to a finite set of historically recognized practices, rather than a broader, more flexible and subjective principle of individual autonomy. *Michael H. v. Gerald D.*, the adulterous paternity case, illustrates another, more extreme application of this approach. In that case Justice Scalia and Chief Justice Rehnquist argued that substantive due process rights ought to be determined by the most narrow specific practice for which there is historical precedent. If that position is the ultimate conceptual destination of the no-right approach to overruling *Roe*, then *Griswold* is surely wrong as well, for contraception has a similarly checkered legal past.

But it might not stop there. If rights recognized by inference are to be determined by reference to specific historical precedent, then perhaps *Brown v. Board of Education* must also be overruled. *Brown* involved the extension of the equal protection clause and not the judicial recognition of an entirely new category of right under the broad term "liberty." But if specific historical practice determines the extent of equal protection rights, then constitutional law would be frozen at the historical practice of segregation that prevailed in 1868. That argument would permit little, if any, latitude for judicial recognition of evolving standards. The constitutionality of a practice would become a function of its longevity and pervasiveness rather than its intrinsic consistency with evolving norms. Even the most oppressive and odious practices, like apartheid, would be immune to judicial intervention.

The problem with the no-right position thus is twofold. First, if *Roe* is to fall while *Griswold* stands, the absence of any real distinction between the two cases means that at least the privacy-rights corner of the constitutional realm would be at the mercy of a kind of judicial anarchy. Second, the most likely attempt at defining a distinguishing principle—recourse to historical practices—in addition to being unworkable on its own terms would threaten to deconstruct more than just privacy rights. This second point was debated in oral arguments in *Webster*. Solicitor General Charles Fried disclaimed any intention to "unravel the fabric of unenumerated privacy rights.... Rather, we are asking the Court to pull this one thread." Counsel for appellees in *Webster* trenchantly rejoined, "It has always been my personal experience that when I pull a thread, my sleeve falls off."[6]

It remains to be seen whether the sleeve will fall off, though the thread is being tugged vigorously. The next case to bring *Roe* before the Court was *Planned Parenthood of Southeastern Pennsylvania v. Casey*. Although many observers assumed that a majority of Justices were prepared to overrule *Roe*, and the parties in *Casey* specifically asked the Court to consider that question, the Court instead followed another course. *Casey* did not expressly overrule *Roe*—at least it did not overrule what Justices O'Connor, Kennedy, and Souter termed *Roe*'s "core holding." Instead those Justices' opinion redefined *Roe* and tried to articulate a new constitutional standard for abortion rights.

Part Five

. . . .

REDEFINING ABORTION RIGHTS:
PLANNED PARENTHOOD OF SOUTHEASTERN
PENNSYLVANIA V. CASEY

18. *Casey*'s Undue Burdens

. . . .

On June 29, 1992, nineteen and a half years after *Roe*, the Court handed down its eagerly awaited decision in *Planned Parenthood of Southeastern Pennsylvania v. Casey*. The Court in *Casey* confronted the large issue of whether to overrule *Roe*, the even broader issue of judicial recognition of substantive due process rights, and the somewhat narrower issue of the constitutionality of the specific provisions of Pennsylvania law. While narrowly reaffirming *Roe*'s "essential holding" (which preserves viability as the legal boundary of the right to abortion) and declining to repudiate the doctrine of substantive due process as we know it, the Court in *Casey* effectively overruled *Roe*'s trimester framework. Although it was not endorsed by a majority of the Justices, *Casey*'s new standard for testing the constitutionality of abortion restrictions is whether they impose an "undue burden" on the right to abortion—defined as having the purpose or effect of placing "substantial obstacles" in the woman's path. This redefined abortion right has a much smaller scope than *Roe*; its authors voted to uphold measures that the Court had previously held unconstitutional.

Casey, actually two consolidated cases, involved challenges by five abortion clinics and a physician (representing himself and a class of physicians who provide abortion services) to five provisions of Pennsylvania's Abortion Control Act of 1982, as amended in 1988 and 1989. Those provisions, several of which previously had been held unconstitutional by the Supreme Court, imposed the following requirements: The informed-consent provision required women seeking abortions to be provided with specified information concerning abortion (some of which must be provided by the physician) at least twenty-four hours before the procedure. The parental-consent provision required the informed consent of at least one parent twenty-four hours before a minor could have an abortion, subject to a judicial bypass procedure. The notice-to-spouse provision required women seeking abortions, subject to certain exceptions, to certify that they had notified their spouse. The medical emergency provision offered an exception to all the foregoing requirements in the event of an emergency posing a significant threat to maternal health. And the fifth provision required abortion facilities to file certain reports with the state.

Casey revealed a Court that is divided into three camps on the question of abortion. The controlling faction consists of a new coalition of moderate conservatives—Justices O'Connor, Kennedy, and Souter—who took the most unusual step of jointly writing the defining opinion. Portions of that opinion were joined by Justices Blackmun and Stevens, forming a majority of the Court (five Justices to four) on four issues: upholding "the essential holding of *Roe v. Wade*," reaffirming the Court's commitment to substantive due process, upholding Pennsylvania's medical emergency definition, and striking Pennsylvania's notice-to-spouse requirement. Justices Stevens and Blackmun, the Court's remaining liberal faction, did not join those portions of the O'Connor-Kennedy-Souter joint opinion that spelled out the new "undue burden" standard and applied it to uphold the informed-consent, waiting-period, and parental-consent requirements. (Justice Stevens, however, did join the joint opinion's affirmance of the reporting requirement's constitutionality.) Those portions of the joint opinion thus were not joined by a majority of Justices and therefore do not constitute an opinion of the Court with respect to the issues of the new standard and the constitutionality of the requirements for informed consent, waiting period, one-parent consent, and reporting. The additional votes to uphold those four provisions of the Pennsylvania law were supplied by the Court's conservative, anti-*Roe* camp—Chief Justice Rehnquist and Justices White, Scalia, and Thomas—but for a different reason. Because they voted to overrule *Roe* completely, they would sustain the constitutionality of the entire Pennsylvania law.

In many respects *Casey* exemplifies much of what is wrong with the abortion debate in America. First, the fragmentation of the Court reflects the disarray between the warring factions in society at large. And just as both sides in the abortion debate appear to be largely shouting past each other, the divisions on the Court appear to have crippled its ability to reason coherently about abortion rights. Whether one is pro– or anti–abortion rights, an objective critical reading of the joint opinion reveals serious flaws and inconsistencies.

The *Casey* decision also fails to provide a principled resolution of the abortion dilemma from either side's perspective. States remain unable to ban previability abortion, and legal abortions presumably will continue to occur in enormous numbers. *Casey's* compromise "undue burden" standard, however, invites states to impose various measures intended to burden a woman's choice—provided they do not do so "unduly." In other words, the only devices the state is precluded from using in its effort to influence women to change their minds about abortion are those that act directly, openly, and straightforwardly to protect previability fetal life. The net consequence vindicates no recognizable moral principle. But it will aggravate the trend toward arbitrariness and inequality in access to abortion, create delay and thus increase the medical risk of abortion to women, and interfere in women's health care. One need not be a supporter of abortion rights to be disturbed by such a result.

Finally, *Casey* raises at least as many questions as it answers. Although the joint opinion begins by asserting that "Liberty finds no refuge in a jurisprudence of doubt," the new undue burden standard is if anything even less determinate and more fact intensive than was *Roe's* trimester framework. At least that framework offered points of reference for each trimester, such as the protection of maternal health as a legitimate state objective in regulating second-trimester abortions. Under *Casey* courts and legislators are left to guess how much burden is "undue"—an approach that guarantees continued litigation as states probe the frontiers of the new standard.

19. The Joint Opinion in *Casey*

. . . .

The joint opinion in *Casey* consists of six parts. Part I briefly describes for the Court the background to the cases, notes the uncertainty surrounding *Roe*'s continued vitality, and describes *Roe*'s "essential holding" as including three branches. The first is that women have a right to choose abortion before viability, and that the state's interest in fetal life "is not strong enough to support a prohibition of abortion or the imposition of a substantial obstacle to the woman's effective right to elect the procedure." Second, the state may prohibit postviability abortion provided the law contains exceptions for pregnancies that threaten the woman's life or health. Third, "the state has legitimate interests from the outset of pregnancy in protecting the health of the woman and the life of the fetus that may become a child."[1]

Part II asserts the Court's commitment to substantive due process. Part III, which together with Part II forms the basis for the Court's reaffirmation of *Roe*'s central holding, discusses the considerations that apply to the Court's decision whether to overrule precedent. Part IV, joined only by Justices Kennedy, O'Connor, and Souter, develops the new undue burden standard. Part V applies the new test to the Pennsylvania law. Part VI offers a closing benediction.

RIGHTS IN THE ABSTRACT: SUBSTANTIVE DUE PROCESS, *STARE DECISIS*, AND UPHOLDING *ROE*'S CENTRAL HOLDING

One of many striking points about *Casey* is the contrast between the joint opinion's professions of fidelity to liberty and substantive due process in the abstract and its actual application of the

new standard. Another is the contrast between the joint opinion's extensive analysis of the reasons why the principle of "*stare
decisis*" (the Court's obligation to follow its own precedent)
requires preservation of *Roe* and the joint opinion's willingness
both to redefine *Roe* and to overrule *Roe*'s progeny. These inconsistencies are even more glaring in the light of the Court's
repeated invocation of the need for certainty, continuity, and
steadfastness in the protection of liberty.

Part II of the joint opinion explicitly embraces a noninterpretivist approach to substantive liberty under the Constitution.
The joint opinion for the Court expressly rejects the view,
advanced by Justice Scalia and Chief Justice Rehnquist in
Michael H. v. Gerald D., "that the Due Process Clause protects
only those practices, defined at the most specific level, that were
protected against government interference by other rules of law
when the Fourteenth Amendment was ratified." *Casey*'s joint
opinion states that "such a view would be inconsistent with our
law. It is a promise of the Constitution that there is a realm of
personal liberty which the government may not enter." The joint
opinion also cites the Ninth Amendment in concluding, "Neither the Bill of Rights nor the specific practices of the States at
the time of the adoption of the Fourteenth Amendment marks
the outer limits of the substantive sphere of liberty which the
Fourteenth Amendment protects."[2]

The Court proceeded to rebut one of the objections to noninterpretivist judicial review—its inherent open-endedness. The
joint opinion recognizes that "adjudication of substantive due
process claims may call upon the Court in interpreting the Constitution to exercise that same capacity which by tradition courts
have always exercised: reasoned judgment." Quoting Justice
Harlan's opinion in *Poe v. Ullman*, the joint opinion points to both
the method and sources that inform the exercise of that judgment: "'Due process has not been reduced to any formula; its
contents cannot be determined by reference to any code. The best
that can be said is that through the course of this Court's decisions it has represented the balance which our Nation, built upon
postulates of respect for the liberty of the individual, has struck

between that liberty and the demands of organized society.'"[3]

Application of that judgment, the joint opinion concludes, means that the Constitution prohibits the state from resolving the profound moral, philosophical, and spiritual questions raised by abortion "in such a definitive way that a woman lacks all choice in the matter."

> These matters, involving the most intimate and personal choices a person may make in a lifetime, choices central to personal dignity and autonomy, are central to the liberty protected by the Fourteenth Amendment. At the very heart of liberty is the right to define one's own concept of existence, of meaning, of the universe, and of the mysteries of human life. Beliefs about these matters could not define the attributes of personhood were they formed under compulsion by the State.[4]

The joint opinion goes on to recognize the profound implications of pregnancy and the harm of unwanted pregnancy. The Court also noted how particular circumstances affect the abortion decision and the extent to which reasonable people can disagree about abortion. And the Court observed that "in some critical respects the abortion decision is of the same character as the decision to use contraception" upheld in *Griswold* and other cases; and, the Court added, "We have no doubt as to the correctness of those decisions." Part II concludes, "It was this dimension of personal liberty that *Roe* sought to protect," and "the reservations any of us may have in reaffirming the central holding of *Roe* are outweighed by the explication of individual liberty we have given combined with the force of *stare decisis*."[5]

Turning to the doctrine of *stare decisis* in Part III, the Court identified four pragmatic considerations, that customarily persuade the Court to overrule its own precedent, and one extraordinary concern presented by *Roe*. The four considerations are: (1) "whether the rule has proved to be intolerable simply in defying practicable workability," (2) "whether the rule is subject to a kind of reliance that would lend a special hardship to the consequences of overruling and add inequity to the cost of repudiation," (3) "whether related principles of law have left the old rule no more than a remnant of abandoned doctrine," (4) "whether facts have so changed or come to be seen so differently, as to have robbed the old rule of significant application or justification."[6] The extraordinary consideration is whether overruling *Roe* would create the impression that the Court had yielded to public opposition.

On the first consideration the Court concluded summarily that "Although *Roe* has engendered opposition, it has in no sense proven 'unworkable.'" The Court's conclusion that *Roe* represents only a "simple limitation beyond which a state law is enforceable," refers to *Roe* in the sense of its "essential holding," and not *Roe*'s trimester framework.[7]

The Court's reasoning on the "reliance" consideration is somewhat unusual. That interest most commonly arises in the context of rules governing commercial transactions and interests in property, "where advance planning of great precision is most obviously a necessity...." While recognizing that "abortion is customarily chosen as an unplanned response to the consequences of an unplanned activity or to the failure of conventional birth control," the Court nevertheless found a substantial reliance interest created by *Roe*:

> ...For two decades of economic and social developments, people have organized intimate relationships and made choices that define their views of themselves and their places in society, in reliance on the availability of abortion in the event that contraception should fail. The ability of women to participate equally in the economic and social life of the Nation has been facilitated by their ability to control their reproductive lives.... The Constitution serves human values, and while the effect of reliance on *Roe* cannot be exactly measured, neither can the certain cost of overruling *Roe* for people who have ordered their thinking and living around that case be dismissed.[8]

On the third consideration the Court held, somewhat backhandedly, that *Roe* remains good law: "No evolution of legal principle has left *Roe*'s doctrinal footings weaker than they were in 1973. No development of constitutional law since the case was decided has implicitly or explicitly left *Roe* behind as a mere survivor of obsolete constitutional thinking." The Court explained that this conclusion followed even if *Roe* is considered from a variety of perspectives. If *Roe* is regarded as an offspring of *Griswold*, the scope of that liberty has been preserved by post-*Griswold* applications of the liberty of intimate relationships, the family, and procreation. If *Roe* is considered as resting on concepts of individual autonomy and bodily integrity, that foundation is reinforced by later cases limiting government power to mandate medical treatment or prohibit its refusal. Even if *Roe* is regarded as unique, a majority of Justices have repeatedly reaffirmed *Roe*'s central holding. Finally, even if *Roe*'s central holding is found to be wrong, "that error would go only to the strength of the state interest in fetal protection, not to the recognition afforded by the Constitution to the woman's liberty." That latter interest, the Court noted, fits comfortably within a long line of cases protecting individual liberty in making certain kinds of important decisions. And the strength of the woman's interest is illustrated, the Court reasoned, by considering the alternative: without constitutional protection of a woman's liberty, the state presumably "might as readily restrict a woman's right to choose to carry a pregnancy to term as to terminate it, to further asserted state interests in population control, or eugenics, for example."[9]

On the fourth consideration—whether a change of facts has weakened the rule—the Court noted that some of *Roe*'s factual assumptions required modification. Abortion is now safer later in pregnancy, and viability sometimes is achieved earlier, than was the case in 1973. But these changes affect only the time when competing interests arise, not the underlying balance struck by the Court between them. Thus, whenever viability may occur, it remains the defining moment when the state's interest in protecting fetal life becomes constitutionally sufficient to support the prohibition of nontherapeutic abortion.* Changed factual

---

*This conclusion reflects a change in at least Justice O'Connor's view of *Roe*'s trimester framework as being on a collision course with itself. At one time she predicted that abortion would become safer later and later while viability was reached

circumstances thus do not support the overruling of *Roe*.

Lastly, the Court reasoned that *Roe*'s status as a landmark case which sought to resolve an intensely divisive and furious national controversy gave it a "rare precedential force to counter the inevitable efforts to overturn it and to thwart its implementation."[10] The Court worried that overruling *Roe*, unjustified by any change in *Roe*'s factual or legal underpinnings, but in the face of intense public pressure, would seriously weaken the Court's legitimacy. The Court pointed to only two previous reversals of comparable magnitude.

One example was the Court's 1937 abandonment of the *Lochner*-style judicial mandate of laissez-faire economic policy. That shift occurred amidst the hard lessons of the Great Depression and the confrontation precipitated by the Roosevelt Court-packing plan. The Court in *Casey* observed that although "the Court lost something" by its failure to see earlier the fallacies upon which *Lochner* rested, "the clear demonstration that the facts of economic life were different from those previously assumed warranted the repudiation of the old law."[11]

The second example is *Brown v. Board of Education*'s rejection of the equal protection rule of "separate but equal" under the 1896 case of *Plessy v. Ferguson*. Once again, whatever the Court's earlier understanding, it had become apparent by 1954 that separate was inherently unequal and that segregation constituted "a badge of inferiority." Thus, *Casey* explains, "While we think *Plessy* was wrong the day it was decided,...the *Plessy* Court's explanation for its decision was so clearly at odds with the facts apparent to the Court in 1954 that the decision to reexamine *Plessy* was on this ground alone not only justified but required."[12]

But "because neither the factual underpinnings of *Roe*'s central holding nor [the Court's] understanding of it has changed (and because no other indication of weakened precedent has been shown) the Court could not pretend to be reexamining the prior law with any justification beyond a present doctrinal dispo-

---

earlier and earlier in pregnancy. Apparently she has come to accept that medical science has gone as far as it can for the foreseeable future in pushing back the point of viability.

sition to come out differently from the Court of 1973." Overruling *Roe* on that unprincipled basis, the Court feared, would "seriously weaken the Court's capacity to exercise the judicial power and to function as the Supreme Court of a Nation dedicated to the rule of law." The Court's legitimacy would be undermined, the Court reasoned, were it to "surrender to political pressure" and unjustifiably repudiate the principle upon which the Court staked its legitimacy in the first place.[13] Having confronted the difficult abortion issue and resolved the conflicting claims as best it could in 1973, the Court in 1992 could see no good reason for reconsidering its earlier resolution and much harm from doing so.

THE REDEFINITION OF *ROE*: THE "UNDUE BURDEN" STANDARD

Casey thus began with a ringing defense of the underlying concept of substantive due process and individual liberty in the realms of intimate relations, family, marriage, and procreation, and a passionate plea that overruling *Roe* would seriously undermine the foundation of the Court's moral authority. That prelude would lead one reasonably to expect a forceful reaffirmation of *Roe* and a clear message to the states that the Court will no longer tolerate their efforts to subvert that decision. What follows in the joint opinion, however, is a substantial downsizing of *Roe*. The result is to overrule important post-*Roe* case law and to invite the states to continue the cat-and-mouse game of testing *Roe*'s newly contracted limits. The contrast between Parts II and III of the joint opinion and Parts IV and V is, to borrow William Manchester's metaphor from another context, "like a spectacularly successful football rally followed by a lost game."[14]

In Part IV the joint opinion retains viability as the point beyond which the state may prohibit nontherapeutic abortion for several reasons. First, as the Court reasoned in *Roe*, the fetus's capability for independent life gives the state's interest in preserving life overriding force. Second, as a matter of fairness, a woman who waits until viability to have an abortion "has con-

233

sented to the State's intervention on behalf of the developing child."[15] Third, the competing interests raised by the abortion issue require line-drawing, and the line drawn by the Court must be reasoned and not arbitrary.

Before viability, however, the joint opinion gives much more weight to the state's interest in preserving potential life than did *Roe* and post-*Roe* cases. The joint opinion repudiates *Roe*'s command that the only legitimate previability state intervention is to protect maternal health. Instead the joint opinion expressly allows the state deliberately to make the woman's right more difficult to exercise from the earliest moments of pregnancy. The abortion right under *Casey* thus is no longer, as the Court previously had described it, "a right to decide whether to have an abortion 'without interference from the State'";[16] rather, it is now a right to seek an abortion *in spite of* interference from the state.

The only substantive limit imposed by *Casey* on the state is that its interference not constitute an "undue burden." The joint opinion explains that standard as follows:

> A finding of an undue burden is a shorthand for the purpose or effect of placing a substantial obstacle in the path of a woman seeking an abortion of a nonviable fetus. A statute with this purpose is invalid because the means chosen by the State to further the interest in potential life must be calculated to inform the woman's free choice, not hinder it. And a statute which, while furthering the interest in potential life or some other valid state interest, has the effect of placing a substantial obstacle in the path of a woman's choice cannot be considered a permissible means of serving its legitimate ends.[17]

This approach collapses the usual two-step fundamental rights analysis—finding a burden and then asking whether the state is advancing a compelling interest through a tightly drawn law—into a single, more difficult step.

Although the joint opinion says the state may seek to inform, not hinder, the woman's choice, the joint opinion's application of the standard demonstrates that the opinion cannot mean what it says. As Justice Scalia observed in his separate opinion, what the joint opinion really means is that the state may not *"unduly"* hinder the woman's decision. In effect, the state may seek to influence, persuade, or otherwise interfere in the woman's decision on grounds that not only are unrelated to her health but may in fact be detrimental to it, provided the state doesn't go too far. Just how far the state may go is uncertain, but the joint opinion's view of the various provisions of the Pennsylvania law suggests that the state may go quite far indeed.

APPLICATION OF THE STANDARD: MEDICAL EMERGENCY

The Court upheld Pennsylvania's medical emergency exception to the other requirements of the Abortion Control Act. That exception is available to a woman when an immediate abortion is necessary "to avert her death or for which a delay will create serious risk of substantial and irreversible impairment of a major bodily function."[18] The trial court had found that the exception's definition of a medical emergency was "inconsistent with the generally accepted definition of medical emergency in the medical profession" and would chill the physician's exercise of medical judgment with the threat of loss of license or criminal prosecution. The district court concluded that the law singled out the abortion procedure from all other treatments for allowing state-mandated delays that could cause a risk of an impairment of a bodily function, as long as the risk was not "serious," the impairment not "substantial and irreversible," and the bodily function not "major."[19]

Rather than come to grips with those fundamental objections, the joint opinion focuses instead on three specific examples of serious conditions which the trial court found were not covered by the statutory exception: preeclampsia, inevitable abortion, and premature ruptured membrane. The Supreme Court, adopting the court of appeals' interpretation that those conditions were covered, concluded that the medical emergency exception consequently did not impose an undue burden. The Court thus upheld the statute's implicit position that physicians must

235

adhere to the other provisions of the law, even if to do so would be medically contraindicated and would create some risk of impairment of the woman's bodily functions.

In effect, the joint opinion allows states not only to attempt to interfere with the woman's choice but to do so in a way that jeopardizes her health and forces doctors to disregard their best medical judgment—provided once again that the state does not go too far (for example, by perpetuating certain very serious conditions such as preeclampsia). This outcome is directly at odds with one of the central premises in *Roe* and every subsequent case until *Webster* (apart from the parental consent and notice cases)—that the previability abortion decision and procedure is a matter between the woman and her doctor, and that the state may not interfere in that relationship or in the doctor's medical judgment in a way that does not protect the woman's health. Indeed, the pre-*Webster* Court had also prohibited the state from imposing postviability regulations that required the physician to compromise the woman's health.

APPLICATION OF THE STANDARD: INFORMED CONSENT AND TWENTY-FOUR-HOUR WAITING PERIOD

The joint opinion's disposition of the informed-consent and waiting-period provisions further illustrates how *Casey* has diminished *Roe*. A gulf now exists between the Court's abstract commitment to abortion rights and precedent on the one hand, and its actual application of those principles on the other. And comparing the joint opinion's response to those provisions with its treatment of the notice-to-spouse provision highlights the elasticity of the new undue burden "standard."

Pennsylvania's law requires a physician, as opposed to a qualified assistant, to inform the woman of the nature of the abortion procedure, the health risks of abortion and childbirth, and the probable gestational age of the child. The law further requires that the woman be informed, by either the physician or a qualified assistant, of the availability of printed materials pub-

236

lished by the state describing the fetus and giving information about medical assistance for childbirth, about child support from the father, and a list of agencies that provide adoption services. Before having an abortion the woman must certify in writing that she was given this information. The law also requires the woman to wait twenty-four hours after receiving the prescribed information before having an abortion.

In previous cases the Court had rejected both kinds of provisions. The Court earlier held that *Roe* barred the state from mandating specific information to be given to the woman "designed to influence the woman's informed choice between abortion or childbirth." And the Court had concluded that it was not "convinced that the State's legitimate concern that the woman's decision be informed is reasonably served by requiring a 24-hour delay as a matter of course."[20] The joint opinion in *Casey* overruled those previous decisions.

The difference between then and now is the joint opinion's decision that the state may enact measures intended to influence the woman against abortion even before viability. Because the informed-consent requirement mandated communication of information that was, in the joint opinion's view, truthful, not misleading, and rationally related to the state's legitimate interests in fostering informed decision-making and preserving fetal life, the three Justices concluded that it did not impose an undue burden. And the joint opinion concluded that the waiting period, while undeniably burdensome and admittedly not in the woman's medical interests, also was rationally related to the state's interests and not "unduly" burdensome.

To appreciate the implications of these conclusions, one must examine the findings of the district court. First, the district court found that the physician-only requirement, by requiring doctors to perform a task that could as easily (and in some ways better) be performed by trained counselors, would needlessly increase the costs of the procedure by placing additional demands on physicians' already full schedules. Second, the trial court found that mandating the content of the informed-consent dialogue, as opposed to allowing the health-care professional to tailor the dialogue to the specific needs of the individual patient, would be contrary to standard medical practice. Third, the trial court found that the informed-consent requirement would be unnecessary because most women, before scheduling an abortion, concluded that abortion is in their best interest "only after a great deal of careful thought, consultation with a family member or other trusted individual, or a medical provider." Finally, the trial court found that the requirement, far from helping women in their decision, would actually "create undesirable and unnecessary anxiety, anguish, and fear."[21] The *Casey* brief of the American College of Obstetricians and Gynecologists, joined by other health organizations, also argued that the informed-consent provision was "antithetical to informed consent as currently understood and practiced," and that the waiting period "will significantly increase the risk of death and other complications associated with abortions which correlate directly with gestational age."[22]

The contrast between the trial court's findings with respect to the twenty-four-hour waiting period and the joint opinion's treatment of that issue provides an even clearer indication of *Casey*'s compromise of *Roe*. The trial court specifically found that the waiting period served no legitimate medical interest and would be "burdensome" to women in a number of respects. The primary burden would derive from the delays occasioned by the requirement, which could actually range from forty-eight hours to two weeks because many clinics do not perform abortions daily.* The trial court concluded that the requirement "will be particularly burdensome to those women who have the least financial resources, such as the poor and the young, those women who travel long distances, such as women living in rural areas, and those women who have difficulty explaining their whereabouts, such as battered women, school-age women, and working women without sick leave." According to testimony at trial, delay in obtaining an abortion substantially increases the

---

*The court also noted that repeat visits, following twenty-four-hour waits, would subject women to the harassment of anti-abortion protesters outside clinics.

risk of complications and mortality: "Beyond eight weeks gestation, the risk of complications (by approximately 30%) and mortality increase (by approximately 50%) with each additional week of gestation."[23] For some women the delay will push a first-trimester abortion over to the second trimester, substantially increasing cost and risk. Finally, the trial court found that very few women are ambivalent about having an abortion when they come to a clinic and that, in addition to increased medical risk and expense, the waiting period would also adversely affect women's psychological health.

The joint opinion acknowledges that these findings are troubling but finds that the waiting period does not create an "undue" burden. The joint opinion suggests that in most cases the medical emergency exception will take care of increased medical risk. And while the district court had concluded that the waiting period was *particularly* burdensome," the joint opinion decides that "A particular burden is not of necessity a substantial obstacle.... The District Court did not conclude that the waiting period is such an obstacle even for the women who are most burdened by it."[24]

The joint opinion appears to be straining to avoid the obvious meaning of the district court's findings. If a law that substantially increases abortion's cost, stress, and risk of injury or death is not a "substantial obstacle," it is difficult to imagine what is.

The joint opinion's reference to the medical emergency provision as buffering the greater medical risk does not really respond to the record. The testimony showed that the risk to the woman of the abortion procedure itself—that is, the harm the woman might suffer *during and after* the procedure—increases substantially during the kind of delay created by the waiting period. A statutory exception that is available only in the event of an exceptional, emergency complication of *pregnancy* (which necessarily *precedes* the abortion) would appear to be inapplicable to at least some complications of abortion.

The joint opinion leaves open the possibility, however, that a waiting period could be held unconstitutional after adequate experience. The opinion is careful to note that the Pennsylvania law was challenged and enjoined before it had ever been enforced. The evidence of burden, strong as it was, therefore had a speculative aspect. Evidence of actual harm, or stronger evidence of specific prospective harm, might satisfy the undue burden standard. This possibility is reinforced by the joint opinion's conclusion, discussed immediately below, that the notice-to-spouse requirement *did* impose an undue burden.*

Even so, the joint opinion remains troubling. First, it contrives a problem with the trial court's use of the term "particularly burdensome" rather than the new test of "unduly burdensome." The joint opinion's semantic hairsplitting on a matter of such gravity is unsatisfactory. "Particularly burdensome," read in the context of the trial court's opinion, obviously means *especially* burdensome. Second, it would be a disturbing constitutional rule indeed that required women actually to suffer admittedly predictable physical or psychological complications before an undue burden could be shown. The joint opinion's disposition of the waiting-period requirement tends in that direction, though its treatment of the notice-to-spouse provision goes the other way. Third, the joint opinion does not adequately reconcile upholding the informed-consent provision with striking down the notice-to-spouse requirement. While the evidence on notice-to-spouse appeared clearly burdensome, there also was ample evidence of harm from the waiting period. This inconsistency casts doubt on the coherence of the undue burden standard.

To be sure, the informed-consent and waiting-period requirements may not be problematic for many patients. Many abortion providers give their patients far more information than the Pennsylvania law requires. Dr. William Harrison of Fayetteville, Arkansas, for example, gives his abortion patients a booklet about abortion that even includes drawings of the stages of fetal development. And overnight use of laminaria, as recommended by Hern's treatise, involves repeat clinic visits. Nevertheless, the

*As this book went to press, however, the Court let stand the Fifth Circuit's ruling in *Barnes v. Moore*, which rejected a challenge to Mississippi's informed-consent and waiting-period requirements. Dr. Helen Barnes's attorneys unsuccessfully tried to distinguish *Casey* by emphasizing the law's impact on rural women, arguing that "Mississippi ain't Pennsylvania."

evidence in *Casey* showed that Pennsylvania's requirements would pose a serious problem for *some* women—typically the vulnerable, the abused, the young, and the poor. As the Court recognized with respect to the notice-to-spouse provision, a law's constitutionality is to be tested by its impact on the individuals it harms, not those for whom it does not matter.

APPLICATION OF THE STANDARD: NOTICE TO SPOUSE

The Court, speaking through Justices Kennedy, O'Connor, and Souter, held the notice-to-spouse requirement unconstitutional. The provision allows exceptions, in addition to the blanket medical emergency exception, which include reported cases of sexual assault and the woman's fear of bodily injury as a consequence of notifying her spouse. The trial court made extensive findings about the burden imposed by the requirement. The lower court found that while most married women consult their husbands before having an abortion, the high incidence of domestic violence in America and the risk of both physical and psychological abuse—including marital rape—along with the practical unavailability of the statutory exceptions in many instances (because abused women often fear to report the abuse), meant that the notice-to-spouse requirement would preclude some women from having an abortion.

The Supreme Court accepted and supplemented those findings, concluding that the requirement would go beyond making abortion more expensive or difficult, and actually would impose a "substantial obstacle." The Court regarded the notification requirement as tantamount to a veto, because of the potentially devastating consequences for the women it affects. The Court therefore reaffirmed the balance struck in *Planned Parenthood of Central Missouri v. Danforth* between the husband's interest and the pregnant woman's. The Court also specifically noted, "The proper focus of constitutional inquiry is the group for whom the law is a restriction, not the group for whom the law is irrelevant." Because the consequences for most of the affected

241

women are potentially so severe, the Court struck down the provision even though its target class is relatively narrow. Finally, the Court observed that the notice-to-spouse provision reflected an outmoded, patriarchal vision of the family and women's and men's respective roles: "[The statute] embodies a view of marriage consonant with the common-law status of married women but repugnant to our present understanding of marriage and of the nature of the rights secured by the Constitution."[25]

The joint opinion's failure adequately to distinguish the waiting period from the notice-to-spouse requirement, and to explain why time has undermined its precedent in one case and not the other, shows how the abortion conflict has compromised the Court's ability to face facts and reason consistently. *Casey* is thus an example of how constitutional law has become another casualty of the abortion struggle.

Abortion is only one of many areas of constitutional law in which the Court balances interests and harms. For this balancing process to protect constitutional rights, the Court must be willing honestly to recognize real harm when it occurs and accord it due weight in the balance. One way the Court can place a thumb on the scale, and thus short-change constitutional rights, is to discount the existence of real harm to a constitutionally protected interest. This kind of "cheating" is especially objectionable because it compromises constitutional rights in the guise of protecting them.

The joint opinion in *Casey* indulges in this practice by undervaluing harm in two ways when it is more closely linked with abortion. First, the kind of harm likely to follow from mandatory waiting periods has become associated particularly with abortion restrictions because the abortion procedure has been the unique target of this kind of regulation. The problem of domestic violence and sexual abuse, by contrast, is more generalized, well documented, and less related specifically to abortion regulation. The Court thus more readily accepted at face value evidence that notice-to-spouse requirements would cause serious harm to women, while discounting evidence of "abortion-specific" harm inflicted by the waiting-period requirements.

Second, both provisions raise gender discrimination problems. The waiting-period requirement does so in the same way that any restriction on abortion arguably discriminates against women and thus is abortion-specific. But the notice-to-spouse provision's threat to gender equality is not abortion-specific; instead it presents the general problem of seeking to reestablish the husband's dominant position in the marital relationship by vesting him with "this troubling degree of authority over his wife."[26]

There appears to be a thumbprint on the scale. Affected women suffer serious physical and psychological harm from either medical complications of delayed abortion or domestic violence. The record abundantly established that the Pennsylvania law increased both risks. The joint opinion offers no reason to suppose that the seriousness of the harm is a function of its *source*—for example, that a broken nose is constitutionally more significant than a perforated uterus. Similarly, gender discrimination is wrong whether or not an abusive husband's participation is enlisted by the state. It is disturbing to see the Court's sensitivity to such problems *diminish* when they are commonly associated with a burden on constitutional rights. If anything, one would expect the Court to be *more* careful in such a case.

APPLICATION OF THE STANDARD: PARENTAL INFORMED CONSENT AND RECORD KEEPING

The joint opinion's affirmation of the parental-informed-consent and record-keeping requirements comes as no surprise. Pennsylvania's parental-consent provision contains an adequate judicial bypass under *Bellotti*, and the Justices found that application of the informed-consent requirements to the parents created no undue burden. The opinion states that the waiting period was especially appropriate for minors because it created an opportunity for parental consultation. And the joint opinion also easily concluded that the record-keeping requirement, apart from the portion relating to notice to spouse, was constitutional. The opinion reached that conclusion under the *Danforth* standard.

20. The Liberal Camp: The Opinions of Justices Stevens and Blackmun

· ·

Justices Stevens and Blackmun both rejected the joint opinion's characterization of the *Roe* framework. As Justice Stevens put it, there is no contradiction in recognizing, as the Court did in *Roe*, that the state's interest in protecting fetal life throughout pregnancy is outweighed by the woman's interest in personal liberty before viability. Justice Stevens therefore would adhere to the Court's earlier invalidation of state attempts to influence women not to have previability abortions. To him the same result would obtain whether the standard is articulated as the Court did in *Roe* or as the joint opinion did in *Casey*: "A burden may be 'undue' either because the burden is too severe or because it lacks a legitimate, rational justification."[1]

Justice Blackmun's opinion is striking in its personal tone. It reveals how the divisiveness of the abortion debate—and the larger struggle over constitutional interpretation—has penetrated the Court. First, and least surprising, Justice Blackmun vigorously defended *Roe* and criticized the Pennsylvania law on the points discussed above. Second, he congratulated the authors of the joint opinion for their resolute commitment to *stare decisis* and personal liberty: "Make no mistake, the joint opinion of Justices O'Connor, Kennedy, and Souter is an act of personal courage and constitutional principle."[2]

Third, he implicitly and bitterly criticized Chief Justice Rehnquist's opinion in *Webster* as misleading: "At long last, the Chief Justice and those who have joined him admit it. Gone are the contentions that the issue need not be (or has not been) recon-sidered."[3] Blackmun went on to describe Rehnquist's conception of personal liberty as "stunted." And he characterized the Chief Justice's consideration of the woman's interests as follows: "In short, the Chief Justice's view of the State's compelling interest in maternal health has less to do with health than it does with compelling women to be maternal."[4]

Finally, Justice Blackmun summed up his worst fears for the Court, and his message to the nation, in the following truly remarkable passages:

> [In *Webster*], all that remained between the promise of *Roe* and the darkness of the plurality was a single flickering flame. Decisions since *Webster* gave little reason to hope that this flame would cast much light. But now, just when so many expected the darkness to fall, the flame has grown bright.... I fear for the darkness as four Justices anxiously await the single vote to extinguish the light....
>
> In one sense, the Court's approach is worlds apart from that of the Chief Justice and Justice Scalia. And yet, in another sense, the distance between the two approaches is short—the distance is but a single vote.
>
> I am 83 years old. I cannot remain on this Court forever, and when I do step down, the confirmation process for my successor well may focus on the issue before us today. That, I regret, may be exactly where the choice between the two worlds will be made.[5]

21. The Opposition: The Opinions of Chief Justice Rehnquist and Justice Scalia

. . . .

Both Chief Justice Rehnquist and Justice Scalia wrote opinions concurring in the judgment (but not the reasoning of the joint opinion) that upheld the four provisions of Pennsylvania's law, and dissenting from the rest of the decision. They also joined each other's opinion, and both opinions were joined by Justices White and Thomas. All four Justices would expressly overrule *Roe*. Thus they would apply only the very deferential rational basis test to state regulation of abortion. The Pennsylvania measures easily satisfy that standard.

The Chief Justice's opinion made several noteworthy points. First, as Justice Blackmun pointedly observed, Rehnquist was explicit in his intent to overrule *Roe*. This candor is a refreshing change from his strained analysis in *Webster*.

Second, he reviewed the post-*Roe* cases to conclude that "the Court was expanding upon *Roe* in imposing ever greater restrictions on the States," generating increasing confusion and uncertainty.[1] That portion of his opinion misses the beat in several places. While Rehnquist correctly noted that later cases elaborated *Roe*, real uncertainty did not set in until the Court began to dismantle *Roe*. Indeed, Rehnquist's own opinion in *Webster* is one of the most confusing and contradictory in the entire pre-*Casey* lineage of abortion cases. Furthermore, the existence of substantial case law not only reaffirming but expanding abortion rights would seem to argue strongly *against* overruling *Roe*. Stripped to its core, then, his objection was really to *Roe*'s recognition of a fundamental right to abortion—as it has been from the beginning when he dissented in *Roe*.

Third, on that core issue Rehnquist rejected the notion that the line of cases from *Pierce v. Society of the Sisters* to *Griswold v. Connecticut* recognizes a broad "right of privacy." He read those cases instead as protecting a limited catalogue of particular liberties—such as the right to send one's child to private school, to teach a foreign language in a private school, to procreate, to marry, and to use contraceptives. As discussed earlier in this book, this approach is one way to come to terms with the potential boundlessness and questionable foundation of a privacy right; but such a piecemeal approach is itself subject to the criticism of resting on unprincipled distinctions—particularly between *Roe* and *Griswold*.

The Chief Justice nonetheless offered several bases for distinguishing *Roe*. One is that abortion, unlike "marriage, procreation and contraception," uniquely "involves the purposeful termination of potential life."[2] Another is that "the historical traditions of the American people [do not] support the view that the right to terminate one's pregnancy is 'fundamental.'"[3] While those observations may support a distinction between abortion on the one hand and marriage and procreation on the other, contraception is another matter. Indeed, in view of the development of "contraceptive" devices (such as the IUD) and drugs that operate by preventing the implantation of fertilized ova, the distinction between contraception and abortion is becoming increasingly porous. For example, a recent study indicates that RU-486 may be an effective "morning-after" pill—or "emergency postcoital contraception."[4] Moreover, because the history of regulation of contraceptives in some respects resembles that of abortion, it is difficult to say that the "historical traditions of the American people" support the view that the right to contraceptives is any more "fundamental" than the right to abortion.

Rehnquist made several telling criticisms of the Court's view that overruling *Roe*'s core holding would compromise the Court's legitimacy. He saw an inherent contradiction between the Court's recognition of its obligation to ignore public criticism and stand by principle on the one hand, and the Court's conclusion that intense opposition to a decision is a compelling reason not to reconsider a previous decision. Under the Court's reasoning, he argued, the Court ought not to have reconsidered *Lochner* "lest it lose legitimacy by appearing 'to overrule under fire.'"[5] After all, opposition to the *Lochner* line of cases produced a far more immediate threat to the Court than anti-*Roe* demonstrations—the infamous Roosevelt Court-packing plan. Nor should the Court have overruled *Plessy,* under the *Casey* majority's approach, because of its intensely divisive nature. The Chief Justice also pointed out that the Court's purported refusal to surrender to political pressure overlooks what is nowhere more obvious than in the abortion debate: there are at least two sides to every controversy. The Court in *Casey* failed to explain why its refusal to overrule *Roe* completely does not equally undermine the Court's legitimacy by showing the Court's submission to those who *favor* the decision.

Justice Scalia's opinion is characteristically pellucid, forceful, and, if one takes the radical step of accepting his premises of constitutional interpretation, sometimes compelling. His criticisms of the joint opinion's efforts to achieve a compromise on *Roe,* its proffered "standard," and its discussion of *stare decisis* expose the joint opinion as more political expedience than reasoned adjudication.

Justice Scalia's approach to the Constitution is rigorously interpretivist. As discussed earlier in this book, such an approach places him far outside the mainstream of the Court's constitutional doctrine. He readily agreed that the power of a woman to abort her unborn child is a "liberty" in the absolute sense, and one of great importance to many women. But he disagreed that it is a liberty protected by the Constitution. He reasoned: "(1) the Constitution says absolutely nothing about it, and (2) the longstanding traditions of American society have permitted it to be legally proscribed." He rejected (unconvincingly in view of his definition of tradition in *Michael H. v. Gerald D.* and his tendency toward literal textualism) the Court's argument that adherence to tradition would require it to uphold laws against

248

interracial marriage, pointing out that the text of the Constitution—the equal protection clause of the Fourteenth Amendment—cuts off any tradition in that regard. "The enterprise launched in *Roe*, by contrast, sought to *establish*—in the teeth of a clear, contrary tradition—a value found nowhere in the constitutional text." In Justice Scalia's view, the Court was not exercising "reasoned judgment" in *Roe*; instead, the only defense of *Roe* that some of the best legal minds in the country have been able to offer is to "rattle off a collection of adjectives [about privacy, intimacy, and personal choice] that simply decorate a value judgment and conceal a political choice." But "those adjectives might be applied, for example, to homosexual sodomy, polygamy, adult incest, and suicide, all of which are equally 'intimate' and 'deep[ly] personal' decisions involving 'personal autonomy' and 'bodily integrity,' and all of which can be constitutionally proscribed because it is our unquestionable constitutional tradition that they are proscribable."[6]

Justice Scalia also targeted for more effective criticism several specific passages of the joint opinion. He demonstrated the circularity and fuzziness of the undue burden standard and pointed out the extent to which it undermines *Roe*. He explained that under the undue burden standard the right to an abortion has ceased to resemble other recognized constitutional rights. He compared the Pennsylvania waiting period, for example, which consciously and deliberately seeks to restrict constitutionally protected conduct, to a "state law requiring purchasers of religious books to endure a 24-hour waiting period, or pay a nominal tax of 1¢." Would the Court uphold such legislation on the ground that it did not impose a "substantial obstacle" on First Amendment rights? Because the joint opinion fails to admit that the undue burden standard is a constitutional anomaly created "to preserve some judicial foothold in this ill-gotten territory," Justice Scalia concluded that "the three Justices show their willingness to place all constitutional rights at risk in an effort to preserve what they deem the 'central holding in Roe'...."[7]

He also criticized the joint opinion's application of the undue burden standard, the net result of which is to authorize "the district judge to give effect to his personal preferences about abortion."[8] To the extent that Scalia found any guidance at all in the joint opinion's test, it is to allow the state to implement any regulation restricting abortion that it chooses, provided the effect is not to reduce significantly the number of abortions. In other words, the state can pursue its interest in protecting fetal life by any but the most direct and effective means.

Scalia is especially potent in his criticism of the Court's *stare decisis* analysis. He first pointed out that *stare decisis* ought to apply to the doctrine of *stare decisis* itself, with which the Court's "keep-what-you-want-and-throw-away-the-rest version" is patently inconsistent. Second, he reminded the Court that the "arbitrary trimester framework, which the Court today discards, was quite as central to *Roe* as the arbitrary viability test, which the Court today retains."[9] Furthermore, he observed, that framework's "rigidity" provides the only basis on which the Court could possibly say that *Roe* has not proved unworkable. Scalia is persuasive here if one understands the "trimester framework" in terms of the interests it seeks to balance rather than the times when it assumes those interests arise. Indeed, the joint opinion itself concluded that *Roe*'s basic account of those interests remains valid.

Scalia also took issue with the Court's reasoning that *Roe*'s pronouncements have special precedential force because they sought to resolve an intensely divisive national controversy. He reminded the Court that *Roe* not only failed to resolve the dispute but greatly magnified it "by elevating it to the national level where it is much more difficult to resolve." In particular, *Roe*'s effort to preempt the political process "destroyed the compromises of the past, rendered compromise impossible for the future, and required the entire issue to be resolved uniformly, at the national level."[10]

Finally, Justice Scalia lambasted the Court for asserting that to overrule *Roe* "under fire...would subvert the Court's legitimacy." He described the Court's reasoning as perpetuating an "Imperial Judiciary." And he pointed out the inconsistency between the Court's "lengthy lecture upon the virtues of 'constancy'" and the fact that only three Justices now adhere to the new, improved version of *Roe* and that two of them had to retreat from previous positions to do so. For him the *stare decisis* model for *Roe* is neither *Brown* nor the Court's switch on economic substantive due process in 1937, but instead *Dred Scott v. Sandford*—a constitutional decision which engendered widespread and passionate opposition and to which the Court steadfastly clung as smoldering national divisions burst into the conflagration of the Civil War.[11]

Be that as it may, Justice Scalia described what he saw in the joint opinion as a threat more serious than erosion of the Court's image:

> But whether it would "subvert the Court's legitimacy" or not, the notion that we would decide a case differently from the way we otherwise would have in order to show that we can stand firm against public disapproval is frightening. It is a bad enough idea, even in the head of someone like me, who believes that the text of the Constitution, and our traditions, mean what they say and there is no fiddling with them. But when it is in the mind of a Court that believes the Constitution has an evolving meaning; that the Ninth Amendment's reference to 'other' rights is not a disclaimer, but a charter for action; and that the function of this Court is to 'speak before all others for [the people's] constitutional ideals' unrestrained by meaningful text or tradition—then the notion that the Court must adhere to a decision for as long as the decision faces 'great opposition' and the Court is 'under fire' acquires a character of almost czarist arrogance. We are offended by these marchers who descend on us every year on the anniversary of *Roe*, to protest our saying that the Constitution requires what our society has never taught the Constitution requires. These people who refuse to be 'tested by following' must be taught a lesson. We have no Cossacks, but at least we can stubbornly refuse to abandon an erroneous opinion that we might otherwise change—to show how little they intimidate us.[12]

Scalia concluded by returning to the central problem of constitutional interpretation raised by *Roe*. He admonished the

Court to pay less attention to the *fact* of the political pressure surrounding *Roe* than to the *cause* of it: a mode of constitutional analysis that purports to rest not on the text or tradition but instead on "reasoned judgment," which he regards as thin cover for individual Justices' personal "philosophical predilections and moral intuition." Scalia believes "the public *should* demonstrate" when the Court turns from the lawyerly task of interpreting text and traditions (which are "facts to study, not convictions to demonstrate about") to the essentially political task of making value judgments, "to protest that we do not implement *their* values instead of *ours*."[13]

Casey's inconsistencies, while troubling, are not surprising—even to someone who does not embrace Scalia's extreme interpretivism. The forces binding the Court to *Roe* are barely stronger than the forces pushing the Court away. At least two of the authors of the joint opinion, if not all three, probably would have voted against the right recognized in *Roe* were the Court writing on a clean slate. The four dissenters in *Casey* plainly would have done so. That left only two aging Justices fully committed to *Roe*. The Court's heart was thus no longer in *Roe*, and the authors of the joint opinion apparently were writing largely in the service of abstract ideals that they would rather not have applied to the case at hand. Little wonder that those Justices stopped far short of giving *Roe*, or even their new undue burden standard, full effect.

Part Six

. . . .

TAKING STOCK, LOOKING AHEAD

22. Continuing Inequality

. . . .

The Supreme Court's ambivalence about abortion rights has helped to create, for the moment at least, the worst of all possible resolutions of the conflict. *Casey* fails to provide a principled accommodation of either women's rights or the state's interest in fetal life. After *Casey* states will be able to impose all sorts of restrictions that inhibit women's access to abortion; but a great many legal abortions will nevertheless be performed. There are approximately one and a half million legal abortions in America each year. Despite the most creative state legislative efforts to invent burdens on choice that are just shy of "undue," the evidence suggests that many women will have sufficient motivation and resources to overcome government-imposed obstacles to legal abortion. Even if states succeed in actually deterring some women seeking abortion, the United States still will experience an enormous number of abortions annually. From the anti–abortion rights perspective, *Casey* thus may reduce the number somewhat, and to that extent counts as an important moral victory; but the massive slaughter will continue. Pro-abortion rights advocates, of course, will complain that the Court has retreated miles from *Roe*.

From an external perspective, the problem is not that the incidence of abortion may be reduced, or that it has not been reduced enough. Rather, the objection is that the Supreme Court has achieved its compromise by aggravating the inequality and arbitrariness that already characterize the allocation of abortion rights. Whether the Constitution protects a right to abortion is a difficult question; reasonable, well-meaning constitutional scholars can and do disagree about it. But if we are to retain such a right, as the Court held in *Casey*, the most basic principles of both due process and equal protection demand that it not be arbitrarily denied.

The Court's abortion decisions have unfortunately produced exactly that result. Access to abortion today is a function of no principle that really matters in the abortion controversy. Circumstances completely irrelevant to the issues in the debate determine whether a woman is able to terminate her pregnancy voluntarily. If she lives in a large metropolitan area, has money and access to transportation, has the support of friends and family, is sufficiently sophisticated to distinguish a real abortion clinic from a sham, can withstand personal abuse from demonstrators at the clinic, can afford to miss several days from school, home, or work and is self-reliant enough to stick to her decision in the face of the state's efforts to enlist her doctor's help in dissuading her, she probably will succeed in exercising her "rights." On the other hand, women who happen to depend on government-subsidized health care, live in remote or rural areas, are unsophisticated, frightened, and alone, tend to defer completely to express and implied medical opinion, have limited access to transportation, and have difficulty being away from work or home may well wind up unwillingly carrying their pregnancy to term. A minor's abortion rights will be determined by all of these fortuitous circumstances plus the additional variables of whether she can trust her parents to be understanding and supportive, or whether she is resilient and sophisticated enough to endure the hardships of litigation during what is probably the most stressful event in her life.

If abortion rights are about allowing women to determine for themselves what is in their best interests in such an intimate and momentous matter, the Court's abortion rights jurisprudence is largely a failure. The circumstances noted above do not distinguish between those women who genuinely conclude that abortion is best for them, and those who reach the opposite decision. Instead circumstances simply distinguish fortunate from disadvantaged women—not the right from the wrong, but the financially, socially, and personally weak from the strong

Such distinctions in the allocation of constitutional rights are indefensible. In other contexts, if such distinctions create or perpetuate the political, social, and economic isolation of one group from mainstream American life, they might violate the core principle of the Civil War amendments to the Constitution. I have described the Thirteenth, Fourteenth, and Fifteenth Amendments as collectively embodying a "caste-abolition" principle, providing a remedy for conditions or actions "that tend to recreate a caste society in which one group is systematically and grossly disadvantaged, dehumanized, and ostracized."[1] It has been argued that one example is gross inequality in public education, which tends to perpetuate the plight of America's underclass.

Laws that in effect create an "abortion rights lottery," and judicial decisions that uphold such laws, may also violate the caste-abolition principle. Without exploring that possibility in full here, several points are worth noting. First, unwanted parenthood is a problematic ingredient of underclass life, and single mothers are especially hard hit. Second, provisions that create a delay in the abortion process are more burdensome for minorities and the poor—further aggravating their difficult health-care circumstances. Third, funding restrictions may effectively make abortion unavailable to such groups. Fourth, lower-class women may be especially vulnerable to restrictions that prey on the unsophisticated and distressed. Finally, the net effect of the Court's work in this area has been to create a category of second-class rights. Lower-class women are at much greater risk because of their circumstances. They depend more on constitutional rights to protect their choice from interference by the state than do women of independent means. The Court's demotion of the status of abortion rights means that such women are more likely to become second-class citizens in the exercise of their privacy rights.

The Court has not really come to terms with this issue. In *Harris v. McCrae* and *Rust v. Sullivan* the Court unconvincingly argued that the cause of this problem was women's poverty, not the law. In *Casey* the Court could not deny that government had acted, so it denied the effect of government's action. The Court's treatment of the notice-to-spouse requirement effectively rebuts its own analysis of the informed-consent provision.

The Court's approach also fails to respect several important principles behind the anti–abortion rights movement. For those critics who object that *Roe* is a purely political choice imposed on the people, with no basis in the Constitution, the dissenting opinions in *Casey* expose the Court's failure to meet the interpretivist objection to *Roe*. The dissenters also add that the Court has made matters worse by announcing a vague, unworkable, and unprincipled new standard. The most important value judgment—how to balance the competing claims of the woman and the fetus—remains denied to the democratic process.

For pro-life advocates who object to *Roe*'s arbitrary denial of fetal rights, *Casey* is scarcely an improvement. There is simply no principled basis for distinguishing two fetal lives—one saved because the woman lacked the means to negotiate the Court-approved obstacle course to abortion, the other extinguished because the woman happened to have superior determination and resources. If anything, the arbitrariness of that outcome is worse. It is not even justified by the competing consideration of the woman's best interests. And under *Casey* the one thing states cannot do is act directly and effectively to save fetal life by outlawing previability abortion.

23. An Uncertain Future

. . . .

Several developments on the horizon could have an important impact on abortion rights in the United States. One involves possible changes in the membership of the Supreme Court. Another depends on pending federal pro-choice legislation. A third turns on recent litigation in the federal courts, including the Supreme Court, that will affect access to abortion. Finally, several cases in state courts involving reproductive issues may bear, if only indirectly, on abortion rights.

CHANGES ON THE COURT

As Justice Blackmun observed in *Casey*, the ultimate fate of *Roe v. Wade* will be determined by future appointees to the Supreme Court. A Republican presidential victory in 1992 would likely have resulted in the appointment of a Justice or Justices willing to overrule *Roe* entirely and could have solidified an already conservative majority on other issues as well. The Democrats, however, have pledged to appoint pro-choice Justices. Even one or two relatively liberal appointments could preserve what is left of *Roe* and moderate the Court's strong trend to the right. The precise consequences for the future of abortion rights of Clinton appointments to the Court are impossible to predict. Justices have surprised and disappointed their appointers in the past. President Eisenhower, for example, called his nomination of Earl Warren as Chief Justice "the biggest damn-fool mistake I ever made."[1] And some observers were surprised at Justices Kennedy's and Souter's votes in *Casey*. At the least, however, Democratic appointees probably would hold the line on *Roe*. It seems less likely that they would turn back the clock to the pre-*Webster* strict scrutiny of previability restrictions. For one thing, they would probably not form a majority on the Court. For another, the abortion issue has been as painfully divisive for the Court as it has been for the country as a whole, and the Court has lost institutional credibility whichever way it has turned on the issue. It seems doubtful that the Court would be eager to reenter that fray so soon after *Casey*. A likelier scenario would be a more aggressive application of the undue burden standard. *Casey* itself illustrates how malleable that test is. A more moderate Court could reduce the extent of *Casey*'s contraction of abortion rights by showing a greater willingness to find that state laws impose an undue burden on abortion rights.

THE FREEDOM OF CHOICE ACT

Even if the Court does not reinstate *Roe* in full force, Congress and the president may do so. Pro-choice legislation, if upheld and vigorously enforced by the Supreme Court, would have the most immediate and far-reaching effect on abortion rights since *Roe* itself. Abortion rights groups have lobbied for a Freedom of Choice Act (FOCA). Although President Bush had threatened to veto the bill, the 1992 elections substantially enhanced the prospects for pro-choice legislation.

The most likely legislation would "establish, as a statutory matter, limitations upon the power of States to restrict the freedom of a woman to terminate a pregnancy in order to achieve the same limitations as provided, as a constitutional matter, under the strict scrutiny standard of review enunciated in *Roe v. Wade* and applied in subsequent cases from 1973 to 1988."[2] Like *Roe*, pro-choice legislation would limit state laws regulating previability abortions to requirements that are medically necessary to protect the health of women undergoing such procedures. It also would allow states to prohibit postviability abortions not necessary to preserve the life or health of the pregnant woman, to decline to pay for abortions, and to protect individuals unwilling to participate in abortions. Legislative proposals also have considered allowing a variety of restrictive measures. Those measures range from requiring a minor to involve a parent, guardian, or other responsible adult before terminating a pregnancy, to perpetuating *Casey* by allowing states to impose burdensome informed-consent requirements and waiting periods.[3]

But an FOCA would not relieve the federal courts of the burden of abortion litigation, or of substantial control over the content of abortion rights. Courts would be called upon to interpret and to enforce an FOCA's provisions, just as they were busy applying *Roe*'s constitutional standards. For example, the courts would have to determine as a matter of statutory interpretation, as they did between *Roe* and *Webster* as a matter of constitutional interpretation, what it means to restrict the freedom of a woman to choose whether or not to terminate a pregnancy, and which requirements are medically necessary to protect the health of women undergoing such procedures. An FOCA thus would keep the courts at the complex task of case-by-case monitoring of abortion restrictions.

An FOCA would, however, redirect the nature of the legal debate about abortion. Abortion rights under an FOCA would have a legislative rather than a constitutional basis. The interpretivist objections to *Roe* as an antidemocratic, unjustified assertion of judicial power would not apply to an FOCA. As a product of the legislative process, an FOCA by definition would represent the choice of the people and not the courts. Thus Justice Scalia's complaint that the Court has no business developing a national abortion code would be met by a congressional mandate to do just that. What's more, Congress could directly overrule unwelcome judicial pronouncements on an FOCA by passing additional legislation.

Still, abortion rights under an FOCA would not be free from constitutional controversy. Congress's authority is limited to certain specific, albeit broad, powers. Legislation that does not derive from at least one of those powers is unconstitutional. An FOCA most likely would rest on two sources of congressional power: (1) Congress's power under the Fourteenth Amendment to enforce due process and equal protection; and (2) Congress's power under Article I of the Constitution to regulate interstate commerce. Past Supreme Court interpretations of congressional power suggest that an FOCA would be constitutional, particularly as an exercise of Congress's commerce power.

To determine whether an FOCA is within Congress's power under the Fourteenth Amendment, it is first necessary to determine which violation of due process or equal protection it seeks to remedy. Proposed legislation has been less than clear on that point, but legislative findings presumably indicate that an FOCA is a response to: (1) the discriminatory impact of abortion restrictions on poor women and minorities, which raises equal protection concerns; and (2) the adverse effect such laws have on reproductive freedom under the Court's pre-*Webster* interpretation of *Roe*, which involves substantive due process concerns.

The difficult constitutional question presented by an FOCA under this interpretation is whether Congress can give a broader reading to equal protection and due process rights than the Court is currently willing to give. In other words, does the Fourteenth Amendment authorize Congress to prohibit by statute the enforcement of state laws that the Court would not find in violation of that amendment? The Court today probably would not hold a state abortion regulation unconstitutional on the grounds of either equal protection or due process suggested by these findings. Under the equal protection clause, the Court has ruled that laws disproportionately affecting the poor are not subjected to strict judicial scrutiny. The Court has reasoned that the poor are not a "discrete and insular minority," in part because the Court believes that their defining characteristic— their economic condition—is not immutable, unlike race.[4] Laws that discriminate against minorities are strictly scrutinized by the courts and almost always held unconstitutional, but only if such discrimination can be shown to be intentional.[5] Congress at most has found discriminatory *impact*, not discriminatory intent, in restrictive state abortion laws. Note also the absence of express findings that restrictive state abortion laws are a form of gender discrimination. And proposed legislation is explicitly

261

intended to give a wider reach to substantive due process than would the Court today. Both *Casey* and *Webster* reflect the Court's latest interpretation of abortion rights under substantive due process principles, and the narrow scope of that interpretation is exactly what pro-choice legislation is trying to expand. While there is precedent that may support the notion that the Fourteenth Amendment authorizes Congress sometimes to prohibit state laws that the Court would uphold, how the Court would rule on an FOCA is uncertain.[6]

Congress's power to regulate interstate commerce is a much more solid constitutional basis for an FOCA. The Court might conceivably conclude that an FOCA is not within Congress's commerce power, but such a ruling would be a radical departure from precedent. Since 1937 the Court has largely deferred to Congress's determination of the extent of its power under the commerce clause and has relied instead on the political process to set limits.* Typically the Court asks whether the activity regulated by Congress, even if local in nature, has a substantial direct or indirect effect on interstate commerce. Even an activity as local and small scale as growing 239 bushels of wheat for mostly domestic consumption on a family farm has been found to be within Congress's commerce power. In that case, *Wickard v. Filburn*, the Court reasoned that while the scale of the farmer's activity might be trivial and local in itself, when aggregated with the wheat production of everyone else nationally the effect on interstate commerce was real and substantial. Under this "aggregation theory"— reminiscent of the parent's question to his or her child: what if everyone refused to eat their peas and carrots?— almost any activity can be found to have an impact on commerce.

Congress's findings that state abortion regulations have a substantial effect on commerce would seem to be at least as plausible as the conclusion that the production of 239 bushels of wheat has such an effect. Congress has specifically noted in an

---

*Of course, other provisions of the Constitution, such as the First Amendment, limit Congress's commerce power. Regulation of interstate commerce in books plainly is within Congress's commerce power, but the First Amendment would prohibit Congress from imposing a production limit on Bibles.

FOCA bill that restrictive abortion laws: would increase the number of "illegal or medically unsafe abortions, often resulting in physical impairment, loss of reproductive capacity or death to the woman involved"; would interfere with physicians' ability to provide health services; and would "obstruct access to and use of contraceptive and other medical techniques that are part of interstate and international commerce...."[7] The conclusion that laws restricting access to abortion would, in the aggregate, have a real and substantial effect on the national economy seems entirely reasonable given the million and a half legal abortions performed annually in the United States. Indeed, opponents of abortion rights are quick to point out that legal abortion is big business. Representative Henry Hyde has complained that "The abortion debate has been bitter and vulgar because a vast abortion industry wants to protect its $500 million annual income."[8]

One might suspect, however, that in enacting an FOCA Congress would be more concerned about civil liberties than about commerce. Even if that is so, the Court has ruled that such noneconomic considerations do not negate what would otherwise be a valid exercise of the commerce power. The Court has upheld federal civil rights legislation enacted under Congress's commerce power in several cases. For example, in *Heart of Atlanta Motel, Inc. v. United States* and *Katzenbach v. McClung* the Court upheld Congress's commerce power to prohibit discrimination in places of public accommodation, in those cases a 216-room motel and a 220-seat, family-owned barbecue restaurant. The Court reasoned that racial discrimination in such places would have a deterrent effect on interstate travel by minorities, which would have a ripple effect on the national economy under the Court's aggregation principle.

If Congress's commerce power extends to racial discrimination at Ollie's Barbecue (which received only about $70,000 worth of food that had moved in interstate commerce and apparently did not cater to interstate travelers), it seems to follow that the power also reaches abortion rights. Congress has noted in an FOCA bill that state laws restricting abortion rights would force women to travel to, and burden the medical resources of, states

263

with more liberal laws. That finding is supported, for example, by the formation of "Overground Railroad" operations in the wake of *Webster* and *Casey* to assist women seeking abortions in obtaining transportation and accommodations while traveling to obtain legal abortions.[9]

DEVELOPMENTS AFFECTING ACCESS: CLINIC BLOCKADES

At least two other developments may have an important impact on women's access to abortion services. The first is the Supreme Court case of *Bray v. Alexandria Women's Health Clinic*, which ruled that a federal civil rights statute does not apply to blockades of abortion clinics. The second involves the federal "gag rule," which restricted the information that health-care providers may offer patients at federally funded family planning clinics.

In *Bray* a federal district court enjoined Operation Rescue from blockading abortion clinics in the Washington, D.C., metropolitan area. *Bray* is one of a number of such cases that have arisen in the federal courts in the last several years. The central legal question is whether blockades of abortion clinics violate rights under federal law, so that the clinics can seek relief in federal court, or whether their judicial remedies are limited to those provided under state law. Thus, although these cases do have an important practical impact on access to abortion, the legal question is the jurisdiction of federal courts to hear blockade cases rather than the status of abortion rights themselves.

The federal law in question was originally enacted as the Ku Klux Klan Act of 1871, part of the post–Civil War civil rights legislation. "The central theme of [its] proponents was that the Klan and others were forcibly resisting efforts to emancipate Negroes and give them equal access to political power. The predominant purpose of [the law] was to combat the prevalent animus against Negroes and their supporters."[10]

The law allows a civil claim to parties injured by "two or more persons in any State or Territory [who] conspire or go in disguise on the highway or on the premises of another, for the purposes of depriving, either directly or indirectly, any person or class of persons of the equal protection of the laws, or of equal privileges and immunities under the laws...." The plaintiffs in *Bray*, nine clinics which provide abortion-related services and various women's rights organizations, alleged that Operation Rescue and certain individuals had conspired to deprive women of their constitutionally protected right to travel from one state to another to obtain an abortion and their privacy right to abortion, and had also violated the plaintiffs' rights under state tort law, including the law of trespass and nuisance. The trial court agreed with the plaintiffs on their travel, trespass, and nuisance claims, and enjoined defendants from blockading or impeding access to the plaintiffs' facilities.*

The trial court also specifically found that the defendants' actions created a substantial risk of physical and mental harm to clinic patients. In addition to the stress and anxiety caused to women who attempted to brave the demonstrators and enter the clinics, the court found that the demonstrators sometimes succeeded in closing clinics temporarily and thus caused substantial harm to those "patients requiring the laminaria removal procedure or other vital medical services...[who] must either postpone the required treatment and assume the attendant risks or seek the services elsewhere. Uncontradicted trial testimony established that there were numerous economic and psychological barriers to obtaining these services elsewhere."[11]

Several legal issues confronted the Supreme Court in *Bray*, where the United States sided with Operation Rescue. The Court has previously held that a claim under the statute must involve some invidiously discriminatory class-based animus. The situation most clearly within the contemplation of the statute, as mentioned above, would be racial bias against black Americans. One issue in *Bray* thus was whether the defendants' conduct targeted a class protected by the 1871 law. The plaintiffs contended that the targeted class was women, and the class-

---

*The trial court declined, on First Amendment grounds, to enjoin the defendants from activities that tend to intimidate, harass, or disturb patients or potential patients.

based animus was thus gender discrimination. The trial court and the court of appeals agreed, and concluded that gender-based animus is covered by the law. The Supreme Court has not yet decided whether gender bias falls within this 1871 law, though one case expressed doubt whether discriminatory animus other than racial bias would be within the statute.[12] Most courts of appeals to consider the question, however, have ruled that the law does apply to gender-based animus.[13]

Defendants and the United States argued that *Bray* does not involve gender bias, and the Court need not decide whether the law applies to it. Operation Rescue argued that it has nothing at all against women as a class, and that its quarrel is rather with anyone—male or female—who helps or participates in abortions. In other words, the defendants argued that the plaintiffs' claim was an improper attempt "to dress up opposition to an activity—the practice of human abortion—to look like opposition to a class." And the United States argued that opposition to abortion is not the legal equivalent of discrimination against women.

Had the Court found that Operation Rescue's activities do involve bias against women, and that the 1871 law covers gender bias, it would have also had to determine whether the defendants' conduct violates a right protected by the statute. The law does not itself provide substantive rights; instead it allows a claim for a violation of an independently existing right. The Court in the past has also interpreted the statute to require proof of a conspiracy "aimed at" or intended to deprive plaintiffs of rights constitutionally protected against private interference. The plaintiffs argued in the trial court that Operation Rescue interfered with two rights: the right to interstate travel and the right to abortion.

The Supreme Court has held in a series of cases that the right to interstate travel is a fundamental right of American citizenship. In *Doe v. Bolton*, the companion case to *Roe v. Wade*, the Court ruled that an in-state residency requirement for access to abortion violated that right. And the Court had earlier held in *United States v. Guest* that interstate travel is a right constitutionally protected against private as well as government interference. Several courts of appeals have held that the private blockading of abortion clinics serving an interstate clientele also violates that right for purposes of the 1871 law.

There is evidence that a substantial portion of abortion services involves interstate travel. For example, the Alan Guttmacher Institute reports that 26 percent of the women from a ten-state area travel to other states to obtain abortion services.[14] Several factors can lead women to travel interstate for abortion: the unavailability of abortion services (either any at all or the kind needed) in their community, the growing differences in abortion laws from state to state, concerns for confidentiality, and a desire to escape harassment.[15] The defendants argued that the court of appeals' holding would produce absurd results, rendering virtually any activity at a site serving interstate commerce, such as a sit-in or picketing at a bus terminal or lunch counter, a constitutional violation. And the United States argued that the Court ought to require a showing that the defendants actually intended to interfere with women's interstate travel.

The trial court in *Bray* declined to decide the plaintiffs' claim that Operation Rescue interfered with the privacy right of abortion. The court reasoned that such a claim was "problematic"— because the plaintiffs had not shown any state involvement and because *Webster* had cast doubt on the status of abortion rights—and that resolution of the question was unnecessary in view of the court's ruling on the travel issue. The defendants argued to the Supreme Court that whatever is left of abortion rights, such rights apply only to state interference, not private action. The plaintiffs, while arguing that the 1871 law expressly provides a claim against certain private conduct, asserted that because the lower courts did not rule on the privacy claim, the issue was not properly before the Supreme Court.

As this book went to press, the Supreme Court handed down its decision in *Bray*. Speaking through Justice Scalia, the Court found no indication of bias against women. Instead it concluded that the clinic blockaders were expressing their opposition to abortion and not to women: "Whatever one thinks of abortion, it cannot be denied that there are common and respectable reasons for opposing it, other than hatred of or condescension toward (or indeed any view at all concerning) women as a class—as is evident from the fact that men and women are on both sides of the issue, just as men and women are on both sides of petitioner's unlawful demonstrations." The Court also ruled, as it has on other occasions in the equal protection context, that the intent element cannot be met by showing that the decision-maker acted voluntarily with awareness of the consequences. Instead it must be shown that the action was taken "because of" and not "in spite of" its adverse impact on the particular class. Thus, although only women can become pregnant and hence seek abortion, that fact alone does not satisfy the Court's intent test. Next, the Court held that the abortion clinics had failed to show that the blockades were "aimed at" a right constitutionally protected against private conduct. The only right so protected at issue in *Bray* was the right to interstate travel, since the Court concluded that abortion is not such a right. Operation Rescue opposes abortion, not interstate travel, the Court reasoned: the blockades do not erect "actual barriers" to interstate movement, nor do they apply their activity in a discriminatory fashion to women who come from out of state.

The outcome of *Bray* will have an important practical impact on access to abortion services. Operation Rescue and other blockade activities have been found by most courts to inhibit women's access to abortion. Indeed, such activities have interfered with women's health care generally, because targeted clinics often provide a range of gynecological services in addition to abortions.

The availability of a federal injunction had played a major role in containing blockade activity. For the time being after *Bray*, clinics will have to take their chances in state courts under state law. State and local courts may be more vulnerable to local political pressure from anti–abortion rights groups. And even if the clinics can obtain injunctive relief, they will have to rely on state and local governments to enforce a court order. In some cases demonstrators have overwhelmed the capacities of local police forces and courts.

The friend-of-the-court brief submitted by the city of Falls

Church, Virginia, in support of the abortion clinics in *Bray*, describes the difficulties faced by localities targeted for Operation Rescue blockades:

> Falls Church, Virginia was the site of Operation Rescue blockades enjoined in this case, and the city...urge[s] the Court to affirm the injunction. Operation Rescue repeatedly summoned hundreds of people to Falls Church to mass around Commonwealth Women's Clinic and seal it off, barring women's access to the clinic for abortions or other medical care. Faced with concerted efforts to incapacitate them, the 30-member Falls Church police force cannot secure access to the clinic premises and adjacent public streets. After entry of the injunction under [the 1871 law], however, the illegal blockades stopped. The federal injunction has been critical to effective law enforcement in Falls Church. Operation Rescue is a nationwide effort, and purely local solutions are unrealistic and inappropriate. Injunctions under state law must be litigated on a case-by-case basis, and pertain only to a particular property. Once one clinic is protected, others in the state bear the brunt of the blockades. Moreover, jurisdiction to prosecute persons in contempt of state court injunctions is only statewide, and many of the blockaders are from out of state.

Falls Church went on to explain that local resources may also be inadequate to process charges against busloads of arrestees. Falls Church, for example, employs only one full-time city attorney and a part-time assistant, who were swamped by arrestees. Similar limitations constrain local courts. Again in Falls Church, the city had to consolidate the defendants' trials and hold them in the community center gymnasium, the only facility large enough to handle the crowd. These problems are nationally significant. The National Abortion Federation reports that between January 1987 and December 1990, 419 clinic blockades resulted in more than 26,000 arrests. The blockades involved destruction of property, invasion of clinics, and overrunning of police lines.[16]

The 1871 statute also prohibits "conspiracies for the purpose of preventing or hindering the constitutional authorities of any

269

State or Territory from giving or securing to all persons within such State or Territory the equal protection of the laws." The Court has not previously interpreted this provision. Although Operation Rescue's campaigns plainly seek to overwhelm local law enforcement authorities and arguably give rise to a "hindrance" claim, the Court held that such a claim had not been properly raised by the *Bray* parties and therefore declined to rule on the question. Justice Scalia's opinion for the Court intimated, however, that "hindrance" claims must also satisfy the class-based animus and "aimed at" requirements which the Court applied to the "deprivation" claim.

Bray does leave besieged abortion clinics and patients with several possible avenues for federal assistance, though none promises immediate relief. One would be to pursue a "hindrance" claim, but the Court's comments make prospects for success doubtful. Another was suggested by Justice Kennedy in his concurring opinion. A federal statute authorizes states to seek federal assistance when state resources are inadequate to protect state citizens and property or to enforce the criminal law. Such a request would allow the attorney general of the United States to make available to the state the full range of federal law enforcement resources, including U.S. marshals. One problem for abortion clinics and patients, of course, would be to persuade the state to make such a request. A third approach would be to seek relief from Congress, for example through amendment to the 1871 statute or a separate statute to cover clinic blockades. Because *Bray* involved a question of statutory and not constitutional interpretation, Congress could in effect overrule the Court's decision. Congress has done so on other occasions, such as the 1991 Civil Rights Act's reversal of a series of narrow Supreme Court interpretations of federal civil rights statutes. To date, however, Congress has considered (but not enacted) legislation that would withhold certain federal funds from local governments that fail to enforce local antiharassment laws against anti-abortion harassment. Legislation of this nature would hardly solve the problems described by Falls Church.

270

DEVELOPMENTS AFFECTING ACCESS: THE GAG RULE

The political process reacted in several ways to the strong public criticism that followed the Supreme Court's 1991 decision in *Rust v. Sullivan* upholding the gag rule. After *Rust* Congress tried to abolish the gag rule, which was imposed by regulations issued in 1988 by the secretary of health and human services under the Reagan administration. Congress can legislate to overturn measures that are adopted by the executive branch through regulation. President Bush vetoed anti-gag-rule bills passed by Congress, however, and the bills' proponents lacked the necessary two-thirds vote to override the presidential veto.

Family planning clinics responded to possible enforcement of the gag rule in a variety of ways. Some simply refused to accept federal funds and planned to reduce their services accordingly. Others tried to circumvent the rule with creative devices. One such device is to segregate federal from privately funded services so that abortion counseling and referral is paid for entirely from private sources. Because creating separate physical facilities for abortion counseling services is beyond the means of most clinics (although arguably required by the regulations), some have tried to segregate services by time. One technique is the "log-out," in which the clinic worker, when asked about abortion, notes the precise time the discussion of abortion begins (that is, logs out) and attempts to pay for that time out of private sources. If these devices are found not to be in compliance with federal regulations, such clinics risk losing their federal funds.

While vetoing legislation to abolish the gag rule, the Bush administration also issued a directive modifying it. The Supreme Court in *Rust* had noted that in medical emergencies the regulations allowed medical personnel to refer patients for an abortion. Thus, under the gag rule as interpreted by the Court, neither doctors nor nurses could provide abortion information and referral except during a medical emergency, in which case apparently either could do so. The 1991 Bush administration directive would allow only physicians to provide abortion information and referral they deemed medically appropriate. The 1991 directive thus opened up the range of information and circumstances—all information medically appropriate—but confined the personnel permitted to give such information and referral to doctors only.

The Bush administration directive prompted another court challenge to the gag rule and a fresh injunction. The United States District Court for the District of Columbia found the regulations invalid on two grounds. First, federal law requires that all legislative-type regulations must first be published in draft form for public comment before taking effect. Although the gag rule itself was issued through proper notice and comment procedures, the 1991 directive was not. The court held that the 1991 directive was a legislative-type rule that must go through the notice and comment procedures. Second, federal statutory (as well as constitutional) law also requires that all regulations have a rational basis. The court found that the 1991 directive's distinction between nurses and physicians lacked a rational basis. Although doctors obviously have more training than nurses, the administration could not rationally assume, the court concluded, that all nurses were unqualified to provide abortion information under medical supervision. Indeed, the Department of Health and Human Services permits nurses in maternal and child health-care programs to provide counseling. The district court therefore enjoined enforcement of the gag rule, and the Court of Appeals for the District of Columbia affirmed the trial court.[17]

The courts' rulings effectively return clinics—at least for the time being—to pre-*Rust* conditions. And because President Clinton has now done away with it, the gag rule thus appears to be a dead letter. But *Rust* remains on the books as the Court's resolution of the constitutional questions raised by that case—with all the troubling implications discussed above.

DEVELOPMENTS IN THE STATE COURTS

Several developments at the state level involve issues related to abortion, particularly the personhood issue, and may shed light on the shape of things to come. Those developments have occurred in three areas: tort claims involving fetal injury and death; criminal prosecution for *in utero* exposure of fetuses to illegal drugs; and disposition of frozen conceptuses. Although the first two developments may undermine *Roe*'s treatment of the personhood issue, that impact is unlikely to occur any time soon; and a recent decision in the third area in a sense reinforces reproductive autonomy.

In discussing the problem of determining when life begins, Justice Blackmun noted in *Roe v. Wade* that only a few states at the time allowed the parents of a stillborn child to sue for wrongful death because of prenatal injuries, and that recognition of such a claim was under criticism. Since *Roe*, however, the claim has been widely accepted: most states now recognize a claim for fetal wrongful death. In most of those states the claim is limited to death caused by injuries sustained by the fetus after viability, though some courts recognize a claim for death from injuries inflicted before viability.

While *Roe v. Wade*, to the extent preserved by *Casey*, would preclude the use of a wrongful fetal death claim to attack voluntary legal abortion (because federal law is paramount to state law), this tort law development nevertheless touches on the personhood conclusion underlying *Roe*. Wrongful death claims, which originally were not recognized by the common law of England or America, are creatures of state legislation. Most state wrongful death statutes speak in terms of a "person" or "human being" or "individual" wrongfully killed. Recognition of a wrongful fetal death claim therefore means that, at least in the limited context of such tort claims, fetuses are legally recognized as "persons." To that extent the Court's conclusion in *Roe* that "the unborn have never been recognized in the law as persons in the whole sense" seems to be called into question.[18] Extending a wrongful death claim to previable fetuses appears to present an even greater challenge to this aspect of *Roe*'s conclusion about fetal personhood.

It has been argued, however, that recognition of such claims is not inconsistent with *Roe*. For one thing, as Justice Blackmun observed in *Roe*, wrongful death claims "appear to vindicate the parents' interest and [are] thus consistent with the view that the fetus, at most, represents only the potentiality of life."[19] Allowing such claims would protect the conceptus and the parents from the intrusions of others. In addition, as one commentator argued:

> In a sense, both the right to have an abortion and the right to bring a cause of action for the wrongful death of a viable or nonviable fetus protects the mother's right to make fundamental choices about reproduction. Where a wrongful death action involves a fetus, the mother, in essence, has suffered an *unwanted* tortiously-inflicted abortion. The mother has thus been deprived of the right to *choose* to carry her pregnancy to term. With an abortion, on the other hand, the mother has exercised her right to choose for herself *not* to carry the pregnancy to term.... Therefore, it makes no more sense to deny a mother-to-be the right to bring suit for the death of a nonviable fetus than it does to force a woman to carry an *unwanted* pregnancy to full term.[20]

The personhood issue—despite, or perhaps because of, its conceptual problems—is the one area which the Supreme Court is most reluctant to revisit. But if the Court were ever to conclude that a fetus is a "constitutional person," even an FOCA could not preserve abortion rights from the fetal claim to equal protection of the laws.

The second development at the state level involves the application of state drug-trafficking laws to pregnant women who expose their offspring to illegal drugs *in utero*. According to one study, at least 167 women in 24 states have been prosecuted under such charges.[21] In Florida, for example, one woman was convicted of "delivering" cocaine to her newborn at birth through the umbilicus. And Connecticut child-welfare officials tried to take another woman's child from her because the woman injected cocaine shortly before going into labor.

These cases present the wrenching problem of protecting newborns from drug exposure, but they also involve the personhood issue. The more areas in which the law recognizes the legal existence of the conceptus—whether as victims of behavior involving tort or as unwilling participants in an illegal drug transaction—the more *Roe*'s conclusion about the legal status of the conceptus becomes open to challenge. So far, the drug cases have been rejected by every appellate court to consider them. The Florida Supreme Court, for example, recently reversed the "umbilicus-delivery" conviction, reasoning that the legislature never intended the drug laws to apply to such cases. And Connecticut's Supreme Court reasoned that the state's child-abuse statute was never intended to cover prenatal conduct. It remains to be seen, however, whether criminal legislation enacted expressly to deal with the problem of intruaterine drug exposure would be upheld. To date, according to the Center for Reproductive Law and Policy, no state has enacted such a statute.[22]

The third development involves the implications of new reproductive technology. New *in vitro* fertilization (IVF) techniques that allow cryogenic preservation of the conceptus at the four- to eight-cell stage of cleavage (often imprecisely referred to as "frozen embryos"), for example, present tough challenges to our legal and ethical systems. IVF involves the removal of ova from the woman, one or more of which is fertilized in a petri dish with the man's sperm and then transferred to the woman's uterus where implantation may or may not occur.

The questions raised by IVF in some respects overlap the abortion debate. For example, similar issues concerning personhood and the legal status of prenatal life arise in the case of IVF. Because the conceptus exists outside the woman's body at the time disputes about its disposition arise, however, the interests involved are not identical to those in abortion. Although the IVF procedure itself is invasive to the woman, involving hormonal injections and the aspiration of ova from her ovaries, at least one court has concluded that "None of the concerns about a woman's bodily integrity that have previously precluded men from controlling abortion decisions is applicable here."[23] And cryogenic storage can result in the preservation of unwanted fertilized ova, raising the difficult questions of what to do with them and who may decide their fate.

275

A detailed discussion of the IVF problem is not possible here, but one recent case is worth mentioning. The Supreme Court of Tennessee recently was faced with a custody battle over seven IVF conceptuses. Because surgery from earlier unsuccessful pregnancies had left Mary Sue Stowe (then Mary Sue Davis) unable to conceive naturally, she and Junior Lewis Davis went through repeated attempts at pregnancy through IVF. When cryogenic preservation of fertilized ova became available, they welcomed the opportunity. The process enabled the clinic they were working with to accumulate more ova for fertilization and thereby increase the chances of successful implantation. But when the Davises' marriage failed, successful implantation had not been achieved. Apparently, neither Mary Sue nor Junior made arrangements for the disposition of the preserved conceptuses.*

That problem surfaced when the couple divorced, with "custody" of the seven preserved conceptuses becoming the principal point of dispute in the divorce proceedings. The nature of the conceptuses was sharply disputed at trial—whether they were "children," "fetuses," "embryos," or "preembryos." As the Tennessee Supreme Court later put it, "semantical distinctions are significant in this context, because language defines legal status and can limit legal rights." The trial court therefore heard testimony from several experts on the nature of the conceptuses. Dr. Jerome Lejune, the French geneticist who identified Downs syndrome, "referred to the four- to eight-cell entities at issue here as 'early human beings,' as 'tiny persons,' and as his 'kin.' "[24] Other, contrary evidence distinguished the early, "preembryonic" stages of conceptus development from the embryonic stage. According to the American Fertility Society, at the eight-cell stage each cell has the potential to become a complete adult; at that point therefore "the developmental singleness of one person

---

*In another heavily publicized case, "an American couple stored embryos in an Australian clinic and subsequently died in a plane crash without leaving directions for the disposition of the embryos. Although a government ethics committee recommended that the embryos be destroyed, the Australian legislature ordered the embryos to be implanted in surrogate mothers and, after birth, be placed for adoption." Lisa Hemphill, "American Abortion Law Applied to New Reproductive Technology," *Jurimetrics*, 32 (Spring 1992), 361, 364.

has not yet been established." By the thirty-two-cell stage, however, "The 32 blastomeres are increasingly adherent, closely packed, and no longer of equal developmental potential. The impression now conveyed is of a multicellular entity, rather than a loose packet of identical cells."[25]

The trial court, persuaded by Dr. Lejune's testimony, reasoned that preembryos and embryos were indistinguishable and that human life begins at conception. The trial court "concluded that the eight-celled entities at issue were not preembryos but were 'children in vitro.'" Under that view the trial court applied the "best-interest-of-the-child" standard typically applicable to child custody proceedings, found that it was in the conceptuses' best interest to have a chance to be born rather than destroyed, and that Mary Sue was willing to give them that chance while Junior was not. While the case was on appeal, Mary Sue said she intended to donate the frozen conceptuses to an anonymous couple.

The Tennessee Supreme Court took a different view. As in the abortion area, the first question was whether the conceptus, called a "preembryo" by the court, is a "person." The Tennessee court looked to several sources to reach essentially the same conclusion reached by the United States Supreme Court in *Roe*. First, a fetus is not a "person" within Tennessee's wrongful death statute unless born alive, contrary to the rule in most other states. Second, other provisions of Tennessee law, including its abortion and homicide laws, do not accord full protection to even viable conceptuses until actually born. And under federal law, specifically *Roe* and even *Webster*, the conceptus is not regarded as a person in the whole sense throughout pregnancy.

Nevertheless, the Tennessee Supreme Court was disturbed by the appellate court's implicit view that the conceptuses were a form of "property." (The appellate court had relied in part on Tennessee statutes governing anatomical gifts and prohibiting experimentation on the tissue of aborted fetuses.) Instead the Tennessee high court reviewed the three major ethical positions that have emerged in the debate over preembryos. One position views the conceptus as a full legal person, which would lead to

277

"an obligation to provide an opportunity for implantation to occur" and would set other limits on handling of the conceptus. At the other extreme is the view that the conceptus is no different from other human tissue, the only legal question being the consent of the person having decision-making authority. The middle view, adopted by the Tennessee court, treats the conceptus with more respect than other human tissue but with less than full legal personhood.

The Tennessee Supreme Court concluded that the preembryos were not, "strictly speaking, either 'persons' or 'property,'" but instead occupied a kind of legal limbo somewhere in between. Ideally, under the court's view, the persons who provide the gametes should arrange by express agreement for the disposition of the preembryos. But in *Davis v. Davis* there was no evidence of an express or implicit agreement. The court saw the key question not as one of providing for storage of the preembryos but rather "whether the parties will become parents." Without an agreement between the parties, the court sought resolution of that dilemma in the right of privacy (in the sense of personal autonomy or the "right to be let alone").*

The privacy right at stake, the Tennessee Supreme Court found, was the right both to procreate and to avoid procreation. Although the IVF procedure is more stressful and traumatic for women than for men, the court found that their respective interests in the decision to become a parent ultimately were equivalent. And the court concluded that no one else had an interest sufficient to warrant interference in the gamete-providers' decision.

The judicial task, under the court's view, is to balance the conflicting interests of the two gamete providers—here Junior Davis and Mary Sue Stowe—on a case-by-case basis. For Junior the burden would be to impose unwanted parenthood on him. Given his circumstances, having "had severe problems caused by

---

*While looking in part to federal law, the Tennessee court was careful to note that the right applied in *Davis* was not identical to the federal constitutional right. The importance of that distinction is that it preserves the state court's decision as a matter of state law, which the United States Supreme Court has no power to dictate.

separation from his parents," he was "vehemently opposed to fathering a child that would not live with both parents"—which would happen if he or Mary Sue had custody or if the recipient couple separated. The interest for Mary Sue was the frustration of having undergone the IVF procedure to no purpose, and the knowledge that the genetic material she contributed would never become children. Between the two, the court concluded that Junior's interest in avoiding unwanted parenthood was more significant. The court noted that the case would be closer if Mary Sue sought to implant the preembryos in herself rather than donate them to another couple, "but only if she could not achieve parenthood by any other reasonable means"—including IVF and adoption.[26] Finally, the court was careful to note that its opinion did not give an automatic veto to the party wishing to avoid parenthood, but rather established a case-by-case balancing test which favored that party, assuming the other party had no other reasonable means of achieving parenthood.

Davis thus is in harmony with Roe. The Tennessee court's analysis of the personhood issue borrowed several leaves from Justice Blackmun's approach in Roe. And the Tennessee Supreme Court's resolution of the case reflects Roe's recognition of a right to reproductive autonomy and its balancing approach to reconciling the competing interests at stake. Davis also shows how Roe can stand for a broader principle of reproductive autonomy than women's freedom to choose. Davis sought to protect that autonomy interest by weighing the nature and extent of the burden imposed on it, regardless of the gender of the person claiming it.

24. Full Circles and Fresh Perspectives

. . . .

In more than one sense, we conclude where we began. Abortion rights continue to be determined more by political power than by constitutional principle. A concentrated twenty-year effort by anti–abortion rights forces to elect officials who would appoint federal judges and Justices opposed to abortion rights produced the *Casey* decision. That decision reflects political compromise more than it does constitutional principle, and comes within a whisper of returning the nation to the pre-*Roe* days of illegal abortion. The political tide turned, however, in the 1992 election. Although the dominant issue in that election was the economy, many voters also listed abortion rights and future appointments to the United States Supreme Court as among their concerns. With a pro-choice president, pro-choice majorities in Congress, and women entering both houses in record numbers, liberal federal abortion rights legislation seems likely; and judicial appointments for at least the next four years also are likely to be pro-choice.

This apparent victory for pro–abortion rights certainly reflects a choice by the people—rather than one mandated by unelected, life-tenured judges—and is therefore immune to the interpretivist objections leveled against *Roe*. Passage of a Freedom of Choice Act and the demise of the gag rule would redress some—but clearly not all—of the arbitrariness and inequality in access to abortion rights.

If these pro-choice promises are fulfilled, America's abortion policy will again be in line with the worldwide trend since World War II toward the liberalization of abortion laws. Although some countries, such as Ireland and Germany, have imposed restrictive laws or agonized over liberalization, many other countries have substantially relaxed their abortion laws. According to a 1990 study by the Alan Guttmacher Institute, "Forty percent of the world's population now lives in countries where induced abortion is permitted on request...." Of those countries, however, "Only the Philippines and the United States have passed restrictive measures at the national level since 1986," the Philippines by constitutional amendment to protect the conceptus from the moment of conception, and the United States by the *Webster* decision (and later the *Casey* decision). AGI also reports that "Between 1986 and 1990, restriction on abortion at the state level increased somewhat in the United States."[1]*

Pro-choice developments, especially enactment of an FOCA, will bring us almost full circle in another sense as well. An FOCA would largely reinstate the abortion policy articulated by the Supreme Court during the post-*Roe*, pre-*Webster* rights elaboration phase. An FOCA would also return the federal courts to the task of further developing that policy, though the source of their authority would be an express legislative mandate rather than an implied constitutional right. It thus appears that, having traveled the road from *Roe* to *Webster* to *Casey*, we may return to *Roe*—albeit under a different license.

But this return to *Roe*, if it happens, does not mean that the abortion conflict has reached a peaceful or principled resolution. There is little indication that warring Americans have found common ground. Instead it appears only that the balance of power is shifting. One side has largely won without necessarily proving itself right—unless by "right" we mean whatever the politically dominant group prefers at any particular moment.

---

*Some of those restrictions—such as detailed informed-consent requirements and mandatory waiting periods—also appear in other countries. Comparative law scholar Mary Ann Glendon has argued that France's imposition of such requirements reflects a more compassionate and humane balance between maternal and fetal interests, especially in light of France's liberal provision of contraceptive assistance and postnatal financial support.[2] While her reference to the overall social support system is well taken, her criticism of the pre-*Casey* constitutional ban on such restrictions overlooks their practical impact on the allocation of abortion rights in this country.

281

Given the passions of extremists on either side, and the size of the canyon that divides them, real reconciliation seems unlikely on our present course.

The polarized atmosphere of the conflict continues to make dialogue about this painful subject difficult. Silencing the opposition has become a common tactic of abortion activists on both sides. For example, as noted earlier, the Democratic party refused to allow Pennsylvania Governor Robert Casey an opportunity to speak against abortion at the 1992 Democratic National Convention. And hecklers shouted him down when he later tried to address a New York City audience at a meeting sponsored by the *Village Voice*. The gag rule reflects the Reagan and Bush administrations' effort, in response to political pressure from the anti-abortion movement, to forbid speech about abortion. The Bush administration's ban on public funding for fetal tissue research—based in part on the dubious assumption that without the ban researchers, doctors, and pregnant women would have an incentive to abort, and contrary to the unanimous recommendation of the National Institutes of Health—also illustrates the conflict's impact on objective scientific research. (Clinton has lifted the ban.) At one time it even seemed possible that anti–abortion rights lawmakers in Congress would attempt the radical measure of silencing the federal courts by withdrawing their jurisdiction to hear abortion rights cases. And harassment by anti-abortion extremists is also a means of preventing patients from communicating with their physicians about abortion.

Early in this book I suggested that we ought to begin searching for new ways to look at the abortion problem, and new means to resolve it. In providing information about abortion and its constitutional implications, I have not tried to describe an alternative approach. But in conclusion I offer a few thoughts toward that end.

The way the abortion debate is typically framed—reproductive choice versus the willful destruction of innocent life—does not leave much room for reconciliation. For each pregnancy there can be only one of two outcomes, and either the woman or someone else gets to choose between them. Each side tries to develop either the ultimate trump argument to demonstrate the rightness of its position, or the most effective strategy to out-flank its opponent. The fruitlessness of the search for the final argument is evident to one who sees validity in the core claims of both sides. Pro-choice extremists cannot convincingly argue that as a community we have no business worrying about conduct that might be, and at least sometimes looks like, the deliberate taking of human life. Pro-life extremists will never convince anyone but themselves that women's claim to reproductive freedom need not be taken seriously. And the harmfulness of the adversarial approach to the abortion issue appears in the Court's arbitrary allocation of abortion rights.

Given the force of the claims on either side, real rapprochement seems unlikely as long as the abortion conflict is considered in its usual terms. Rather than investing all our energy in trying to figure out why or how one side should prevail, a more constructive route might look for a way to live with both some measure of abortion rights *and* opposition to them. *Roe*, of course, sought to achieve a compromise between those competing interests; but its approach is subject to a number of criticisms.

Taking the dispute out of the constitutional context, as an FOCA would do, may actually be a step toward a new approach to resolving the problem. It would restore *Roe*'s attempt to compromise competing interests while largely avoiding the thicket of constitutional interpretation. In particular, an FOCA could not be criticized as an illegitimate judicial usurpation of democratic will. Still, enacting an FOCA is far from an adequate solution. First, that step alone would not remedy the serious problem of unequal access to abortion services. Second, an FOCA would recapitulate the post-*Roe* process of reviewing state legislative efforts to appease the anti-abortion faction while appearing not to cross the legal limit of permissible regulation. In other words, the pressure to limit abortion would persist, the door would remain open for the kind of spurious balancing act demonstrated in *Casey*, and the abortion wars would likely continue in the courts and in the streets. Third, an FOCA has little to offer the other side. It would allow abortions to continue in massive numbers. The only concessions to the pro-life side considered in the FOCA debate have been proposals to permit states to enact the kinds of restrictions that contribute to the present arbitrariness in the allocation of abortion rights.

We thus have reached an impasse in the abortion controversy. Choosing sides requires the unacceptable sacrifice of compelling interests whichever way one's knee jerks, while attempts at compromise have proven unsuccessful. When we come to such a point, perhaps it is time to question our assumptions. A key assumption in the abortion conflict is that the central interests are the ones identified by Justice Blackmun in *Roe*: the woman's liberty interest in reproductive choice on one side, and the state's interest in maternal health and fetal life on the other. If many people find themselves unwilling in good conscience to choose between those interests, and unable to achieve a satisfactory compromise among them, perhaps we have not fully understood the interests at stake. In other words, maybe the abortion issue is like the parable about blind men and the elephant. One grabs a leg and calls the elephant a tree; another seizes the tail and calls it a rope.

The interest in reproductive freedom has been defined in a way that allows it to be denied on an unprincipled and arbitrary basis. This outcome ought to be unacceptable either constitutionally or as a matter of policy. Arbitrary denial of rights violates fundamental constitutional values of equality and due process. The "caste-abolition" principle—if recognized by the courts— may require that if the benefits of abortion rights cannot be made equally available, the burdens of not having them must be equally shared. And no sound policy can justify the increased medical, psychological, and moral risks created by state-mandated delay in abortion. Finally, the Court has been wrong to consider the interest in reproductive freedom as solely the pregnant woman's. If such a right exists, it is the state's concern as well: civil liberties are and ought to be in the best interest of a free society as well as of the individual.

The Court's approach also has given little real vitality to the state's interests as typically defined. First, because of abortion's relatively greater safety than childbirth throughout pregnancy, few pre- or postviability abortion-specific regulations truly advance the interest in maternal health. That interest more often has been invoked as a smokescreen for measures intended to inhibit the choice of abortion. Perhaps the best thing that can be said for *Casey's* joint opinion is that its express approval of deliberate state efforts to burden choice eliminated the need for the pretext of maternal health. States may now openly seek to interfere with women's choice, provided they are not too successful. The best way to protect maternal health plainly would be to prohibit interference with, and to facilitate access to, a full range of health-care options, including abortion.

Second, the state's interest in previability life enjoys little effective protection. *Roe* triggered an enormous increase in the number of legal abortions. The Court's more recent toleration of waiting periods, informed-consent laws, burdensome parental notification and consent laws, and general deference to state legislatures in matters of abortion may interfere with some women's access to abortion services, but it does not advance a coherent pro-life program or notably reduce the number of abortions. The only way to do that would be to allow (or perhaps even to *require*) states to outlaw most if not all abortions. Such proscriptions have proved very difficult to enforce, and abortion has always been practiced, legally or not—but then so has homicide. One might nevertheless agree that, assuming the validity of the pro-life argument, society ought to express disapproval of abortion by outlawing it in most circumstances (even if illegal abortions will continue). But in view of the demand for legal abortion in the United States—one and a half million annually—and recent political developments, it appears unlikely that the agenda of extreme anti–abortion rights advocates will ever be realized. Legal abortion will continue to be performed in the United States in large numbers for the foreseeable future, even under *Casey*.

Third, the conflict is not just between the woman's interests and the state's, but also between the state's two interests themselves. Notwithstanding the arguments of groups such as Feminists for Life about the risks of abortion, most informed opinion recognizes, and experience confirms, that liberal abortion laws protect women's health more than restrictive ones. Yet only very restrictive abortion laws significantly protect fetal life.

Those opponents of abortion who believe it is the murder of innocent children thus will never be satisfied as things now stand. Arguments about privacy, liberty, and women's choice are likely to fall on deaf ears because they do not respond to the concerns of people who hold those beliefs. On the other hand, militant abortion rights advocates also remain frustrated and intransigent. Mutually respectful discourse between opposing extremes has never been part of the abortion debate.

Any workable resolution thus must speak to the moderates on both sides and the undecided in the middle. For more open-minded pro-lifers, this book may provide an appreciation of the force of a woman's claim to reproductive freedom, and the consequences of interfering with that freedom. For pro-choicers interested in better understanding the other side, this book has described constitutional and other objections to that claim, especially those raised by the personhood problem.

Once each side begins to appreciate the other's claims, perhaps we can change the adversarial, interest-group approach that precludes pro-lifers from accepting any abortion rights and pro-choicers from accepting restrictions on those rights. The next step is to question whether *Roe*'s description of either side, and the Court's solutions, are adequate. Given the existence of abortion rights, the problem of their unequal and arbitrary allocation argues forcefully against the kinds of restrictions allowed under the Court's current compromise. And we can't satisfy the moral demands of the abortion-is-always-murder side of the debate without forfeiting the woman's opposing interest. Increased access to contraceptives—urged by Planned Parenthood—would reduce the abortion rate while also promoting choice, but abortion's moral dilemmas would remain. Several interrelated questions therefore arise: First, is there an aspect of our reaction to abortion not adequately described by the usual opposing arguments about "life" and "personhood"? Second, does this newly identified aspect suggest some common ground between moderates on the abortion is-

286

sue? Third, does recognizing this aspect help to accommodate a new understanding of opposition to abortion while also addressing the problems of inequality and arbitrariness?

Stepping away from the shouting mobs, we may find that for many people the answer to each of these questions is yes—but only if they can be honest about their reactions to abortion. It may well be that many people on both sides of the issue share an intuitive, naturally human abhorrence of the deliberate dismemberment of what looks like a tiny human being. This repugnance may be deeply rooted in an empathic kinship with one another that is the source of all that is precious and caring in human relationships when it is present—and all that is horrible and brutal when it is absent. If abortion offends certain fundamental, almost primal, sensibilities, then abortion's *images* assume a special importance. Whether or not the conceptus is a "human life" from fertilization onward, the images of abortion at various stages of gestation certainly are not the same. No wonder that anti-abortion activists wave pictures—and even actual fetuses—from late-term abortions. Those images have an impact that the picture of an eighth-week vacuum aspiration curettage does not. An abortion in the eighth week of pregnancy is simply not the same experience as one in the fifteenth or twenty-second week. The illustrations in Part One show the dramatic changes undergone by the conceptus during that period. If this "repugnance hypothesis" is valid, then our understanding of the interests at stake in the abortion controversy must be refined.

On one side, abortion rights proponents who squarely face abortion's realities may find it deeply disturbing, especially in the second trimester, despite their beliefs about free choice. This aversive reaction may be the only point of concurrence between the two sides in the abortion conflict. I have not met anyone who *likes* abortion. As Sarah Weddington, counsel for "Jane Roe" in *Roe v. Wade*, put it, "I don't hear anyone advertising that a 'neat' thing to do on a sunny Saturday would be to get an abortion."[3] Some people may find it less offensive than others, many may be glad that it is available, and most women who have one apparently do not suffer psychological harm. But few if any individuals

287

feel *good* about it. Abortion at best provides relief, not joy. While people disagree whether abortion is cause for remorse or guilt, few would say it is an occasion for celebration. By contrast, most people would agree that the birth of a child—even in difficult circumstances—usually stimulates the most powerful of all positive human emotions. This is not to deny that some children are born unwanted, bring an unwelcome burden, or suffer neglect or abuse. The point instead is that many people, even if they would vote differently in a referendum on pro-choice legislation, share basic emotional responses to both childbirth and abortion. Progress might be made if we focused for a time on these similarities instead of on our ideological differences.

On the other side, perhaps many of abortion's more moderate opponents do not claim to have a pipeline to the truth about abortion's moral dilemmas or the question of personhood. They may find that the source of *their* discomfort is not in abstract or dogmatic arguments about constitutional law, judicial restraint, state interests, embryology, philosophy, or even religious doctrine. It may instead derive from repugnance. In other words, the more vocal and visible faction of the anti-abortion side may not speak for many opponents of abortion. Given a chance to reflect, many might explain that their opposition is more visceral than ideological.

The repugnance hypothesis is much more than a matter of squeamishness about gory surgical procedures. The images of abortion, especially in the second trimester, distress not so much because they are unpleasant but because they appear profoundly inhumane. For example, Dr. Warren M. Hern's text, *Abortion Practice*, explains that second-trimester dilation and evacuation "is an emotionally stressful experience" even for experienced health-care professionals—who are scarcely fainthearted about surgery or human suffering generally—and cautions that it is necessary to "provide support for those who participate in the procedure."

The repugnance hypothesis tries to express more fully what really bothers people about abortion. It also asks that we be honest with ourselves about what the issues really are. If one thing is clear in the abortion conflict, it is that the conceptus is no one's constituent. When lawmakers enact restrictions on abortion, they are responding to the demands of postnatal people. The repugnance hypothesis suggests that we examine what actually drives those demands and ask whether the state's response fits.

The implications of the repugnance hypothesis are likely to provoke opposition from some quarters on either side of the abortion wars. Any search for a fresh perspective that seeks even partly to bridge the gap by definition threatens the politics of division, extremism, and contention. But if this inquiry offers a real chance of finding new common ground on the abortion issue, we would be socially irresponsible to turn our backs on it. If the image of dismembered tiny human beings is what upsets many people who are troubled by abortion, the problem ought to be honestly acknowledged as part of the state's real interest, and accommodation of that interest ought to be structured accordingly.

These images must first be put in realistic perspective. The late-term "bloody fetus" images sponsored by some anti-abortion activists do not represent what the vast majority of abortions are like in this country (or in most other countries with legal abortion). Just as there appears to be an inconsistency between abstract attitudes about abortion and the actual choices people make, there may also be a wide gap between what distresses many abortion opponents and what most abortion really looks like.

If we concede that the powerful repulsion of abortion is an important issue, and if we come to appreciate the images that provoke that reaction, several general conclusions follow. All of them assume the existence of some right to choose abortion—otherwise we will have sacrificed one of the compelling interests at stake. That is a bridge that the United States, and much of the developed world, has already crossed. The question here is not *whether* we should have abortion rights at all, but *how* we should deal with them.

First, because the repugnance of abortion's images seems to depend on the age of the conceptus, the Court was correct in *Roe* to search for a gestational threshold; but the point at which abortion becomes too much for many people to bear may occur *before* viability. The selection of viability as the legal border was based on an effort to balance the woman's interest in reproductive freedom against the state's interest in protecting fetal life. An approach that sought to accommodate the repugnance hypothesis would search instead for a threshold based on a state interest defined in terms of abortion's severe emotional impact. Determination of that threshold will require careful study, but it probably occurs somewhere in the second trimester.

Second, under its own balancing approach the Court has been incorrect since *Roe* in upholding restrictive measures imposed before that threshold, whether the state interest is protecting the fetus or those deeply disturbed by abortion's images. Up to the legal threshold there is little if any legitimate basis for interfering with women's choice. The repugnance hypothesis would recognize that something is "wrong" with abortion past a certain point, largely because it "feels wrong" to many people. And, at least after viability, the repugnance hypothesis would be augmented by the Court's view of the state's interest in postviability fetal life. Before then, however, all of the powerful arguments against arbitrariness and inequality in the allocation of abortion rights (including the caste-abolition principle), and in favor of recognizing those rights in the first place, would seem to preclude interference. And the state's interest in fetal life would not justify the kind of prethreshold interference in choice approved in *Casey*. Because *Casey* preserves viability as the constitutional boundary, implementing this repugnance approach would require action by the Court.

Third, once the legal threshold is transposed from viability to the new "repugnancy" point, genuinely strict judicial scrutiny should be applied to prethreshold measures. As the Court recognized in *Roe*, some state regulation may be appropriate to safeguard maternal health from unscrupulous and unqualified practitioners and unsafe procedures. But experience has taught that abortion regulations often seek to deter women from choosing abortion rather than to protect women once they make that choice. Strict judicial scrutiny would still be needed to "smoke out" laws that seek to make abortion less available from those that genuinely seek to make it safer. Given the safety of early abortion, very few abortion-specific laws would pass this scrutiny. And, for reasons described earlier, restrictions on abortion funding ought not to be upheld either.

Fourth, assuming the repugnance hypothesis is valid, the foregoing conclusions describe something closer to a real compromise than does *Roe* (or its statutory cousin, the FOCA) or *Casey*. Extreme advocates on both sides of the abortion issue can find fault with *Roe*, *Webster*, and *Casey*. Even moderate elements have cause to complain about the resolutions attempted to date. But the repugnance hypothesis assumes that many people on both sides of the debate who are deeply disturbed by abortions past a certain point in gestation might tolerate them before then. By strongly protecting *really* unrestricted access to abortion up to that point—as opposed to the haphazard, arbitrarily defined access now allowed by the Court—and allowing the state to prohibit it thereafter, perhaps more people on both sides could feel a sense of resolution.

Just as both sides would gain something, both would be required to yield as well. The pro-choice side would have to accept a somewhat narrower gestational window in which abortion may be legally obtained, though that window would be fully open and not partially or occasionally barred. That window very likely would include almost all abortions now legally performed in the United States anyway. And the anti-abortion side would have to give up its incrementalist agenda of sniping at various prethreshold targets and accept free access to abortion during that period in return for an earlier threshold and a clearer description of its interest. In a larger sense, this approach would deny to extremists on either side in the debate the dominant position they have enjoyed—and arguably abused—for the past twenty years.

This approach also is supported by the basic principles of equality, fair treatment, and nonarbitrariness underlying both the equal protection and due process guarantees. The right to abortion would really mean something where it existed, and the point at which prohibition is allowed would be based on a consideration that may resonate strongly with more people. The strict judicial scrutiny of this approach would remove many unequally distributed obstacles to choice, especially if *Harris* is overruled. Indeed, overruling *Harris* might also lead to recognition of a constitutional right to state protection from private interference with choice, such as Operation Rescue's blockade of abortion clinics.

If the repugnance hypothesis is valid, there also might be greater consensus on resolving the conflict, consequently less pressure on the Court to dilute abortion rights, and perhaps even less stigma associated with abortion altogether. Once we recognize common ground, clarify what troubles many people about abortion, and allow that problem to be acknowledged and addressed openly and directly, perhaps abortion—which for the time being apparently is here to stay in any event—will become less controversial. To the extent the controversy can be defused, support for extreme activism, such as harassment of abortion clinics, providers, and patients, probably would decline. And to the extent the medical profession can be left alone, perhaps more doctors would be willing to offer abortion services to their patients. Those developments, along with removal of funding restrictions, would mean that a woman's decision to have an abortion would turn more on her own needs and choice, and on issues that really matter, than on the fortuitous factors that now heavily influence her decision.

Of course this proposal rests on an unproved assumption. And there are objections, some of them forceful. One is that, even assuming an agreement on a common repugnance point, the post-threshold prohibitions on abortion would be no less arbitrary than the current restrictions. Yet any bright-line test is susceptible to such criticism. The fact is, every resolution of the abortion controversy (apart from flat prohibition of all abortion, or abortion on demand throughout pregnancy) involves such a test. The trouble with the current state of abortion law is not that its bright-line viability test produces arbitrariness at that boundary, but rather that the application of that test produces arbitrariness *throughout* pregnancy. If the line is drawn with reference to a consideration or principle that really matters in the debate, it is by definition not arbitrary—abortion after the threshold is different from prethreshold abortion. The problem now is that there is not one threshold but many, and most are drawn with reference to nothing that anyone cares much about in the debate.

A second objection to the repugnance hypothesis is that it violates the principles discussed in connection with the personhood issue. In brief, those principles are that each human being has intrinsically equal moral worth and is entitled to the law's minimal protections, and that neither functional capacity nor appearance are legitimate bases for denying those protections. The repugnance hypothesis does violate those principles if the human community is defined in genetic terms, but so does *any* toleration of abortion except perhaps when necessary to save the woman's life. The repugnance hypothesis may offer an alternative conception of the human community, however, defined in empathic rather than genetic terms. It would also avoid the assertion of personhood status for the zygote, which many people might find intuitively implausible. In any event, the repugnance hypothesis is neither an argument for a right to abortion nor a rebuttal of the strongly pro-life position, whether based on liberal principles or religious dogma. Instead the repugnance hypothesis assumes the existence of some abortion rights—without arguing one side or the other of that dispute—and tries to provide a more realistic accommodation of the interests at stake.

A third objection is that if the problem is abortion's images, then the solution is simply "don't look." This objection misapprehends the repugnance hypothesis. We all form images of things we care about but may never have seen. The repugnance hypothesis, for example, may account for some people's opposition to capital punishment—even though few people have actually witnessed an execution. Indeed, the repugnance hypothesis may state a powerful argument for directing our attention to, not from, the abortion issue. And it may provide important information about how to respond to abortion's dilemmas. As one anti–abortion rights extremist has observed, if we can't bear to look at it perhaps it ought not to be tolerated. But the "it" most people can't bear to look at is not what most abortion looks like. The repug-

293

nance hypothesis seeks to distinguish between image and reality.

Still another objection, more pragmatic than the others, is that a common repugnance point will prove elusive. Why assume a common ground that can be defined with sufficient precision to be workable? At bottom, this argument questions the central assumptions of the repugnance hypothesis. There is no ready response to this kind of skepticism, except to acknowledge that it illustrates the need for further study. It seems doubtful, however, that the repugnance point would involve greater uncertainty or unstructured choice of criteria than has *Roe* or any other Supreme Court abortion decision. As the joint opinion explained in *Casey*, once the Court is in the business of implying such rights, it necessarily must make the best judgments it can; and the Court doubtless can count on the assistance of numerous friends of the court in doing so. As Hern's text on abortion points out, and as other practitioners have informed me, there comes a point at which even abortion practitioners, whom we would expect not to be squeamish, find the procedure very stressful. That point appears to be somewhere between the fifteenth to the eighteenth week of gestation.

The criteria of workability is not precision but practicability. We are now so far from any real common-ground resolution of the abortion problem that it would be cynical to be more demanding of a new approach than we are of the current one. The repugnance hypothesis does not promise complete harmony, it merely asks whether we can do better.

The purpose of this discussion—and of this book as a whole—is not to win an argument but to open real discussion. I have described, in summary fashion, a broad range of responses to the challenges of abortion and their legal, social, and medical impact. I have not tried to advance either the pro-life or the pro-choice agenda. Instead my goal has been to provide a basis for informed appraisal of where we have been, where we now stand, and where we are headed on this issue.

My hope is that we begin to ask ourselves whether our society's approach to abortion is meeting the needs of our people, or whether the costs of the conflict warrant a search for a new perspective. We now stand at the crossroads of profound social choices. The end of the cold war challenges us to find a way to demobilize and offers the opportunity to redirect massive resources to urgent social needs at home. With the end of that ideological conflict, it is much easier to see real people with real needs on both sides of the former Iron Curtain.

Perhaps there is a similar lesson for us on the abortion issue. Perhaps it is possible to get past the hostility and conflict-oriented approach of the abortion wars. Perhaps we can begin looking for ways to talk with and care for, rather than dominate, each other—even in the difficult context of abortion. If we are ever going to face our hard choices, we must begin searching for and listening to the lost voices.

Notes

1. The Nature of the Debate

1. *Philadelphia Inquirer*, "Quaker Overground Railroad Keeps Trucking," *Abortion Report*, July 22, 1991, State Report Section. *Abortion Report* is a daily, on-line reporting service available on Mead Data Central's Lexis-Nexis service, CMPGN library, ABTRPT file.

2. Ronald Dworkin, "The Great Abortion Case," in *A Documentary History of the Legal Aspects of Abortion in the United States: Webster v. Reproductive Health Services*, ed. Roy M. Mersky and Gary R. Hartman (Littleton, Colo., 1990), 1:51 (hereafter Mersky and Hartman).

3. "The Great Divide," *Life*, July 1992, 32, 34.

4. American Political Network, "Pro-life Candidates Look to 'Graphic Ads,'" *Abortion Report*, July 21, 1992, national briefing section; "Bailey Ad Runs Restricted, Supreme Ct. Refusal," *Abortion Report*, November 2, 1992; "Pro-Life Ads: FCC Rules Stations Can Run Warnings," *Abortion Report*, August 24, 1992.

5. "The Great Divide," 32, 34

6. Christopher Leone, "Self-generated Attitude Change: Some Effects of Thought and Dogmatism on Attitude Polarization," *Personality and Individual Differences*, 10 (1989), 1243; Christopher Leone, Lawrence W. Taylor, and Kevin Adams, "Self-Generated Attitude Change: Some Effects on Thought, Dogmatism, and Reality Constraints," *Personality and Individual Differences*, 12 (1991), 233.

7. Alice R. Rossi and Bhavani Sitaraman, "Abortion in Context: Historical Trends and Future Changes," *Family Planning Perspectives*, 20 (1988), 273, 277–281 (describing Ron Lesthaeghe's and Jon Surkyn's research).

8. *Ibid.*

9. *Ibid.*, 279.

10. Richard Lacayo, "Crusading Against the Pro-Choice Movement," *Time*, October 21, 1991, 26,

11. Jerry Adler, et al., "Abortion's Long Siege," *Newsweek*, April 27, 1992, 44.

12. Molly Ivins, "Sex Bullies: What Do the Anti-Abortion, Anti-Gay, Anti-Porn Groups Want? Nothing Less than Sex Control," *Playboy*, 37 (June 1990), 88.

13. Kathryn Kelley, "Sexuality and Hostility of Authoritarians," *High School Journal*, 68 (1985), 173.

14. Rossi and Sitaraman, 277.

15. Susan Faludi, *Backlash: The Undeclared War Against American Women* (New York, 1991).

16. Neil A. Lewis, "Selection of Conservative Judges Guards Part of Bush's Legacy," *New York Times*, July 1, 1992, A9.

17. Brief of American Jewish Congress, et al., in Mersky and Hartman, 5:275.
18. Rossi and Sitaraman, 276.
19. Mersky and Hartman, 5:355.
20. Mersky and Hartman, 5:117–118.
21. Bureau of National Affairs, "ABA Backs Abortion Rights, Right to Die, and Job Protection," *United States Law Week*, 58 (February 20, 1990), 2474.
22. "ABA Takes Pro-Choice Stance," *Abortion Report*, August 12, 1992.
23. Rossi and Sitaraman, 277 (reviewing survey data and concluding that "abortion is not a partisan issue").
24. "Dem. Convention: Without a Podium, Casey Still Speaks," *Abortion Report*, July 23, 1992.
25. Mersky and Hartman, 4:101–105.
26. "Quayle I: From Last Night's Interview with VP Dan Quayle," *Abortion Report*, July 23, 1992.
27. "Bush, Like Quayle, Would 'Support' Family Abortion Decision," *Abortion Report*, August 12, 1992; "Bush: Reax to Abortion Comments on 'Dateline NBC,'" *Abortion Report*, August 13, 1992.
28. Ellen Messer and Kathryn May, *Back Rooms: Voices from the Illegal Abortion Era* (New York, 1988), 31.
29. *Ibid.*, 9–10. Caroline's life was saved by an Episcopal rector, "a gentle Christian man," who arranged for her to receive medical treatment—which involved hospitalization, a dilation and curettage, and a transfusion of five units of blood—and for the church to pay her hospital bill. "He remarked that he had lots of parishioners who had money to fly to Sweden to get an abortion, and it was really criminal that just because I didn't have money I'd had to go through this kind of experience."
30. *Ibid.*, 65–67. Messer and May also include stories from abortion providers and pro-choice activist men.
31. Mersky and Hartman, 8:285 (emphasis in original).
32. Mersky and Hartman, 8:288–289.
33. Mersky and Hartman, 8:304–313.
34. Mersky and Hartman, 3:128–130.
35. Mersky and Hartman, 3:131–132.
36. Mersky and Hartman, 3:133–134.
37. Subcommittee on Regulation, Business Opportunities, and Energy of the House Committee on Small Business, *Hearings on Consumer Protection and Patient Safety Issues Involving Bogus Abortion Clinics*, 102d Cong., 1st Sess., 1991, 4–7 (testimony of Shannon Lock).
38. *Ibid.*, 7–9 (testimony of Lynn Taliento).

2. The Demographic and Social Context

1. Stanley K. Henshaw and Jane Silverman, "The Characteristics and Prior Contraceptive Use of U.S. Abortion Patients," *Family Planning Perspectives*, 20 (1988), 158.
2. The data described in the text can be found in U.S. Bureau of Census, *Statistical Abstract of the United States: 1991*, 111th ed. (Washington, D.C., 1991), Table 102, p. 71 (hereafter *Statistical Abstract*), with sources cited as follows: "1972, Centers for Disease Control, Atlanta, GA, *Abortion Surveillance Summary*, 1972, 1974, and The Alan Guttmacher Institute; 1975–1983, S. K. Henshaw and J. Van Vort, eds..

Abortion Services in the United States, Each State and Metropolitan Area, 1984–1985, The Alan Guttmacher Institute, New York, N.Y., 1988 (copyright); 1984–1987, The Alan Guttmacher Institute, unpublished data."

3. *Ibid.*

4. Jacqueline Darroch Forrest, "Unintended Pregnancy Among American Women," *Family Planning Perspectives*, 19 (1987), 76 ("Only 47% of the abortions that occurred during the period 1977–1981 were reported.")

5. *New Encyclopedia Britannica*, 15th ed., vol. 19 (Chicago, 1984), 966, 1013; *Encyclopedia Americana International Edition*, vol. 27 (Danbury, Conn., 1980), 428; *Echoes from the Holocaust: Philosophical Reflections on a Dark Time*, ed. Alan Rosenberg and Gerald E. Meyers (Philadelphia, 1988), ix.

6. *Preventing Maternal Deaths*, ed. Erica Royston and Sue Armstrong (Geneva, 1989), 107.

7. Stanley K. Henshaw, "Induced Abortion: A World Review, 1990," *Family Planning Perspectives*, 22 (1990), 76, 78.

8. *Ibid.*, 78.

9. Harry L. Shapiro, "An Anthropologist's View," in *Abortion in a Changing World*, ed. Robert E. Hall (New York, 1970), 1:183.

10. Forrest, "Unintended Pregnancy," 76–77 (emphasis added).

11. *Statistical Abstract*, Table No. 103, p. 71. The data for 1987 are not precisely comparable with previous years because of a change in the method of calculation. *Ibid.*, n.2.

12. Kenneth D. Kochanek, "Induced Terminations of Pregnancy: Reporting States, 1987," *Monthly Vital Statistics Report*, 38 (1990), 1, 5–6.

13. Henshaw and Silverman, "Characteristics and Prior Contraceptive Use," 159, 162.

14. *Statistical Abstract*, Table 103, p. 71.

15. Kochanek, "Induced Terminations," 1.

16. Henshaw and Silverman, "Characteristics and Prior Contraceptive Use," 162–163.

17. *Ibid.*, 162–164.

18. *Ibid.*

19. Kochanek, "Induced Terminations," 6.

20. Henshaw and Silverman, "Characteristics and Prior Contraceptive Use," 166–167.

21. Aida Torres and Jacqueline Darroch Forrest, "Why Do Women Have Abortions?" *Family Planning Perspectives*, 20 (1988), 169.

22. U.S. Department of Justice, *Sourcebook of Criminal Justice Statistics* (Washington, D.C., 1990.).

23. U.S. Department of Justice, *Sourcebook of Criminal Justice Statistics* (Washington, D.C., 1988), 214.

24. U.S. Department of Justice, *Sourcebook of Criminal Justice Statistics* (Washington, D.C., 1982).

25. U.S. Department of Justice, *Sourcebook of Criminal Justice Statistics* (Washington, D.C., 1988), 215.

26. Torres and Forrest, "Why," 174.

27. Stanley K. Henshaw, Jacqueline Darroch Forrest, and Jennifer Van Vort, "Abortion Services in the United States, 1984 and 1985," *Family Planning Perspectives*, 19 (1987), 63.

28. *Ibid.*, 66.

29. *Ibid.*, 69.

30. Julie Johnson, Priscilla Painton, and Elizabeth Taylor, "Abortion: The Future Is Already Here," *Time*, May 4, 1992, 26, 29.

31. Henshaw, Forrest, and Van Vort, "Abortion Services," 69.

32. Johnson, Painton, and Taylor, "Abortion," 29.

33. Jacqueline Darroch Forrest and Stanley K. Henshaw, "The Harassment of U.S. Abortion Providers," *Family Planning Perspectives*, 19 (1987), 9, 13.

34. George E. Curry, "Reagan Hails Abortion Foes in Capital March," *Chicago Tribune*, January 23, 1986, 3; Joyce Gemperlein, "Reagan Hails Foes of Abortion," *Philadelphia Inquirer*, January 23, 1986, 4.

35. Forrest and Henshaw, "Harassment," 9.

36. Elizabeth Appley, "Two Decades of Reproductive Freedom Litigation and Activism in Georgia: From Doe v. Bolton to Atlanta v. Operation Rescue," *Georgia State Bar Journal*, 28 (1991), 34, 38.

37. Georgia M. Sullivan, "Protection of Constitutional Guarantees Under 42 U.S.C. Section 1985(3): Operation Rescue's 'Summer of Mercy,'" *Washington & Lee Law Review*, 49 (1992), 237, 238.

38. Priscilla Painton, "Buffalo: Operation Fizzle," *Time*, May 4, 1992, 33.

39. Forrest and Henshaw, "Harassment," 10.

40. Brief of the National Abortion Federation in Bray v. Alexandria Women's Clinic, United States Supreme Court, No. 90-985.

41. Forrest and Henshaw, 13.

42. Johnson, Painton, and Taylor, "Abortion," 28.

43. Forrest and Henshaw, "Harassment," 12.

3. The Medical Context

1. F. Gary Cunningham, M.D., Paul C. MacDonald, M.D., and Norman F. Gant, M.D., *Williams Obstetrics*, 18th ed. (Norwalk, Conn., 1989) (hereafter *Williams*).

2. *Ibid.*, 40.

3. *Ibid.*, 48, 88–90.

4. *Ibid.*, 90.

5. *Ibid.*, 90–91.

6. George W. Corner, M.D., "An Embryologist's View," in *Abortion in a Changing World*, 1:10–11 (presenting photographs of human and rabbit embryos).

7. Carl Sagan, *The Dragons of Eden: Speculations on the Evolution of Human Intelligence* (New York, 1977), 209; Carl Sagan and Ann Druyan, "Is It Possible to Be Pro-Life and Pro-Choice?" *Parade Magazine*, April 22, 1990, 4.

8. Mersky and Hartman, 4:43–45.

9. *Williams*, 8–9.

10. *Ibid.*, 9–10.

11. *Ibid.*, 9.

12. *Ibid.*, 9, 12.

13. Mersky and Hartman, 5:358–360.

14. *Williams*, 746–747.

15. *Ibid.*, 747–748 (emphasis in original).

16. *Ibid.*, 748.

17. Mersky and Hartman, 5:361.

18. *Williams*, 106–107, 751.

19. *Williams*, 489.

20. *Ibid.*, 499–501.

21. Warren M. Hern, *Abortion Practice* (Philadelphia, 1990), 104 (hereafter *Hern*).

22. *Ibid.*, 108.

23. *Ibid.*, 119.

24. *Williams*, 503.

25. *Hern*, 114.

26. *Williams*, 504.

27. *Ibid.*, 504.

28. *Hern*, 122.

29. *Williams*, 504.

30. *Hern*, 122.

31. *Ibid.*, 123.

32. *Ibid.*, 124.

33. *Ibid.*, 139–142.

34. *Ibid.*, 151,

35. *Ibid.*, 135.

36. Stanley K. Henshaw, "Induced Abortion, A World Review, 1990," *Family Planning Perspectives*, 22 (1990), 76, 82.

37. Mersky and Hartman, 3:77.

38. *Ibid.*, 157–170.

39. *Ibid.*, 104.

40. Mersky and Hartman, 5:372–373.

41. Mersky and Hartman, 5:483, 487–488; Hani K. Atrash, et al., "Legal Abortion in the United States: 1972 to 1982," *American Journal of Obstetrics and Gynecology*, 156 (March 1987), 605.

42. Mersky and Hartman, 5:364.

43. *Ibid.*, 367–370.

44. Mersky and Hartman, 5:362, n.7 (brief of the American Medical Association).

45. Mersky and Hartman, 5:488, n.9.

46. *Williams*, 506–507.

47. *Ibid.*, 506.

48. Mersky and Hartman, 5:495.

49. Henshaw, "Induced Abortion," 81.

50. Mersky and Hartman, 5:366.

51. Mersky and Hartman, 5:490.

52. Willard Cates, Jr., and Roger W. Rochat, "Illegal Abortions in the United States: 1972–1974," *Family Planning Perspectives*, 8 (1976), 86, 87.

53. Henshaw, "Induced Abortion," 81, citing a WHO publication, *Preventing Maternal Deaths*, ed. Erica Royston and Sue Armstrong (Geneva, 1989).

54. *Preventing Maternal Deaths*, 110. Marlise Simons, "Abortions Across Latin America Rising Despite Illegality and Risks," *New York Times*, November 26, 1988, 1.

55. Henshaw, "Induced Abortion," 82; *Preventing Maternal Deaths*, 109–110.

56. Henshaw, "Induced Abortion," 81.

57. Mersky and Hartman, 5:364. One study found that abortion deaths are more completely reported than childbirth deaths and that the data are biased toward

overestimating the health risks to women of abortion relative to childbearing. Willard Cates, et al., "Mortality from Abortion and Childbirth: Are the Statistics Biased?" *Journal of the American Medical Association* (hereafter *JAMA*), 248 (July 9, 1992), 192.

58. Mersky and Hartman, 5:374–376.

59. Many studies of the adverse psychological effects of abortion are poorly controlled, compromising the validity of the research because "confounding variables could contribute to or be causing any observed effects." They also fail to evaluate women before the abortion "to establish a baseline for the existence of any psychological disturbance and then reevaluate after the abortion." Moreover, "The five decades of research studying the psychological effects of abortion on women do not examine the same event or medical procedure because of changing technology, legal circumstances, and social climate." The changes include criteria used by physicians to justify abortions; varying illegality and social opprobrium attached to abortion; and the preselection of women granted abortions for psychiatric reasons and for physical reasons. The APA lists other defects. Some studies fail to define adequately the dependent variable of psychological harm. Psychometric difficulties include reliance on case study or anecdotal method, failure to standardize questionnaires or interviews, failure to assess reliability and validity of instruments, and use of tests such as the MMPI without noting whether results indicate pathology. Finally, other design problems include failure to obtain representative samples (for example, racially homogenous or predominantly so, single women, and one socioeconomic class). Samples furthermore are self-selected. Sample sizes often are small and have high attrition rates. Mersky and Hartman 5:436–450.

60. *Brief of the United States Catholic Conference*, Mersky and Hartman, 5:110; *Brief of Covenant House and Good Counsel*, Mersky and Hartman, 3:19–49.

61. *Born Unwanted: Developmental Effects of Denied Abortion*, ed. Henry David, et al. (New York, 1988).

62. Arthur B. Shostak, Gary McLouth, and Lynn Seng, *Men and Abortion: Lessons, Losses, and Love* (New York, 1984), 13.

4. The Historical Context

1. John T. Noonan, "An Almost Absolute Value in History," in *The Morality of Abortion: Legal and Historical Perspectives*, ed. John T. Noonan, Jr. (Cambridge, Mass., 1970), 1–59.

2. Joseph Dellapenna, "The History of Abortion: Technology, Morality, and Law," *University of Pittsburgh Law Review*, 40 (1976), 359.

3. Cyril C. Means, "The Law of New York Concerning Abortion and the Status of the Foetus, 1664–1968: A Case of Cessation of Constitutionality," *New York Law Forum*, 24 (1968) (hereafter Means I), 411; Cyril C. Means, "The Phoenix of Abortion Freedom: Is a Penumbral of Ninth Amendment Right About to Arise from the Nineteenth-Century Legislative Ashes of a Fourteenth-Century Common-Law Liberty?" *New York Law Forum*, 27 (1971), 335 (hereafter Means II).

4. John M. Riddle, *Contraception and Abortion from the Ancient World to the Renaissance* (Cambridge, Mass., 1992), 7.

5. *Born Unwanted*, 10.

6. George Devereaux, *A Study of Abortion in Primitive Societies* (New York, 1955).

NOTES

7. Harry L. Shapiro, "An Anthropologist's View," in *Abortion in a Changing World*, 1:184.

8. Noonan, 3–4.

9. Riddle, 9.

10. Stephen M. Krason and William B. Hollberg, "The Law and History of Abortion: The Supreme Court Refuted," in *Abortion, Medicine, and the Law*, ed. J. Douglas Butler and David L. Walbert, 3d ed. (New York, 1986), 196, 197–198.

11. Riddle, 19.

12. Noonan, 6.

13. Riddle, 20–23.

14. Noonan, 7.

15. Noonan, 9.

16. Cyril C. Means, "A Historian's View," in *Abortion in a Changing World*, 1:17–18 (hereafter Means III).

17. Riddle, 111.

18. Noonan, 21–22.

19. Riddle, 112.

20. Barbara Tuchman, A *Distant Mirror: The Calamitous 14th Century* (New York, 1978), 1–60, 105, 366. See also William Manchester, A *World Lit Only by Fire: The Medieval Mind and the Renaissance* (Boston, 1992).

21. Means III, 18–19,

22. Noonan, 32.

23. *Ibid.*, 33–34; Means III, 18–19.

24. Noonan, 39–45.

25. Mersky and Hartman, 2:288.

26. Means II, 337.

27. *Ibid.*, 340.

28. *Ibid.*, 343.

29. Mersky and Hartman, 2:291.

30. Robert M. Byrn, "An American Tragedy: The Supreme Court on Abortion," *Fordham Law Review*, 41 (1973), 807, 818–819.

31. Robert A. Destro, "Abortion and the Constitution: The Need for a Life-Protective Amendment," *California Law Review*, 63 (1975), 1250, 1269–1270.

32. Dalton's treatise provides: "Note also in murder or other homicide, the party killed must be in *Esse, sc. in rerum natura*, For if a man kill an infant in his mothers wombe, by our law, this is no felony: neither shall he forfeit anything for such offense: and whether (upon a blow or hurt given to a woman with child) the child die within her body, or shortly after her deliverie, it maketh no difference." Quoted in Means II, 345.

33. Quoted in Means II, 346.

34. Krason and Hollberg, 204.

35. Means hypothesizes that Coke's position derived from the tension between Coke's opposition to abortion and his disapproval of the ecclesiastical courts' supremacy over offenses under canon law. Coke believed that ecclesiastical courts should be allowed to impose only spiritual sanctions, such as excommunication; but he also may have feared that secular penalties were necessary to deter abortion. According to Means, "the mideaval Church, through its ecclesiastical courts, punished abortion, whenever committed during pregnancy, as a purely spiritual offense, by purely spiritual penalties." Means also observes that in the chapter of Coke's trea-

tise that contains an apparently comprehensive list of "Misprisions divers and severall," no mention is made of abortion at all. Means II, 346–348.

36. Quoted in Means II, 343.

37. Quoted in Means II, 349.

38. Sir James Fitzjames Stephen, A History of the Criminal Law of England (London, 1883), 1:54.

39. Means II, 350.

40. Curiously, while Means criticizes Coke for misstating the law to suit his antiabortion agenda, Blackstone cites Coke as recording the *liberalization* of the common law's treatment of abortion.

41. William Blackstone, *Commentaries on the Laws of England* (1765), 1:125–126 (facsimile of first edition, Chicago, 1979) (citations omitted).

42. William Blackstone, *Commentaries on the Laws of England* (1769), 4:198 (facsimile of first edition, Chicago, 1979).

43. Edward Jenks, A *Short History of English Law: From the Earliest Times to the Year 1919*, 2d rev. ed. (Boston, 1922), 151.

44. Means II, 377–378.

45. James C. Mohr, *Abortion in America: The Origins and Evolution of National Policy, 1800–1900* (New York, 1978), 23–24.

46. Mersky and Hartman, 2:299–301.

47. 50 Mass. 263, 267 (1945). Among the authorities reviewed by the court was Chitty on Criminal Law, published shortly before Lord Ellenborough's Act was passed, which cited a case in which the indictment alleged an assault on a woman pregnant and big with child. The Massachusetts court regarded the indictment in that case as alleging, in effect, that the pregnancy was sufficiently advanced for the child "to be regarded in law as having a separate existence, a life capable of being destroyed; which is equivalent to the averment that she was quick with child." Further, defendant's conduct amounted to an aggravated assault on the woman.

48. 2 Zabriskie 52 (1849). The court acknowledged that two contemporary writers, Russell on Crime and Roscoe's Evidence, both suggest that procuring an abortion is a crime at common law; but, the court pointed out, neither takes account of the quickening doctrine and both rely on Chitty.

49. Abrams v. Foshee, 3 Iowa 274 (1856); Smith v. Gaffard, 31 Ala. 45 (1857); Smith v. State, 33 Maine 48, 55 (1851); Mitchell v. Commonwealth, 78 Ky. 204 (1879).

50. 13 Pa. State Rep. 630, 632 (1850).

51. Mohr, 20–21.

52. *Ibid.*, 25.

53. Mohr, 28 (quoting act).

54. Mohr, 35.

55. Means I, 437, 443–453. Although Mohr questions some of Means's more extreme arguments (including the proposition that the new law did not really intend to treat abortion differently from other procedures), he ultimately concludes that "the basic insight that emerges from [Means's] discussion seems undeniably on the mark: the evolution of abortion policy in the United States was inextricably bound up with the history of medicine and medical practice in America, and would remain so through the rest of the nineteenth century." Mohr, 31.

56. Mohr, 26.

57. *Ibid.*, 43.

58. *Ibid.*, 43–44.

59. Means I, 441–443.

60. One particularly notorious abortionist was Ann Lohman, operating under the name of Madame Restell, whose New York clinic eventually established branches in Boston and Philadelphia, dispatched salesmen to peddle pills on the road, and advertised extensively her "treatment of cases of female irregularity" and her cures for "complaints incidental to the female frame." Mohr relates that her annual advertising budget alone is estimated to have reached $60,000 by 1871. Mohr, 52.

61. Mohr, 89.

62. Brief of 281 American Historians, Mersky and Hartman, 8:107, 117.

63. Indeed, a note at the end of the court's opinion in *Parker* states that "by *St.* 1845, c. 27, provision is made for the punishment of the offence [pre-quickening abortion] with which the defendant was charged in this case." 50 Mass. at 268. And the court in *State v. Cooper* stated, "If the good of society requires that the evil [of abortion] should be suppressed by penal inflictions, it is far better that it should be done by legislative enactments" than by the judiciary. The New Jersey legislature accepted the court's invitation. As noted at the end of the *Cooper* court's reported opinion. "This decision induced the legislature to amend the criminal code, so as to make the offense in question [attempting pre-quickening abortion] a crime." 2 Zabriskie at 58.

64. Mohr, 196–225.

65. Mohr, 224–225. These provisions raised a practical problem for the prosecution that resulted in few women being actually convicted. The woman's testimony often would be important in proving the abortionist's guilt. Under the laws of many states, however, and as a matter of federal constitutional law after the Supreme Court's 1964 decision in Malloy v. Hogan, 378 U.S. 1 (1964), applying the Fifth Amendment's privilege against self-incrimination to the states, her testimony could not be compelled. Consequently, prosecutors often were forced to grant the woman immunity in return for her testimony. B. James George, Jr., "The Evolving Law of Abortion," in *Abortion, Society, and the Law,* ed. David F. Walbert and J. Douglas Butler (Cleveland, 1973) 3, 11–12 (hereafter "Evolving Law").

66. Mohr, 226.

67. The abortion issue was thrust into the public's attention in the early 1960s by Sherri Finkbine's case. The twenty-nine-year-old Phoenix, Arizona, hostess of a children's television show and mother of four children had taken thalidomide, without a prescription, while pregnant with a fifth child. When she learned of the severe birth defects the drug could cause, she applied to her local hospital's committee for certification that an abortion was medically necessary. (Arizona law did not then allow deformity of the child as a ground for abortion.) A routine audit by the county medical association, however, interceded and caused the case to wind up in litigation. With time running out as Ms. Finkbine entered her third month of pregnancy, the Finkbines were denied legal access to abortion in Arizona. As the public watched their ordeal, and their case was debated in the press, they frantically considered seeking an abortion in Japan and ultimately went to Sweden. Ms. Finkbine encountered more delay there, and when she finally had the procedure it was found that the fetus was indeed seriously deformed. Marian Faux, *Roe v. Wade: The Untold Story of the Landmark Supreme Court Decision That Made Abortion Legal* (New York, 1988), 43–51.

68. Mohr, 253.

69. *Ibid.,* 256.

70. Roe v. Wade, 410 U.S. at 143.

71. George, "Evolving Law," 7–10.
72. *Ibid.*, 19.
73. *Ibid.*, 23–26.

6. The Background to Roe

1. Thomas Grey, "Do We Have an Unwritten Constitution?" *Stanford Law Review,* 27 (1975), 703, 706, n.9.

2. Marshall reasoned that Article III, which grants judicial power extending to "cases" "arising under this Constitution" and "controversies" between citizens and their government, implies an authority to decide all matters arising in such cases and controversies. That is, the power of judicial review inheres in the uniquely judicial function of deciding actual cases and controversies. Marshall also relied on the supremacy clause of Article VI, which provides that "This Constitution, and the Laws of the United States which shall be made in Pursuance thereof...shall be the supreme Law of the Land...." Marshall reasoned that a legislative act not made "in Pursuance thereof," i.e., consistently with the Constitution, was not law at all. And Marshall also invoked the oath of office clause of Article VI, under which "judicial Officers" "shall be bound by Oath or Affirmation, to support this Constitution." There is much to question in *Marbury,* from Marshall's participation in a case in which he had personal knowledge, to his arguably contrived interpretation of the Judiciary Act and Article III, to his reliance on an oath of office taken by legislators and executive officials alike, to his assumptions that there is something compelling about judicial, as opposed to legislative, judgment on the constitutionality of laws. Nevertheless, almost two hundred years of constitutional law have firmly established the power of judicial review.

3. The idea of judicial review was hardly radical or even novel at the time. A plan to include the judiciary in the executive's veto process through the establishment of a Council of Revision was proposed at the Constitutional Convention. Although that proposal was defeated, the records of the Constitutional Convention, the state ratifying conventions, and the *Federalist Papers* all reflect recognition of and some support for judicial review. Indeed, at the time *Marbury* was decided, the assertion of authority to declare an act of Congress invalid was hardly noticed in the controversy surrounding the Court's assumption that it could, were the jurisdictional grant constitutional, order the secretary of state to deliver Marbury's commission. Today judicial review is firmly established as part of our constitutional heritage. A century and a half after *Marbury,* in response to the contention that Arkansas's governor and legislature were not bound by the Supreme Court's ruling in Brown v. Board of Education, 347 U.S. 483 (1954), the Court stated that *Marbury* "declared the basic principle that the federal judiciary is supreme in the exposition of the law of the Constitution, and that principle has ever since been respected by this Court and the Country as a permanent and indispensable feature of our constitutional system." Cooper v. Aaron, 358 U.S. 1, 17 (1958).

4. The most narrow conception of the scope of judicial review would confine it to determining whether the formal processes specified in the Constitution have been complied with (e.g., origination in the proper house of Congress, enactment by both houses, presentment to and signature by the president or override of a presidential veto), leaving determination of the constitutionality of a law's substance to the polit-

ical process. Under this view, the judges would ask only whether a law was duly enacted. If so, the legislators' (and the executive's, absent a veto) implicit judgment that a law's substance was constitutional would be final, subject to a check only at the ballot box. Marshall's opinion in *Marbury* implicitly rejects this view, and the Court has never openly endorsed it. As discussed below, however, in a number of areas the Court has declined to subject legislation to very searching scrutiny, thereby greatly circumscribing the substantive reach of judicial review in such areas.

5. 17 U.S. (4 Wheat.) 316, 415, 427 (1819). For analysis of the distinction between constitutional provisions that merely allocate power between the state and federal governments, and those that also protect individual rights, see Dennis v. Higgins, 498 U.S. 439, 111 S.Ct. 865 (1991).

6. Grey, 706.

7. While society might not always agree on the merits of particular constitutional disputes, it at least can agree on a process for resolving them. The kind of process in which society might place its faith would have the attributes of a court: an independent, multimember body trained in the use of precedent and legal reasoning. Charles Black, *The People and the Court: Judicial Review in a Democracy* (Westport, Conn., 1960), 34–55.

8. Alexander Bickel, although warning that excessive reliance on judicial review tends to weaken a sense of constitutional responsibility in the democratic process, nevertheless concluded that judicial review is needed to derive, enunciate, and apply our "enduring values." Alexander M. Bickel, *The Least Dangerous Branch: The Supreme Court at the Bar of Politics* (Indianapolis, 1962). And Michael Perry has suggested that courts are functionally equipped to assist in the moral evolution of our national community by participating in the deliberative resolution of our fundamental political and moral problems. Michael J. Perry, "Noninterpretive Review in Human Rights Cases: A Functional Justification," *New York University Law Review,* 56 (1981), 278.

9. Grey, 713 n.46.

10. In 1761, referring to the collection of documents and principles in which the English constitution is embodied, James Otis argued to a Massachusetts court that "an act against the Constitution is void: an act against the natural equity is void: and if an act of Parliament should be made [violating these principles], it would be void." Quoted in Daniel A. Farber and Suzanna Sherry, *A History of the American Constitution* (St. Paul, Minn., 1990), 67.

11. *Ibid.,* 68.

12. Under the English tradition, acts of Parliament are supreme; and the judiciary lacks the power to declare them invalid. Some opposition thinkers, however, including Sir Edward Coke, took a contrary view. Coke declared in Dr. Bonham's Case, 77 Eng. Rep. 646, 652 (K.B. 1610), that "when an act of Parliament is against the common right and reason, or repugnant, or impossible to be performed, the common law will controul it, and adjudge such Acts to be void," Quoted in Farber and Sherry, 67.

13. 3 U.S. (3 Dall.) 386, 388 (1798).

14. *Ibid.,* 398 (emphasis added).

15. John Hart Ely, *Democracy and Distrust* (Cambridge, Mass, 1980).

16. United States v. Carolene Products, 304 U.S. 144, 152 n.4 (1938).

17. Nixon v. Herndon, 273 U.S. 536 (1927) (exclusion of blacks from Democratic primary).

18. James L. Huston, "The Creation of the Constitution: The Integrity of the Documentary Record," *Texas Law Review,* 65 (1986), 1, 34.

19. The problem of an ambiguous historical record is illustrated in the debate over whether the Fourteenth Amendment was intended to apply the first eight amendments of the Bill of Rights to the states. As in the abortion debate, historical evidence can be marshaled by either side. Compare Adamson v. California, 332 U.S. 46, 92 (1947) (Black, J., dissenting), with Charles Fairman and S. Morrison, "Does the Fourteenth Amendment Incorporate the Bill of Rights?" *Stanford Law Review,* 2 (1949), 5, 140.

20. Michael McConnell, "On Reading the Constitution," *Cornell Law Review,* 73 (1988), 359, 362.

21. Philip Kurland, "The Origins of the Constitution," *William & Mary Law Review,* 27 (1986), 839, 842.

22. The practice of selective invocation of historical sources has long been familiar to the Supreme Court. For example, although Chief Justice Marshall observed in *McCulloch* that the First Congress established a national bank, he conveniently neglected to mention in *Marbury* that it was also the First Congress that enacted the Judiciary Act of 1789, Section 13 of which he held unconstitutional in *Marbury v. Madison.* More recently, compare the Court's conclusion in *Marsh* that the presence of legislative chaplains in the First Congress substantiates the practice's constitutionality with the Court's suggestion in *New York Times v. Sullivan* (holding that the First Amendment limits state defamation law) that the Alien and Sedition Act, also enacted by the First Congress, was unconstitutional.

23. Corfield v. Coryell, 6 Fed. Cas. 546, 551 (No. 3230) (C.C.E.D. Pa. 1823).

24. 83 U.S. (16 Wall.) 36, 77 (1872).

25. 198 U.S. 45, 53 (1905).

26. For example, see Adair v. United States, 208 U.S. 161 (1908) (invalidating federal legislation that prohibited employers from requiring employees to agree not to belong to labor unions); Coppage v. Kansas, 236 U.S. 1 (1915) (same, with respect to state laws); Adkins v. Children's Hosp., 261 U.S. 525 (1923) (invalidating federal minimum-wage legislation for women and children in the District of Columbia); Tyson & Bro.—United Ticket Offices v. Banton, 273 U.S. 418 (1927) (invalidating legislation regulating the price of theater tickets); Morehead v. New York ex rel. Tipaldo, 298 U.S. 587 (1936) (invalidating state law mandating minimum wages for women).

27. For example, see Hammer v. Dagenhart, 247 U.S. 251 (1918) (holding the Child Labor Law of 1916 invalid as not within Congress's commerce power); A.L.A. Schechter Poultry Corp. v. United States, 295 U.S. 495 (1935) (invalidating, on the same basis, the National Industrial Recovery Act of 1933 as applied to a poultry company that sold its products within New York City); Carter v. Carter Coal Co., 298 U.S. 238 (1936) (invalidating, on the same basis, the Bituminous Coal Conservation Act); United States v. Butler, 297 U.S. 1 (1936) (invalidating, on the same basis, the Agricultural Adjustment Act of 1933).

28. For example, see Houston, East & West Texas Railway Co. v. United States, 234 U.S. 342 (1914) (upholding federal authority to regulate railroad rates, even for purely intrastate hauls, when railroads discriminated against interstate hauls); Hipolite Egg Co. v. United States, 220 U.S. 45 (1911) (upholding the Pure Food and Drug Act); Muller v. Oregon, 208 U.S. 412 (1908) (upholding maximum-hour legislation for women working in laundries).

29. For example, in *Coppage v. Kansas* the Court rejected the contention that legislation prohibiting employers from requiring employees to promise not to join unions was necessary to protect the relatively weak bargaining position of individual employees: "Since it is self-evident that, unless all things are held in common, some persons must have more property than others, it is from the nature of things impossible to uphold freedom of contract and the right of private property without at the same time recognizing as legitimate those inequalities of fortune that are the necessary result of the exercise of those rights." 236 U.S. 1, 17 (1915).

30. The problems of underpaid and overworked workers or unemployment increasingly came to be seen "not as an inescapable corollary of personal freedom or an inevitable result of forces beyond human control, but instead as a product of conscious governmental decisions to take *some* steps affecting the affairs of economic life"—such as enforcing laws protecting private property and contract and immunizing the owners of capital by recognizing the corporate form. Laurence Tribe, *American Constitutional Law*, 2d ed. (Mineola, N.Y., 1988), 579.

31. Although the Court's 1934 ruling in Nebbia v. New York, 291 U.S. 502 (1934), upholding a New York law establishing minimum milk prices, presaged the end of economic substantive due process, the Court held unconstitutional in 1936 a state law setting minimum wages for women, Morehead v. New York, ex rel. Tipaldo, 298 U.S. 587 (1936), and from 1935 to 1936 struck several important pieces of New Deal legislation. A.L.A. Schechter Poultry Corp. v. United States, 295 U.S. 495 (1935) (National Recovery Act); United States v. Butler, 297 U.S. 1 (1936) (Agricultural Adjustment Act); Carter v. Carter Coal Co., 298 U.S. 238 (1936) (Bituminous Coal Conservation Act).

32. Justice Roberts, the author of *Nebbia v. New York*, who provided the fifth vote to uphold the new, broad interpretation of Congress's power under the interstate commerce clause, explained years later: "Looking back, it is difficult to see how the Court could have resisted the popular urge for uniform standards throughout the country—for what in effect was a unified economy." Owen J. Roberts, *The Court and the Constitution* (Cambridge, Mass., 1951), 61.

33. For example, see West Coast Hotel v. Parish, 300 U.S. 379 (1937) (upholding minimum-wage legislation and overruling *Adkins v. Children's Hospital*); United States v. Carolene Products Co., 304 U.S. 144 (1937) (upholding the Filled Milk Act of 1923); Williamson v. Lee Optical Co., 348 U.S. 483 (1955) (upholding a law prohibiting an optician from fitting or duplicating eyeglass lenses without a prescription from an ophthalmologist or optometrist); Ferguson v. Skrupa, 372 U.S. 726 (1963) (upholding a law prohibiting anyone but a licensed attorney from engaging in the business of "debt adjusting").

34. West Coast Hotel Co. v. Parrish, 300 U.S. 379, 391 (1937) (emphasis added).

35. Wickard v. Filburn, 317 U.S. 111 (1942) (upholding the application of the Agricultural Adjustment Act to a farmer's production of 239 bushels of wheat for mostly domestic consumption); Heart of Atlanta Motel, Inc. v. United States, 379 U.S. 241 (1964) (upholding application of Title II of the Civil Rights Act of 1964 to a 216-room motel); Katzenbach v. McClung, 379 U.S. 294 (1964) (upholding application of Title II of the Civil Rights Act of 1964 to Ollie's Barbecue restaurant, a family-owned restaurant with a seating capacity of 220 which served primarily local customers and received only $70,000 worth of food that had moved in interstate commerce); Perez v. United States, 402 U.S. 146 (1971) (upholding application of Title II of the Consumer Credit Protection Act to a loan shark); Russell v. United

States, 471 U.S. 858 (1985) (upholding application of a federal criminal statute to arson of an apartment building); Preseault v. Interstate Commerce Commission, 494 U.S. 1 (1990) (upholding federal legislation preserving for possible future railroad use rights-of-way not currently in service and authorizing interim use as hiking trails).

36. Barron v. Mayor and City Council of Baltimore, 32 U.S. (7 Pet.) 243 (1833).

37. Adamson v. California, 332 U.S. 46 (1947) (Black, J., dissenting).

38. Adamson v. California, 332 U.S. 46 (1947) (Frankfurter, J., concurring); Duncan v. Louisiana, 391 U.S. 145 (1968) (Harlan, J., dissenting).

39. 302 U.S. 319, 325 (1937).

40. 410 U.S. at 152.

41. Grey, 717.

42. 410 U.S. at 153.

43. 277 U.S. 438, 478 (1928) (the framers of the Constitution "sought to protect Americans in their beliefs, their thoughts, their emotions and their sensations").

44. 316 U.S. 535, 541 (1942).

45. The equal protection clause of the Fourteenth Amendment provides that no state shall "deny to any person within its jurisdiction the equal protection of the laws." Unless a statute is based on certain kinds of classifications (like race or gender) or impairs fundamental rights (like the right to privacy), the Supreme Court generally will uphold it against an equal protection challenge if there is any conceivable rational basis for the law (note the similarity to the substantive due process analysis discussed above). Dandridge v. Williams, 397 U.S. 471 (1970) (upholding Maryland's limit of $250 per month per family on payments under Aid to Families with Dependent Children, as rationally related to the state's interests in maintaining a fair balance between the economic status of wage-earners and welfare families and in promoting family planning; poverty is not a special classification and there is no fundamental right to welfare). This is a very easy test to meet. The Supreme Court has held that the due process clause of the Fifth Amendment generally (though not always) applies similar principles to action by the federal government. Bolling v. Sharpe, 347 U.S. 497 (1954).

46. The Court did not hold in *Skinner*, however, that involuntary sterilization is itself unconstitutional. Nor has the Court always been sensitive to the need for judicial protection of procreational interests. Indeed, Buck v. Bell, 274 U.S. 200 (1927), upheld Virginia's involuntary sterilization of Cassie Buck because, as Justice Holmes wrote, "society can prevent those who are manifestly unfit from continuing their kind.... Three generations of imbeciles are enough." *Ibid.*, 207.

47. 367 U.S. 497, 522, 548 (1961) (Harlan, J., dissenting).

48. 381 U.S. 479, 486 (1965) (Goldberg, J., concurring).

49. *Roe v. Wade*, 410 U.S. at 167–170 (Stewart, J., concurring).

50. There was no opinion joined by a majority of the Court concerning the prohibition on sales to minors; four Justices would have recognized a minor's right to exercise some choice in such matters, while three other Justices concurring in the judgment would have allowed government to regulate the sexual activity of minors but found the means chosen by the state in *Carey* to be so arbitrary as to be a denial of due process. 431 U.S. 678, 688–689 (1977).

51. 478 U.S. 186, 192 (1986), *quoting* Palko v. Connecticut, 302 U.S. 319, 325 (1937).

52. *Ibid.*, 199 (Blackmun, J., dissenting) (citations omitted).

53. Justice Scalia's opinion attempted to distinguish Stanley v. Illinois, 405 U.S.

645 (1972), in which the Court held that an unwed father, who had established a significant parental relationship with the illegitimate child, was entitled to a hearing on fitness as a parent. To Justice Scalia, *Stanley* rested "not upon such isolated factors [as paternity and establishment of a significant relationship] but upon the historic respect—indeed, sanctity would not be too strong a term—traditionally accorded to the relationships that develop within the unitary family." 491 U.S. 110, 123 (1989) (plurality opinion). In other words, what was legally important to Justice Scalia and Chief Justice Rehnquist in *Michael H.* was not the strength of the biological father's relationship with his daughter but the state's interest in protecting what gave the *appearance* of being a traditional unitary family—the daughter's mother, the husband, and the daughter herself—regardless of the realities of the underlying relationships. Justices O'Connor and Kennedy joined all of Justice Scalia's opinion except the portion limiting the scope of protected liberty interests to the most narrowly defined historical precedent possible.

7. Roe v. Wade *and* Doe v. Bolton

1. Faux, *Roe v. Wade*, 39.
2. *Ibid.*, 18.
3. *Ibid.*, 24.
4. 410 U.S. at 118–119.
5. *Ibid.*, 124.
6. *Ibid.*, 136.
7. *Ibid.*, 140.
8. *Ibid.*, 150.
9. *Ibid.*, 153. These assumptions and conclusions were challenged by anti-abortion *amici* in *Webster.*
10. *Ibid.*, 158.
11. 492 U.S. 490, 569 n.13.
12. 410 U.S. at 159, 162.
13. *Ibid.*, 163–164.
14. *Ibid.*, 211–213 (Douglas, J., concurring).
15. *Ibid.*, 221–222 (White, J., dissenting).
16. *Ibid.*, 172–174 (Rehnquist, J., dissenting).
17. 410 U.S. 179, 183 (1973).
18. *Ibid.*, 192.

8. *Criticisms of* Roe

1. Arnold H. Loewy, "Why *Roe v. Wade* Should Be Overruled," *North Carolina Law Review*, 67 (1989), 939, 942 n.21.
2. Sidney Callahan, "Context of the Abortion Debate," in Mersky and Hartman, 2:17, 19.
3. *Ibid.*, 21.
4. *Ibid.*, 23.
5. The philosophical basis for this argument can be found in Judith Jarvis Thompson, "A Defense of Abortion," *Philosophy and Public Affairs*, 1 (1971), 47, in which she defends abortion rights in at least some contexts (at least when the

woman did not voluntarily or casually risk pregnancy) on the grounds that the state lacks the authority to appropriate the woman's body for childbearing purposes.

6. Mersky and Hartman, 1:57–58 and n.7.

7. Callahan, 27.

8. *Ibid.*, 27.

9. Mersky and Hartman, 1:51, 54.

10. *Ibid.*, 55.

11. *Ibid.*, 56–57.

12. *Ibid.*, 59–60.

13. *Ibid.*, 60–61.

14. John Noonan, "The Root and Branch of Roe v. Wade," *Nebraska Law Review*, 63 (1984), 888.

15. Robert H. Bork, *The Tempting of America: The Political Seduction of the Law* (New York, 1990), 110.

16. *Ibid.*, 114.

17. Robert H. Bork, "Neutral Principles and Some First Amendment Problems," *Indiana Law Journal*, 47 (1971), 1, 2.

18. Herbert Wechsler, "Towards Neutral Principles of Constitutional Law," in *Principles, Politics, and Fundamental Law* (Cambridge, Mass., 1961), 3, 27.

19. Bork, "Neutral Principles," 3.

20. *Ibid.*, 8.

21. Grey, 706–718.

22. Laurence H. Tribe, *Abortion: The Clash of Absolutes* (New York, 1990), 86–96.

23. Mohr, 258–259.

24. Brief of International Women's Health Organizations, Mersky and Hartman, 7:3, 16.

25. Craig v. Boren, 429 U.S. 190 (1976); Mississippi University for Women v. Hogan, 458 U.S. 718 (1982).

26. Geduldig v. Aiello, 417 U.S. 484, 496 n.20 (1974). On one hand the Court has upheld against gender discrimination challenges to government action that withholds "benefits" on the basis of pregnancy (for example, excluding pregnancy-related claims from coverage under a government disability insurance policy, or excluding pregnancy-related absences from a paid sick-leave policy). On the other hand the Court has regarded the imposition of "burdens" as gender discrimination (for example, denying accumulated seniority to women returning to work after pregnancy while granting seniority to other workers returning from sick leave). General Elec. Co. v. Gilbert, 429 U.S. 125 (1976); Nashville Gas Co. v. Satty, 434 U.S. 136 (1977).

27. For whatever it is worth, "nearly a thousand law professors and the nation's leading organization of lawyers" have endorsed recognition of a constitutional right to privacy that includes a woman's right to choose whether to bear a child. Tribe, *Abortion*, 82. The position of the American Bar Association is described earlier. The "nearly a thousand law professors" refers to the 885 American law professors who filed a Brief for a Group of American Law Professors, Mersky and Hartman, 6:513.

28. Walter Dellinger and Gene Sperling, "Abortion and the Supreme Court: The Retreat from Roe v. Wade," *University of Pennsylvania Law Review*, 138 (1989), 83, 97–98 n.51.

29. John Hart Ely, "The Wages of Crying Wolf: A Comment on Roe v. Wade," *Yale Law Journal*, 82 (1973), 920, 923.

30. *Ibid.*, 933–946.

31. *Ibid.*, 934–935.
32. *Ibid.*, 935–936.
33. Dellinger and Sperling, 109–110.

9. A Search for Balance

1. 410 U.S. at 162–165.

10. Regulation of the Medical Aspects of Abortion

1. Planned Parenthood of Central Missouri v. Danforth, 428 U.S. 52, 64 (1976).
2. *Ibid.*, 63.
3. Colautti v. Franklin, 439 U.S. 379, 388–389 (1979).
4. *Ibid.*, 387–394.
5. City of Akron v. Akron Center for Reproductive Health, 462 U.S. 416, 438–439 (1983).
6. Planned Parenthood Ass'n of Kansas City, Mo., Inc. v. Ashcroft, 462 U.S. 476. (1983).
7. Simopolous v. Virginia, 462 U.S. 506, 514 (1983).
8. 439 U.S. 379, 380 n.1, 393–398.
9. 428 U.S. 52 (1976).
10. 462 U.S. at 482–486.
11. Thornburgh v. American College of Obstetricians and Gynecologists, 476 U.S. 747, 769 (1986) (emphasis added).
12. *Ibid.*, 766.
13. *Ibid.* (quoting Bellotti v. Baird, 443 U.S. 622, 655 [1979]).
14. Planned Parenthood Ass'n of Kansas City, Mo., Inc. v. Ashcroft, 462 U.S. 476 (1983).

11. Direct Regulation of the Woman's Decision

1. The Supreme Court upheld in *Planned Parenthood of Central Missouri v. Danforth* a Missouri requirement that a woman, before having an abortion in the first trimester, must certify in writing that "her consent is informed and freely given and is not the result of coercion," 428 U.S. at 65–66.
2. City of Akron v. Akron Center for Reproductive Health, Inc., 462 U.S. 416, 442–446 (1983).
3. 476 U.S. 747, 761 (1986).
4. *Planned Parenthood of Central Missouri v. Danforth*, 428 U.S. at 71.
5. *Planned Parenthood of Central Missouri v. Danforth*, 428 U.S. at 75.
6. 443 U.S. 622, 634–635 (1979).
7. By 1983, when the Court next considered the parental-consent issue in two cases decided the same day, the Court was becoming increasingly fragmented in its conception of a woman's privacy rights. In *City of Akron v. Akron Center for Reproductive Health, Inc.*, the Court held unconstitutional Akron's ordinance requiring all minors under fifteen years of age to obtain either consent of one parent or a court order. 462 U.S. 416 (1983). The ordinance's defect was that it did not meet the requirements set forth in Justice Powell's opinion in *Bellotti v. Baird*, under which a minor must be

allowed to prove either that she is informed and mature enough to make her own decision or that abortion would be in her best interests. Justice O'Connor, then newly appointed, dissented (joined by Justices White and Rehnquist). Her approach would determine the validity of all abortion regulation by asking whether the regulation "unduly burdened" the woman's choice.

In *Planned Parenthood Ass'n of Kansas City, Mo., Inc., v. Ashcroft*, the Court upheld Missouri's statute, which, as interpreted by the Court, required consent of one parent or a court order based either on a finding of competence or that abortion would be in the minor's best interests. 492 U.S. 476 (1983). In an opinion joined only by Justice Powell and Chief Justice Burger, the Court upheld the statute under the *Bellotti v. Baird* standards. Justices O'Connor, Rehnquist, and White concurred in the result under Justice O'Connor's new "no undue burden" standard, which is discussed in more detail below. 492 U.S. at 505 (O'Connor, J., concurring).

8. The Court upheld Utah's parental-notice requirement on narrow grounds in H.L. v. Matheson, 450 U.S. 406 (1981). The Utah law required the physician to notify the parents or guardian of the pregnant minor if possible, or her husband if she is married, Noting the legitimate state interest in preserving parental authority and requiring parental consultation in the abortion decision, and that the statute required only notification and not consent, the Court upheld the Utah statute as applied to an unmarried, presumably immature minor living with and dependent upon her parents.

Justice Powell's concurring opinion (joined by Justice Stewart) pointed out that *Bellotti* would require a judicial bypass procedure for a minor mature enough to make the abortion decision herself or if notification were not in her best interests, but those facts were not shown on the record in *H.L. v. Matheson*. 450 U.S. at 419–420 (Powell, J., concurring). Justice Stevens concurred in the judgment and would have gone further in upholding the parental-notice requirement even as applied to mature minors. Justice Marshall (joined by Justices Brennan and Blackmun) dissented on the grounds that the statute unjustifiably and sweepingly interfered with the woman's decision, the physician's judgment, and the family's privacy. *Ibid.*, 425 (Marshall, J., dissenting).

9. 497 U.S. 417 (1990).

10. 497 U.S. 502 (1990).

12. The Public Funding of Abortion

1. In Maher v. Roe, 432 U.S. 464 (1977), the Court upheld a Connecticut statute limiting Medicaid funding to abortions that are "medically necessary" (a term defined to include psychiatric necessity). The Court reasoned that the law would not be unconstitutional under *Roe v. Wade* unless it affirmatively restricted the woman's right to choose whether to terminate her pregnancy. Any obstacle to the woman's choice, the Court concluded, lay in her indigency and not in the Connecticut statute.

2. Pub.L. No. 96-123, Sec. 109, 93 Stat. 929. Harris v. McRae, 448 U.S. 297 (1980).

3. Two other abortion funding cases merit mention. In Poelker v. Doe, 432 U.S. 519 (1977), relying on *Maher v. Roe*, the Court upheld a St. Louis ordinance providing publicly funded hospital facilities for childbirth but not for nontherapeutic abortion. In Beal v. Doe, 432 U.S. 438 (1977), the Court upheld Pennsylvania's interpretation of Title XIX of the Social Security Act, 42 U.S.C. §1396 *et seq.*, as not requiring states that participate in the Medicaid program to fund *all* abortions

(including those not medically necessary) permissible under state law. The Court in *Harris v. McRae* also held that Title XIX does not require a participating state to fund medically necessary abortions for which federal reimbursement would be unavailable under the Hyde Amendment. 448 U.S. at 306–311. See also Williams v. Zbaraz, 448 U.S. 358 (1980) (same).

4. For discussion of the Court's negative rights paradigm in the context of a constitutional claim to equal educational opportunity, see Donald P. Judges, "Bayonets for the Wounded: Constitutional Paradigms and Disadvantaged Neighborhoods," *Hastings Constitutional Law Quarterly*, 19 (1992), 599. Portions of the discussion in the text of the negative rights paradigm first appeared in that article; other portions first appeared in Judges, "Confirmation as Consciousness-Raising: Lessons for the Supreme Court from the Clarence Thomas Confirmation Hearings," *St. John's Journal of Legal Commentary*, 7 (1991), 147. See also Judges, "Light Beams and Particle Dreams: A Reexamination of the Individual versus Group Rights Paradigm in Affirmative Action," *Arkansas Law Review*, 44 (1991), 1007, 1039–1046 (consideration of impact of paradigm dominating affirmative-action debate on that group). For a brief description of the philosophical origins of the negative rights idea, see Robin West, "Foreword: Taking Freedom Seriously," *Harvard Law Review*, 104 (1990), 43.

5. 448 U.S. at 315–318.

6. See Tribe, *American Constitutional Law*, 1346–1347.

7. See, for example, Williams v. Walker-Thomas Furniture Co., 350 F.2d 445, 449 (D.C. Cir. 1965) ("where the element of unconscionability is present at the time a contract is made, the contract should not be enforced"); Henningsen v. Bloomfield Motors, Inc., 32 N.J. 358, 404, 161 A.2d 69, 95 (1960) ("attempted disclaimer of an implied warranty of merchantability and of the obligations arising therefrom is so inimical to the public good as to compel an adjudication of its invalidity"); Tunkl v. The Regents of the Univ. of Cal., 60 Cal. 2d 92, 98, 383 P.2d 441, 447, 32 Cal. Rptr. 33, 39 (1963) (even though hospital may be selective in admitting patients, it cannot contract to release itself from negligence).

8. The Court reaffirmed this principle in *Webster v. Reproductive Health Services*, upholding a prohibition on the use of public facilities or employees to perform abortions not necessary to save the mother's life. 492 U.S. 490 (1989). The Court has also applied this approach in the First Amendment area, reasoning that the First Amendment constitutes only a prohibition on certain kinds of government restrictions on speech, not an entitlement to the means to exercise one's free speech rights. See, for example, Regan v. Taxation with Representation of Wash., 461 U.S. 540, 548–551 (1983) (sustaining the Internal Revenue Code's distinction between nondeductibility of contributions to tax-exempt organizations that engage in lobbying and deductibility of contributions to organizations that do not engage in lobbying).

9. See McCulloch v. Maryland, 17 U.S. (Wheat.) 316 (1819); Ely, *Democracy and Distrust*, 135–136 (Court's job when detecting a law depriving one of constitutional entitlement is to unblock the stoppage). To be sure, as explained below, the Court has not included the poor in that category. For criticism of that conclusion, see Judges, "Bayonets for the Wounded."

14. The Webster Case

1. 492 U.S. 490, 501 (1989).

2. The preamble has, however, prompted creative arguments about when one is eligible to apply for a driver's license, to purchase alcoholic beverages, and to claim a tax deduction for dependents.

3. 492 U.S. at 524 (O'Connor, J., concurring).

4. *Ibid.*, 513, plurality opinion.

5. Mersky and Hartman, 5:40–43.

6. This presumption was not challenged by the parties in the Supreme Court. Justice O'Connor observed in her concurring opinion (which disagreed with the Chief Justice's reading of the remainder of the statute as posing an opportunity to reconsider *Roe*'s trimester framework) that the presumption arguably would have created a conflict with *Roe* and the Court's post-*Roe* abortion decisions. 492 U.S. at 526–527.

7. *Ibid.*, 517–519 (plurality opinion).

8. *Ibid.*, 520.

9. Justice O'Connor's reference to the conclusion that the second-trimester hospitalization requirement in *Akron* was not an undue burden reflects her view of the Court's holding in that case, not her agreement with that holding. In fact, she dissented in *Akron*.

10. *Ibid.*, 537 n.* (Scalia, J., concurring in part and concurring in the judgment).

11. *Ibid.*, 531.

12. *Ibid.*, 541 n.1 (Blackmun, J., concurring in part and dissenting in part).

13. *Ibid.*, 552–553.

15. *1989 Post-*Webster *Cases*

1. 497 U.S. 417, 110 S.Ct. 2926, 2940 (1990).

2. *Ibid.*, 110 S.Ct. 2945–2946.

3. *Ibid.*, 2944–2945.

4. Justice Kennedy's separate opinion in *Hodgson* (joined by the Chief Justice and Justices White and Scalia) invoked "our most revered institutions" in concluding that the two-parent notification requirement would be constitutional standing on its own: "Minnesota has done no more than act upon the common-sense proposition that, in assisting their daughter in deciding whether to have an abortion, parents can best fulfill their roles if they have the same information about their child's medical condition and medical choices as the child's doctor does; and that to deny parents this knowledge is to risk, or perpetuate, estrangement or alienation from the child when she is in the greatest need of parental guidance and support. The Court does the State, and our constitutional tradition, sad disservice by impugning the integrity of these elemental objectives." 110 S.Ct. at 2964 (Kennedy, J., concurring in the judgment in part and dissenting in part).

5. It lies somewhere between the preponderance-of-the-evidence standard (i.e., simply more likely than not, or by 51 percent) usually applicable in civil cases and the most demanding beyond-a-reasonable-doubt standard applicable in criminal cases. In Cruzan v. Director, Missouri Dept. of Health, 497 U.S. 261, 110 S.Ct. 2841 (1990), the Court held that a state could require proof by clear and convincing evidence of the intent of an unconscious patient in a permanent vegetative condition to have life-sustaining forced nutrition and hydration removed.

6. Cross v. Ledford, 161 Ohio St. 469, 477, 120 N.E.2d 118, 123 (1954), quoted in

Ohio v. Akron Center for Reproductive Health, 497 U.S. 502, 110 S.Ct. 2972, 2981–2982 (1990).

7. Addington v. Texas, 441 U.S. 418 (1979) (civil commitment proceedings); Santosky v. Kramer, 455 U.S. 745 (1982) (termination of parental rights).

8. 110 S.Ct. at 2984 (Scalia, J., concurring).

16. Rust v. Sullivan

1. The discussion of *Rust* comes largely from Judges, "Confirmation as Consciousness-Raising," 157–159.

2. The Supreme Court declined to review (and therefore let stand) the decision of the United States Court of Appeals for the Second Circuit in Planned Parenthood of America, Inc. v. Agency for International Development, 915 F.2d 59 (2d Cir. 1990), *cert. denied*, 111 S.Ct. 2257 (1991). The Second Circuit upheld an AID policy that precluded assistance to foreign nongovernmental organizations that perform or promote abortions or abortion-related services (including abortion counseling), even if provided with separate funds.

3. 42 C.F.R. §§ 59.8(a)(2), 59.8(b)(5) (1991).

4. 111 S.Ct. 1759, 1772–1773, 1776 (1991) (emphasis added).

5. *Ibid.*, 1777.

6. *Ibid.*, 1785 (Blackmun, J., dissenting).

7. 111 S.Ct. at 1773.

8. Rust v. Sullivan, 889 F.2d 401, 415 n.1 (2d Cir. 1989) (Cardamone, J., concurring), *aff'd*, 111 S.Ct. 1759 (1991).

9. 111 S.Ct. at 1785 (Blackmun, J., dissenting).

17. Webster *and the Overruling of* Roe

1. *Planned Parenthood Ass'n of Kansas City, Mo., v. Ashcroft*, 462 U.S. at 505 (O'Connor, J., concurring).

2. 492 U.S. at 526.

3. *Planned Parenthood Ass'n of Kansas City, Mo., v. Ashcroft*, 462 U.S. at 505; *City of Akron v. Akron Center for Reproductive Health, Inc.*, 462 U.S. at 452.

4. Guam Soc'y of Obstetricians & Gynecologists v. Ada, 776 F. Supp. 1422 (D. Guam 1990), *aff'd* 962 F.2d 1366 (9th Cir.), *cert. den.*, 113 S.Ct. 633 (1992); Sojourner T. v. Edwards, 772 F. Supp. 930 (E.D. La. 1990), *aff'd*, 974 F.2d 27 (5th Cir. 1992), appeal pending.

5. New York v. Ferber, 458 U.S. 747 (1982); Osborne v. Ohio, 495 U.S. 103 (1990).

6. "Transcript of Oral Argument Before Court in Abortion Case," *New York Times*, April 27, 1989, B12.

19. The Joint Opinion in Casey

1. 112 S.Ct. at 2804.

2. *Ibid.*, 2805.

3. *Ibid.*, 2806, quoting *Poe v. Ullman*, 367 U.S. at 542 (Harlan, J., dissenting from dismissal on jurisdictional grounds).

4. *Ibid.*, 2806–2807.

5. *Ibid.*, 2807–2808.

6. *Ibid.*, 2808–2809.

7. *Ibid.*, 2809.

8. *Ibid.*, 2809.

9. *Ibid.*, 2811.

10. *Ibid.*, 2815.

11. *Ibid.*, 2812.

12. *Ibid.*, 2813. Plessy v. Ferguson, 163 U.S. 537 (1896).

13. 112 S.Ct. at 2814–2815.

14. William Manchester, *The Glory and the Dream: A Narrative History of America, 1932–1972* (New York, 1973), 87.

15. 112 S.Ct. at 2817.

16. *Ibid.*, 2819, quoting *Planned Parenthood of Central Missouri v. Danforth,* 428 U.S. at 61.

17. 112 S.Ct. at 2820.

18. *Ibid.*, 2822, quoting 18 Pa. Cons. Stat. § 2303 (1990).

19. 744 F. Supp. 1323, 1346–1347 (E.D. Pa. 1990).

20. *Akron I*, 462 U.S. at 444, 450.

21. 744 F. Supp. at 1354.

22. Brief of the American College of Obstetricians and Gynecologists, the American Medical Women's Association, the American Psychiatric Association, the American Public Health Association, the Association of Reproductive Health Professionals, the National League for Nursing, and the National Medical Association as *amici curiae* in support of petitioners, March 3, 1992, § II. B.

23. 744 F.Supp. at 1344, 1352.

24. 112 S.Ct. at 2825–2826.

25. *Ibid.*, 2829, 2831.

26. *Ibid.*, 2831.

20. *The Liberal Camp*

1. 112 S.Ct. at 2843 (Stevens, J., concurring in part and dissenting in part).

2. 112 S.Ct. at 2844 (Blackmun, J., concurring in part and dissenting in part).

3. *Ibid.*, 2853.

4. *Ibid.*

5. *Ibid.*, 2844, 2855 (citations omitted).

21. *The Opposition*

1. 112 S.Ct. at 2855, 2858 (Rehnquist, C.J., concurring in the judgment in part and dissenting in part).

2. *Ibid.*, 2859, quoting *Harris v. McRae,* 448 U.S. at 325.

3. 112 S.Ct. at 2859.

4. Anna Glasier, et al., "Mifepristone (RU 486) Compared with High-dose Estrogen and Progestogen for Emergency Postcoital Contraception," *New England Journal of Medicine,* 327 (1992), 1041.

5. 112 S.Ct. at 2863–2864.
6. 112 S.Ct. at 2874–2876 (Scalia, J., concurring in the judgment in part and dissenting in part).
7. *Ibid.*, 2878.
8. *Ibid.*, 2880.
9. *Ibid.*, 2881.
10. *Ibid.*, 2882.
11. *Ibid.*
12 *Ibid.*, 2883–2884 (internal citations omitted).
13. *Ibid.*, 2884–2885.

22. *Continuing Inequality*

1. Judges, "Bayonets for the Wounded," 603.

23. *An Uncertain Future*

1. Geoffrey R. Stone, et al., *Constitutional Law,* 2d ed. (Boston, 1991) lxxii.
2. S. 25, 102d Congress, 2d Sess. § 2(b) (1992).
3. *Ibid.*, § 3(b)(3).
4. Dandridge v. Williams, 397 U.S. 471 (1970).
5. Washington v. Davis, 426 U.S. 229 (1976).
6. Section 5 of the Fourteenth Amendment authorizes Congress to enforce by appropriate legislation the provisions of Section 1, which contains the equal protection and due process clauses. Although there is precedent to support the view that Section 5 authorizes Congress to invalidate state laws that the Court would uphold under Section 1, the reach of that proposition is uncertain. Provided Congress clearly expresses its intention to rely on its Fourteenth Amendment powers, the real constitutional conflict here is between the Congress and the federal courts, not between Congress and the states. The reason is that the Fourteenth Amendment expanded federal power at the expense of state power, but it did not expand legislative power at the expense of the judiciary. John E. Nowak and Ronald D. Rotunda, *Constitutional Law,* 4th ed. (St. Paul, Minn., 1991), 909–918; Gregory v. Ashcroft, 111 S.Ct. 2395 (1991); Fitzpatrick v. Bitzer, 427 U.S. 445 (1976).

In *Katzenbach v. Morgan,* 384 U.S. 641 (1966), the Court upheld section 4(e) of the Voting Rights Act of 1965, which invalidated New York laws imposing literacy requirements on certain voters, even though the Court had previously upheld state literacy requirements. The Court in *Morgan* gave a broad reading to Congress's power under the Fourteenth Amendment and deferred to Congress's finding that the New York literacy test was invidiously discriminatory. The later case of *Oregon v. Mitchell,* 400 U.S. 112 (1970), however, apparently cut back somewhat on *Morgan.* In *Mitchell* the Court struck down the provision of the Voting Rights Act Amendments of 1970 which reduced the voting age in state and local elections from eighteen to twenty-one. There was no opinion for the Court in *Mitchell;* the Justices wrote five separate opinions. A majority of Justices expressed the view that Section 5 of the Fourteenth Amendment does not give Congress carte blanche to define the scope of Section 1. Justice Stewart, along with Chief Justice Burger and Justice Blackmun, read *Morgan* only as upholding a congressional conclusion that denying an ethnic group the right to vote violates the equal protection clause.

Morgan and *Mitchell* leave the scope of congressional power under Section 5 unclear. Both cases involved congressional efforts to expand equal protection rights beyond the minimum set by the Court, rather than to limit such rights as interpreted by the courts. In any event, *Morgan* "provides strong support that section 5 of the fourteenth amendment does give Congress broad power to ban state laws authorizing discriminatory acts...." (Nowak and Rotunda, *Constitutional Law*, 916), and it may allow Congress, in some undefined circumstances, to invalidate a state law when the courts would not. In another context the Court recently gave a broad interpretation to Congress's Section 5 powers. In *Metro Broadcasting, Inc. v. FCC*, 497 U.S. 547 (1990), the Court held that Section 5 (as well as the commerce clause) empowers Congress to enact affirmative-action laws that would be invalid if enacted by states.

7. S. 25, § 2(a)(2).

8. "Role of Abortion Issue in the 1992 Campaign," *Abortion Report*, September 30, 1992.

9. Since 1937 the Supreme Court has limited Congress's commerce power in only one area; and an FOCA appears to steer clear of that area. In a series of cases between 1976 and 1992 the Court has attempted to give some content to the Tenth Amendment, which provides that "powers not delegated to the United States by the Constitution, nor prohibited by it to the States, are reserved to the States respectively, or to the people." Unlike the Court's pre-1937 approach, the issue has not been whether certain subjects are within commerce but whether the Tenth Amendment precludes Congress from regulating certain subjects that clearly are commerce. Those cases involve application of various federal regulatory measures to the states, including federal wage and hour guidelines applied to state employees and federal low-level radioactive waste regulations. The Court has had a difficult time developing a workable Tenth Amendment standard, and has even given up on occasion and handed the problem back to the political process. See, for example, Garcia v. San Antonio Metropolitan Transit Authority, 469 U.S. 528 (1985).

Most recently, the Court has drawn the constitutional line at federal laws that "commandeer" the legislative or regulatory process of the state. New York v. United States, 112 S.Ct. 2408 (1992). In other words, the Court today will uphold congressional authority to apply generally applicable laws, such as wage and hour laws, to states, but will strike down federal measures that in effect coerce the state government to pass and to enforce federally prescribed laws and regulations. The Court's objection is that such laws shift the political burden from federal legislators to state officials, who must take the political heat for unpopular measures they have no choice in adopting. An FOCA does not direct states to enact any laws or regulations; its effect is just the opposite: it *prohibits* states from enacting specified laws. Because an FOCA does not commandeer state governments to carry out a federal legislative agenda, but instead directly enacts federal policy on its own, the Tenth Amendment would appear to present no obstacle.

10. United Brotherhood of Carpenters & Joiners of America v. Scott, 463 U.S. 825, 836 (1983).

11. National Organization for Women v. Operation Rescue, 726 F. Supp. 1483, 1489 (E.D. Va. 1989). aff'd., 914 F.2d 582 (4th Cir. 1990), *rev'd in part and vacated in part sub nom.*, Bray v. Alexandria Women's Health Clinic, No. 90-985, 1993 WL 3819 (U.S. 1993).

12. *United Brotherhood of Carpenters & Joiners of America v. Scott*, 463 U.S. at 836 n.11.

13. See *National Organization for Women v. Operation Rescue*, 914 F.2d at 585 (citing cases).

14. Stanley Henshaw and Jennifer Van Vort, "Abortion Services in the United States, 1987–1988," *Family Planning Perspectives*, 22 (1990), 102, 105.

15. Brief for the National Abortion Federation and Planned Parenthood Federation of America, Inc., as *amici curiae* in support of respondents, *Bray v. Alexandria Women's Health Clinic*, No. 90-985.

16. Brief of National Abortion Federation.

17. National Family Planning and Reproductive Health Association v. Sullivan, No. 92-935, 1992 U.S. Dist. LEXIS 9421 (D. D.C. July 1, 1992), *aff'd.*, No. 92-5252, 1992 U.S. App. LEXIS 28469 (D.C. Cir. November 3, 1992).

18. 410 U.S. at 162.

19. *Ibid.*, 162.

20. Barbara E. Lingle, "Allowing Fetal Wrongful Death Actions in Arkansas: A Death Whose Time Has Come," *Arkansas Law Review*, 44 (1991), 465, 485–486.

21. Mark Hansen, "Courts Side with Moms in Drug Cases," *ABA Journal*, 78 (November 1992), 18.

22. *Ibid.*

23. Davis v. Davis, 1992 WL 355059, at 14 (Tenn. June 1, 1992). At the time this book went to press, the court's opinion in *Davis* had not been released for publication and was available only on on-line computerized legal research services. The citation here is to Westlaw.

24. *Ibid.*, 4.

25. *Ibid.*, 4–5, quoting American Fertility Society, "Ethical Considerations of the New Reproductive Technologies," *Fertility & Sterility*, 53 (June 1990), 315.

26. *Davis v. Davis*, 1992 WL 355059, at 15–16.

24. Full Circles and Fresh Perspectives

1. Stanley K. Henshaw, "Induced Abortion: A World Review, 1990," *Family Planning Perspectives*, 22 (1990), 76, 79.

2. Mary Ann Glendon, *Abortion and Divorce in Western Law* (Cambridge, Mass., 1987), 17–19.

3. Sarah Weddington, "Abortion: The New Focus," in Mersky and Hartman, 1:3, 14.

Table of Cases

322

Index

AAA Women for Choice, 26
Aborted Women, Silent No More,
23–25
Abortion: access, *see* Access to abortion; characteristics of patients,
34–37; and civil rights, 264;
demographics of, *see* Demographics of abortion; disposing of
remains, 175n; historical context
of, 83–110; and hospitalization,
173–174; and human emotions,
288–295; and maternal health,
see Maternal health; and medical
emergency, *see* Medical emergency; as medical emergency,
235–236; and nativism, 104;
physical consequences of, 73–79;
psychological effects, *see* Psychological effects of abortion; public
facilities for, *see* Public facilities;
reasons for, 37–40; reform movement, 108–109; regulation of, *see*
Government regulation of abortion; therapeutic, 89, 90; timing
of, 33–34
Abortion clinics, 264–270, *see also*
Bogus abortion clinics; hindrance
claim, 270
Abortion cost, 43. *See also* Funding
of abortion.
Abortion debate: adversarial
approach, 7–9; advertising, 6;
future of, 258–295; images of,
5–6; intractable nature of, 4; as

legal issue, 9–15; and parental
consent, *see* Parental consent;
personal experience, 19–27; personhood issue, *see* Personhood
issue; rhetoric of 4–5; stereotypes,
15–19
Abortion in America (Mohr), 84,
100
Abortion magnets, 108
Abortion Practice (Hern), 66–73,
288, 294
Abortion procedure, 66–73;
amnioinfusion procedures, 70;
antiprogesterone, 66, 73; dilation
and evacuation (D & E), 70–72;
early abortions, 69; and government regulation, *see* Government
regulation; hysterectomy, 66, 69;
hysterotomy, 66; inducing labor,
66; laminaria, 67; laparotomy, 66;
mechanical stimulation, 69; medical induction, 69–70; menstrual
extraction, 68; RU-486, 66, 73,
247; vacuum aspiration, 68
Abortion versus childbirth health
risks, 17, 49, 74–79
Abortionist versus pregnant woman,
laws against, 102–103
Abortionists, 44–45, 240; and repugnance hypothesis, 288–289, 294
Abortionist's Case, 91
Access to abortion, 42–47, 264–270;
and harassment campaigns,
43–47

325

A NOTE ON THE AUTHOR

Donald P. Judges is associate professor of law at the University of Arkansas School of Law. Born in Baltimore, he attended the Johns Hopkins University and studied law at the University of Maryland, where he was graduated first in his class and was editor in chief of the law review. After a clerkship on the U.S. Court of Appeals for the Fifth Circuit and five years as an associate in the Washington law firm of Arnold & Porter, he turned to the teaching of law. Mr. Judges writes frequently on constitutional issues and has received several awards and prizes, including the Joseph Bernstein Award for Legal Writing.